TENACIOUS

TENACIOUS

The Art of Relentlessly Pursuing Your Wildest Dreams

by Scott Scovill

Tenacious: The Art of Relentlessly Pursuing Your Wildest Dreams

Copyright © 2026 by Scott Scovill

All rights reserved. No part of this publication may be reproduced, stored in a retrieval system, or transmitted in any form by any means, electronic, mechanical, photocopy, recording, or otherwise, without the prior permission of the publisher, except as provided by USA copyright law.

No patent liability is assumed with respect to the use of the information contained herein. Although every precaution has been taken in the preparation of this book, the publisher and author assume no responsibility for errors or omissions. Neither is any liability assumed for damages resulting from the use of the information contained herein.

This book is intended for informational purposes only. It is not intended to be used for the sole basis for medical or health decisions, nor should it be construed as advice designed to meet the particular needs of an individual's situation.

Certain names and identifying details have been changed whether or not so noted in the text.

Published by Forefront Books, Nashville, Tennessee.

Distributed by Simon & Schuster.
Library of Congress Control Number: 2025927312

Print ISBN: 978-1-63763-387-8
E-book ISBN: 978-1-63763-388-5

Cover Design by Faceout Studio, Amanda Hudson
Interior Design by PerfecType, Nashville, TN

Printed in the United States of America

DEDICATION

This book is dedicated to everyone who strives to be the best version of themselves they can be. You make the world a better place for everyone, not just you. Thank you.

I'd like to also dedicate the very first copy to roll off the presses to my mom, Jean. Her love and support are both foundation and fuel for the adventure otherwise known as Scott's life. I love her to the moon and back!

CONTENTS

Foreword by Storme Warren   9
Introduction   13

Chapter 1: Trying   19
Chapter 2: Hard Wiring   39
Chapter 3: Don't Stop Believing   55
Chapter 4: When Sparks Fly   69
Chapter 5: First Steps   79

Interlude I: Failing   107

Chapter 6: With or Without U2   115
Chapter 7: Rolling with the Stones   145

Interlude II: Arriving   173

Chapter 8: Building to a Crescendo   183
Chapter 9: Heartbreak and Silver Linings   221

Interlude III: The Spoils!   251

Chapter 10: A Look in the Mirror   257
Chapter 11: Orchestrating Joy   291

Epilogue   319
Acknowledgments   327

FOREWORD

My name is Storme Warren. I host a radio show on the Garth Brooks–owned channel called *The Big 615* on the TuneIn platform. I have been hosting TV and radio shows around the globe for more than forty years.

I moved to Nashville in the fall of 1993. I knew just a handful of people in the country music industry. I quickly discovered that if I wanted to fit in and make a long run at this town, I was going to need some help. That help came in the form of friendships I still have to this day. I always tell young people moving to town that Nashville is a two-way street. That advice isn't a strategy or game plan, just the truth. If you help people out, they hopefully will help you out when the need arises. It's a simple mantra to live by. Not just in the music industry but in life as well. I've watched too many people try to move to Nashville and take the bull by the horns. They don't last very long. Nashville isn't Los Angeles or New York where that kind of attitude is almost necessary. Nashville runs on relationships.

When I first met Scott Scovill I was just twenty-three years old. I had recently moved to town from LA. I landed a freelance job as a field producer for *TNN Country News*, a daily country music show on the since-defunct cable channel The Nashville Network. When June of 1994 rolled around, it was time to buckle in and get ready to cover

Fan Fair (now known as CMA Fest). So much was happening at once that we needed clones to cover the myriad performances and events. Before that day, I had only witnessed Fan Fair as, well, *a fan*. Trying to cover their performances and get frenzied artists to do interviews was a different beast.

On the first day, I had already covered two fan club parties and an artist's number one celebration prior to racing to the main stages at the Nashville fairgrounds. This was where literally everybody who was anybody performed. A who's who for all of country music. The shows moved fast. Each artist would get about three songs, and then, without missing a beat, the adjacent stage would fire up with the next artist. All day long, Thursday through Sunday, it was relentless. I needed to find a solution to cover everything happening at once. The answer came through Scott Scovill. He was directing every performance from a simple white rental trailer parked backstage. He had a crew of camera operators capturing the shows and sending the content through long cables into his humble "control room." There wasn't enough space in the trailer for Scott to sit and direct the shows. Instead, he worked outside, with the back doors flung wide open. There, he stooped over a small video switcher . . . all day long, in the Nashville summer heat and humidity.

That is where I first introduced myself to Scott. I told him where I worked and explained my dilemma. He looked up from his monitor and offered, "If you have some tape, I'll just record a copy of the shows on my extra deck here." My eyes brightened. "You'd do that?" I asked.

He said, "Of course. I'll start now, and you can just grab the tapes tonight, pending CMA's approval."

Scott and I created a smooth system that made covering the performances seamless. While I was backstage interviewing the stars, he recorded the shows and made notes about what highlights happened when. It was like a gift from heaven.

That relationship grew over the years. When the event moved from the hot, stinky fairgrounds to the footprint of downtown Nashville, we began to evolve into a whole new world. And that is the real essence of Scott. *Evolution.* He traded in his tiny system for multiple huge video systems and several bigger Jumbotron screens. Fast-forward to today, and Scott now has dozens of these screen systems onstage and on tour with artists like Luke Combs, Garth Brooks, and Brad Paisley. If you've sat in the nosebleed sections of a country tour over the past thirty-plus years, chances are you were able to watch those shows because of Scott's work. From tours to music videos to corporate events, before you knew it, his Moo TV was everywhere. Scott now has more companies than Moo TV, but let's save those stories for another time. This book is not about what he's done, but instead it's about what *you* can do if you embrace his brand of tenacity.

Scott and I have remained dear friends for over three decades. We've shared the high points of this industry together. And a few low ones too. Scott would take me to Nashville Predators NHL hockey games, as he was and still is an avid fan. And he's not a bad player himself.

Speaking of playing, one aspect of his well-rounded career as an entrepreneur is his love and talent for not only capturing country music but performing it as well. Over the years he quietly escaped the day-to-day chaos of his traveling video circus and started playing his own shows in Europe. Very few people, including myself, knew he had this side of him.

Music is Scott's passion. Every aspect of it. He's a songwriter, singer, producer, and a true craftsman who treats every tentacle of his incredibly diverse career with that same passion.

Not long ago, Scott reached out to ask me if I would introduce him at a Nashville show where his band was playing for charity. For the first time, Scott was performing in the town that built him. He was nervous despite years of performing overseas. He'd recorded multiple albums and played around the world, but this show was different. Even the biggest superstars will tell you that playing in Nashville can be intimidating. It's often a jaded audience very much used to seeing talented musicians on a daily basis. I had never seen Scott perform before that night.

After I introduced him, much the same way I'm introducing him to you here, I was filled with pride. Proud of our relationship spanning thirty years. Proud of his courage to play in Nashville and expose this other side of him to his longtime friends and family. Proud of his willingness to capture the opportunities life presents and make the most of them.

Scott is a true inspiration. If he ever fell, he'd get back up. The Covid pandemic nearly destroyed his business. Artists weren't touring—therefore, no need for his services. But he somehow figured out how to change direction and survive for eighteen months. He took a financial beating, nearly going bankrupt, but he never gave up hope—he never lost the optimism that is his true secret sauce.

If you can dream it, you can do it. That's Scott. I feed off his energy and drive to constantly create new avenues for his business and for his creative spirit. His enthusiasm is contagious, as you'll see.

If you know Scott, you're a lucky individual. I am a lucky man. If you don't yet know him, you're about to become lucky as well.

Enjoy this journey of reading this book as much as I have enjoyed knowing him.

My friend, Scott Scovill.

—Storme Warren
Host of *The Big 615* on TuneIn and emcee of festivals and songwriter shows around the globe

INTRODUCTION

Hi, I'm Scott! I'm one of the billions of humans you share this planet with. I wrote a book! Isn't that cool? I sure think so and my publisher does too. How amazing is that? And now you are reading it. *Wow!* To me this is all very exciting. I'm not famous. I don't have millions of followers. I don't even have a jet! So who am I?

Well, for starters, I'm a guy who, at one time, was so afraid to try that I didn't. I'm a guy who let my fear of failure drag me to the ground. I'm a guy whose life became smaller and less than I ever imagined. It was a sneaky little trip to rock bottom. I hardly saw it coming until it was too late. *Boom!* And there I sat, ashamed.

But while I was wallowing in my humiliation, something wonderful happened. During a chance encounter, I caught a glimpse of a life that seemed like an absolute dream. It sparked something in me, and that spark inspired me to make a real effort. In a fateful moment, I promised myself that I would not only risk failure and try, but that I'd keep trying until I achieved that dream. I swore to myself that I would be relentless no matter how many times I failed and no matter how much it hurt. I decided to be *tenacious*! I didn't know the word back then. Not really. But this word has led to—and now defines—a lifetime of success. Developing tenacity has helped replace my shame with pride. Today I live a life that is incredible to me. And here's the coolest part: I'm sharing this with you because the most powerful transformative force in my life is something you can develop too. Allow me to elaborate.

I've had the pleasure of working with and getting to know many people who I find to be exceptional—people who have achieved awesome feats. People whose lives I admire. Many of them were born into some kind of advantage. Some possessed a brilliant photographic memory from the start. Others have amazing, natural athletic ability. Some are musically pitch-perfect. And still others have been gifted with stunning natural beauty. Fascinatingly, all these people, whose lives I admire, have one thing in common: They are fiercely, relentlessly tenacious. Remarkably, if you ask them what made the difference for them (and I have), they would each tell you it was tenacity! They acknowledge that their talents played a part in their success but swear that it's their unwavering willingness to keep trying—especially after failing—that got them to where they are. All of them encountered people along the way who had more talent than they did. But despite that talent, those others fell to anonymity because they gave up. My notable friends all insist that being tenacious in their lives changed everything.

Unlike the talents and advantages that these people were born with, tenacity is 100 percent developable. By contrast, if you weren't gifted with intelligence, could you work hard at becoming smarter? Studies say yes, though only by a small percentage. And if you had no natural musical or athletic ability, could you work hard at developing some skill? Again, the answer would be yes, but chances are low of you becoming a true master of that skill. On the other hand, tenacity—*the* quality my friends most often cite as the key to their exceptional lives—is 100 percent something you *can* develop! Unlike the skills you were or weren't born with, you can go from having zero tenacity to being totally tenacious in record time. I know, as I have lived at both ends of this spectrum.

My life, while far less noteworthy than my famous friends, stands as a glowing example of this. That is why you must read this book. Because you will see that I'm a lot like you, and I have one message I desperately want to share with you: *Being tenacious can make all the difference for you*; it is *the* key that can unlock your dreams if you decide to pursue them!

Developing tenacity—the determination to never quit, no matter what—turned *everything* around for me. Where I was once immobilized by fear, I now lead a life I would never have dared to dream. Today, despite lacking the advantages I listed above, I am a successful entrepreneur with multiple award-winning companies and more than two hundred great employees. I have my own tour bus and driver that I use on the weekends to visit my friends and clients as they perform shows around the country—artists that include Dierks Bentley, Brad Paisley, and Luke Combs. I sit on the board of directors for the Academy of Country Music (ACM). I've won multiple creative honors, including a CMA (Country Music Association) Touring Award for Video Director of the Year. I do a good deal of public speaking. I make albums and spend my summers performing as a singer throughout Europe, at times for crowds of over ten thousand. I have been an executive or co-executive producer on a couple of films, including one starring Jennifer Garner. I've been to every continent, visited sixty countries, and even went on an Antarctic expedition! Last but not least, I managed to write this book! Not bad for a kid who was too afraid to do his homework—a kid who failed out of college with no credits. Trust me when I tell you that being tenacious was at the root of all my success.

I'm a bit embarrassed to list my accomplishments here, but how else would you know what tenacity helped me achieve? As I write these words, I confess that I am so very far from perfect. I'm a tad dysfunctional at times. I don't always do the right thing. My doubts and fears have been known to get the best of me in the moment. But when I find something that is important to me, I push through all of that. When something really matters, I am doggedly tenacious. And because of this, I am successful, happy, and truly proud. I love my life!

All this from being tenacious. And now that you and I have met, you can know my secret too.

With this one key ingredient I've managed to live a life where I no longer let my fears paralyze me. A life where I am not ashamed to fail. A life that is fulfilling and makes me truly content. I want you to have that, too, and you can!

A little foreshadowing: In addition to sharing my own insights on the subject, I have asked some of my famous friends to share stories about how being tenacious played a role in their life. In chapter 1, for instance, you will meet Olympic gold medalist Scott Hamilton. His incredible story is fraught with tenacity. Aside from his natural physical ability, Scott had the advantage of disadvantages! You heard that right. The cards stacked against him as a young boy were tremendous, yet out of that struggle his tenacity was born.

Are you struggling? If so, great. Being in the midst of the grind is a perfect time to grow your tenacity! Or are you someone who has no struggles at all? If that is the case, let's roll up our sleeves and find a dream worth struggling for. Scott Hamilton will tell you he is grateful for his challenges. They were a key ingredient in the recipe of his amazing life. I feel the same way about mine.

You will find that Scott, and all of the guests in this book, are relatable people, very much like you and me. If their fame makes that connection seem like a stretch for you, fear not. This book mainly focuses on the example of little ol' me. Although trying was exceptionally hard for me at first, you'll see that it kept getting easier. I quickly found that fear—the foundation of my dysfunction—was powerful only because I let it be. When I finally decided to try, it wasn't that scary. Trying again and again slowly became easier and easier. There are books about this written by psychologists and college professors. They might have a fancier, more elaborate solution to your woes. I have read a few of their books and they are great but, of course, less personal. This book is my story, and for me, its truth is brutally simple: If you want a better life, then find something you aspire to and resolve to pursue it.

Decide to try.

Then keep trying.

Repeat.

This is *tenacity*.

So that's it. No need to read the book . . . all you have to do is try. That's the message! Want a refund? Well, if just "deciding to try" is a simple concept (and it *is* simple), then why the heck aren't we all living our very best, most courageous lives?! The reasons we fail to be tenacious are different for each of us. Past trauma, fear, doubt, learned behavior—these forces can be overwhelming. They got the best of me for years. But I found a way through, and that's exactly why you should read on. I invite you to learn from my successes and, more importantly, from my failures. Then, let my guests inspire you. Take the journey with us. Let us help you along the way. You are ready for change, I am sure of it; you did, after all, pick up this book.

It's time to flex your tenacity, chase your dreams, and live your best life!

Scott

(Scan the QR codes like the one here for extra content. This QR links to a pic of Storme and some fun pics of me. One waist-deep in snow in Antarctica, one in Kathmandu, Nepal, with the Himalayas in the distance behind me, and one on a camel in Morocco. Life is an adventure, go places!)

*All photos and supplemental material can be found on TENACIOUSBOOK.COM

CHAPTER 1

Trying

> Defeat is not the worst of failures. Not to have tried is the true failure.
>
> —George E. Woodberry

"Scott Scovill, please report to the guidance counselor's office."

The sound of my name crackling through the classroom speaker startled me. My head had been resting on the desk. As usual, I was half-listening to the lesson, mostly daydreaming. I looked up, and my teacher gazed back with disappointment. She seemed unfazed that I was getting the call. That made one of us. I had spoken to the guidance counselor only once or twice before. What did she want? My teacher motioned toward the door. I stood up, wiping the sleep from my eyes. I could feel the stares as I walked from my seat at the back of the class to exit at the farthest corner.

As I made my way down the empty hall, I could conjure no reason for being summoned. I supposed it was due to the culmination of my years underperforming and skipping school. Perhaps the guidance counselor was the latest to join the ranks of those trying to "reach" me and inspire me to be better. (Sigh.) Good luck with that.

Her cramped little office was overstuffed with books and files. There was barely enough room for a guest chair. I took a seat, ready for her to make her best attempt at fixing me. Sure, I knew I was a mess, mostly failing my senior year. But being a mess was working out fine so far. Her eyes were pinned on me. Sizing up the situation, she seemed sad, unsure of what she should say. There we sat in uncomfortable silence.

"I don't think you are going to be able to graduate."

I knew this was false. Teachers were always underestimating my ability to pass tests. Who could blame them? I often fell asleep in class, and I hardly ever did my homework.

"Well, I appreciate your concern, but I doubt I'll have any trouble passing my exams."

She shook her head. "I'm so sorry, you slipped through the cracks. Your situation is so unique, we never thought to look at the advanced placement students." She paused. She was clearly troubled. I had no idea what she was talking about.

"Even though you tested well enough to take advanced classes, you have been promoted to the next grade level only because you passed the finals. But per New York State guidelines, passing your finals isn't the only requirement to graduate. You need a passing *average* to get state credit. Your semester grades this year have been so low, you do not have that passing average, and thus, you will not get state credit for many of your classes. You now need every single credit this year or you will be held back and have to repeat your senior year."

What? Could this be true? We were in the last half of the second semester. I realized that even with great scores on my finals, getting a passing average in most of my classes would be incredibly difficult. My chest tightened. An advanced placement student flunking the twelfth grade? Repeat my senior year while my friends moved on to college? She had my attention now. I sat in shock, not knowing what to say.

The counselor continued, "I am so sorry we didn't realize this sooner. We just didn't think this was possible with an advanced placement student. The good news is that you have a chance, but you truly need to get a passing average in every class. I've spoken with all your teachers, and we have come up with a system so you can make up for past work and raise your semester grades. It will require a lot of effort, but you have an opportunity to turn this around."

In that moment, my heart sank as low as it could. Passing tests was easy for me. Heck, I could ace them. But doing homework and actually applying myself? That was all but impossible for me. Discovering at this moment that I needed to make up work—that I had to actually *try*—felt like a death sentence. I knew what'd happened whenever I had to try in the past. Tears welled in my eyes, I felt flush and started sweating.

It was happening to me already. I was broken.

What was this? The Averill Park School system, my teachers, and classmates were great, so why couldn't I do the work? The answer is a bit complicated. To get to the root of the issue, we'd have to dig deep.

Hitting Rock Bottom

Despite being broken in this way, I was otherwise happy and healthy. By all accounts, I had a pretty good life. I grew up in the farmlands, way back in the woods, in beautiful northern New York. Mine was a fairly normal childhood. I had divorced parents but lots of love, a good share of friends, and plenty of hobbies. As a typical country boy, my hair was too long, my high-water jeans were too short, and my face was usually dirty. I spent countless hours in the woods with my pals, fishing and sleeping under the stars. We made campfires to keep warm and to reheat whatever we had absconded with from our mothers' pantries. It was magical.

At home, I loved the game *Dungeons and Dragons*, reading about science, model trains, playing Atari, and listening to music. Oh, I loved music. It was a pretty great childhood when I think back on it. So what do I mean when I say I was broken?

Well, I had one particularly troublesome dysfunction that would rear its ugly head whenever I tried to do my homework. I would, with good intentions, sit down to do the work, but an emotional reaction would always ensue. It's hard to describe this reaction, but my best attempt is to say that an intense frustration and hopelessness would build within me from the moment I faced the simple challenge of the work. There was a tightness in my chest, and my brain would become a swirling storm of emotion. I would get so wound up that I wouldn't be able to continue. It hurt to even think about it. As I failed to overcome these feelings, they would intensify. My state would quickly devolve into confusion, and tears of guilt would flow. I would end up a sobbing mess, completely overwhelmed. Why did I feel this way? I truly wanted to do well. I wanted to be a good student. Instead I failed.

Back in the eighties, people didn't look for complicated reasons to explain a lack of scholastic success. You were either a good student or a bad student; I was the latter. Nowadays, someone like me might be diagnosed with ADHD and put on medication that, for better or worse, would rewire their brain. Who knows, maybe that would have helped me in the short term. But would I be as happy as I am today? I doubt it, though we'll never know. And that's OK with me. I've pondered what my life would be like without this early struggle, so much so that I probably could've written another book exploring exactly what was wrong with me.

The good news is that we don't need to go there in these pages. I know where my trauma and dysfunction originated. In fact, we all have our problems. *But the beautiful thing about this book is that it's about solutions.* No matter your struggles, burdens, or distractions, it aims to show you that time and time again, being tenacious can get you through.

So, back to my school dilemma, let's review: I wasn't doing my homework. When you don't do your homework, you typically get really bad grades; I did just that. But I'd get a good grade on the final. As such, the teachers would reason that I had learned enough, and they'd promote me to the next grade. Naturally, I didn't feel like I had failed the class. This, coupled with the fact that I was a reasonably well-behaved kid, allowed me to get by for years without doing my homework. Getting by kept my dysfunction from coming to a head—until that defining moment in the guidance counselor's office.

I was terrified by the realization that I absolutely had to do the work. How could I ever get past my inability to even try? I'm sure that everyone reading this can relate to the fear of inadequacy. To the feeling that you simply cannot overcome a challenge. That you will fail if you try. All too often, fear wins before we try. The sad thing is that this seemingly proves our fears were correct. I've heard that Henry Ford used to say, "Whether you think you can, or you think you can't—you're right." Think about that.

I suddenly realized I had painted myself into a corner. To graduate, I would have no other option but to try, even though trying was inexplicably painful for me.

Applying myself was brutal. I worked as hard as my dysfunction allowed. All the while, a voice in my head screamed, *You can't! Don't try! You will fail!* Yet I knew I couldn't quit this time. As awful as it felt to think about pushing myself past my perceived limits, the thought of not graduating was worse. Imagining that failure was so horrific, it literally made me sick to my stomach.

I turned in a lot of papers with smeared ink from my crying. I gave up trying some days to escape the pain, only to find myself drowning in guilt for giving up. I was overwhelmed with the dread of not passing and the daily reality of my failures. I know this doesn't make much sense to those of you who've never experienced such a mental block, but it was all so real to me.

Good Guidance

The school implemented several measures to help me. I ate my lunch in the working study hall so I could try and catch up on back assignments. I also stayed after hours every day and was often the only kid in the science lab, steaming up those plastic goggles with my tears. This was a lonely and particularly rough time. I fought hard to keep those tears from betraying the cool facade I had maintained for years. A senior crying over his classwork? We all remember how judgmental classmates could be back in high school. I was mortified and determined to never let them see my weakness. Yet I failed at that too, and at times they did see the outpourings of my frustrations. It was demoralizing.

I stayed after school every day to complete labs or English papers. With each droplet into a vial and each pen stroke, I felt like I was falling short, still unable to do enough. I was finishing the work, slowly, but the anxiety made it so hard to focus, I wanted to explode. This went on for months.

At times the struggle was too much. I'd go into cocoon mode and stop working, taking a day or two to resume the fight. Even then, I would try only because I could see no other path, not because I wanted to. These weren't intentional acts of tenacity; they were more like the desperate actions of a cornered animal.

As I was struggling through all of this, I learned that some of my classmates were placing bets as to whether or not I would graduate. The shame I felt upon hearing this walled me off from everyone. I felt trapped in a cage—and everyone was peering in. I feared that this ugly feeling of shame would stay with me for the rest of my life.

Though I did my best, in the end I doubted it was enough. I expected the worst. Beyond the shame of failing, I anticipated going through another year of high school. Another whole year of this torture. Frankly, I wasn't sure I was up for it. Would I drop out? The previously broken kid was now completely shattered.

The judgment finally came. My teachers sat me in a room, all looking at me. I felt so small and exposed. I took a deep breath, bracing for their final reproach. To my shock, they told me that they had decided to pass me. It didn't seem right to me. I wasn't even happy at first. They explained that my struggle was evident and that they were impressed I worked so hard to overcome whatever demons were holding me back. They admitted that, at times, I came up short, but based on my test grades, they knew I had learned the material. Finally, they felt that whatever I was facing would not be resolved by humiliating me and keeping me for a redundant senior year. As their words settled in, I felt the weight of a mountain lift off of my shoulders. I would graduate, dodging ultimate failure yet again.

What Trying Has to Do with It

In the introduction, I described being tenacious as trying and never giving up. Already in this chapter, I have admitted to giving up many times, even *cocooning* for days after failing. How is this an example worth sharing? After all, I was a quitter a thousand times over. Here's the thing: I may have stopped trying in the moment, but every time I fell I would lick my wounds and march back into battle. I gave up in the moment, but I never quit for long. Unbeknownst to me, I was discovering my own tenacity. It was still in its infancy, far more forced than intentional, but I was trying. I was trying, and, despite painfully failing, I was trying again.

I had fallen short despite my best efforts, and even the teachers admitted as much. The magical thing, in hindsight, is that I was learning something far more important than those twelfth-grade lessons. The teachers saw it too. I was finally trying to apply myself.

This is what being tenacious looks like in real life. In the wild. It's probably not the story of the gifted athlete who works hard every day, getting incrementally better as they march unhindered to Olympic glory. If such a perfect athlete exists, they have exceptional resolve and dedication. Good for them! But that is not a story of tenacity. No, real-life stories of tenacity are uglier—full of flaws, shortcomings, and pain.

My journey was riddled with angst. I remember fellow students asking me if I was OK after seeing my red eyes and tear-stained cheeks. I also remember falling into my mother's arms after losing a battle with an assignment—a great shame for an eighteen-year-old man. No, there is no tenacity without struggle, hardship, and failure. This is why tenacious stories are the best. They are so hard-fought that not giving up is what makes them *special*. This is why being tenacious can make all the difference in your life—and it's achievable through one simple act. *Not giving up* can make your life amazing. Have I mentioned that before? Spoiler alert: Developing tenacity can be brutal at first, but stick with it. It truly gets easier with practice—way easier!

> My heroes are the ones who survived doing it wrong,
> who made mistakes but recovered from them.
> —Bono

Throughout this whole senior-year saga, I wasn't chasing a dream. I was just trying to elude a catastrophe. This impending catastrophe literally forced me to take my first steps toward tenacity, changing my path forever. Did anything else keep me going besides the fear of flunking? Yes, there were countless moments of near defeat, but there were also moments of victory. When I finished a paper, a lab, or a report, the feeling of handing in that work was intoxicating. The relief was so real. These little victories bolstered my spirits, helping me head right back into the fight.

Remember, stories of tenacity are messy, sometimes riddled with less-than-perfect outcomes. Brush off the mess and embrace the moments of triumph. Pride is fuel!

Feeling Tenacious

Does relentlessly trying sound like it could work for you? Or does it sound like too simple a solution? Remember the Henry Ford quote? "Whether you think you can, or you think you can't—you're right." Well, there is your answer. If you believe in being tenacious, it *will* work. Mind you, while the concept really is incredibly simple, the execution can be brutally hard.

Think back to a time when you didn't give up on something important. A time when you were overwhelmed but persevered nevertheless and made it through. Did your career challenge you in ways that you were not prepared for? Was it your health or the health of a loved one that held you back? Perhaps an important relationship was on the rocks? Did you work through it? Was it hard? Was it messy? Did you fail and stop trying but then decide to step up and try again? That was being tenacious!

Let's build from that success and put the same kind of continuous effort into making your dreams come true! Can you think of a tenacious story in your own life? No? Are you sure? If not, no worries. If you don't feel as if you've been particularly tenacious, then this book is especially for you. I wasn't back then either. We will grow tenacity together!

My good buddy, Olympic hero, and figure skating legend Scott Hamilton knows something about being tenacious. Ladies and gentlemen, I have asked Scott to tell you about his journey with tenacity in his own words, and he has graciously agreed. Take it away, Scott!

SCOTT HAMILTON
ON BEING TENACIOUS

There is something truly wonderful about time. It affords you the opportunity to look back and see your life as it has been lived up to this point and to understand how resilient we can be.

But none of that can happen without truly participating in the contest called *life*. And the crazy thing is, the longer we live, the more we realize how life isn't designed to be fair.

Being adopted at six weeks of age wasn't a choice I had, but rather something that would remain a puzzle throughout all my days. Wrestling with identity and the feelings of abandonment versus being chosen would show up in many aspects of my journey. I think what got me through all of that was the undeniable understanding that I was loved completely and that my parents would sacrifice anything to allow me to thrive and survive.

At four years of age, my parents realized that I wasn't growing and didn't seem to be developing like other children. They came to the opinion that it must be medical, so for the next few years I was mostly in and out of hospitals. There were tests and more tests. Some invasive, some tedious, and some "icky." At the end of four years, we still had no answers, just advice: "Go home, live as normal a life as you can, and let's see what happens next." Not much of an answer, it was more like its own form of surrender.

It was in living a normal life that I was given a chance to participate in a local learn-to-skate program with over a hundred *well* kids. I was a lot more comfortable with sick kids since I spent so much more time with them, but here I stood, the sick kid among a throng of well ones.

Having a history of being the shortest and weakest in my class, my self-esteem was predictably low. I was always the last one chosen for playground games and often bullied for being so little—and also for being adopted.

But skating was the great equalizer. Each week I would show up and get better. Pretty soon I realized that I could skate as well as the well kids, and after a few weeks more, I was skating as well as the best athletes in my grade. That first taste of identity and purpose ignited my confidence like nothing else I had ever experienced. I was actually good at something. Little did I know that the instinct of tenacity guided me through that first part of my life. Skating gave me so much and laid the groundwork for everything else I would later endure.

Being a male figure skater in a small town came with its own challenges. "Hey, Twinkle Toes, show us something pretty." "Hey, Ballerina, don't forget to point your toes." So once again, I had to rise above a challenge. I soon made the decision to start playing hockey. I had to shut down those kids' taunts. I knew I could skate better than all of them, so playing hockey gave me the power to show them up. It also shut them up.

I played for three seasons, or, more appropriately, two neck braces. Ultimately, it was time to focus on figure skating again. I had earned everyone's respect, so it felt right to get back to doing what I was more suited to do. I was always going to be much too small to be competitive in hockey.

Failing in skating was emotionally difficult and something I hadn't anticipated. I hated the figure eights I needed to do to qualify for competitions, and they hated me back. Failure after failure changed my outlook and my hopes for skating at a high level, but it was my mother who always saw something more in me than I did. She would tell our neighbors, "We are going to the Olympics someday," and my response was always, "Based on what exactly?" But practice took care of some of that, and I was able to qualify for the 1973 US Figure Skating Championships in the "novice" level.

I choked, fell five times in my three-minute program, and finished dead last. So I decided to be even more tenacious the next season. I fell only twice that time but finished ninth out of ten.

Fast-forward two years. My mother was diagnosed with cancer. Our family was broke, and I was given one more year to skate.

Something happened in that time. My regular coach retired and a new coach took his place. He was much more of a disciplinarian, and, since I had nothing to lose, I submitted to his authority.

My mom arrived at nationals with her arm in a sling due to the surgery she'd undergone to remove her left breast and lymph nodes in her left arm. She said it was mainly to keep people from bumping into her, but I knew she was in a great deal of pain. She was also wearing a wig because she had lost her hair to chemotherapy. But the most noticeable thing about her at that competition was the joy she displayed at the events.

As I went out to do my long program, I saw the huge smile on her face and the obvious pride she felt watching me take to the ice for what I thought was my last competition ever. Somehow, I won the Junior National Title, and the reason my mother was so joyful that whole week was because she knew my skating life wasn't over. On her way to Colorado Springs for the competition, she was asked to stop in Chicago to meet with a wealthy couple who loved skating and wanted to sponsor me.

So now I was turning eighteen, was going to be sponsored, and would have my own apartment to live in. I affectionately call that the "trifecta for disaster."

I was so bad that year that once again I returned to my losing ways, finishing very close to the bottom in the final results. It was humiliating, but what made this failure the worst embarrassment ever was that it would be the last time my mother would ever see me skate in competition. She lost her battle to cancer three months later, and the devastation was beyond anything I had ever experienced. My brother and I were in her hospital room until around three in the morning on her last night. I was awakened at 8:30 a.m. by my brother-in-law. All he could say was, "Your mother is gone." And all I could think to reply was, "I know." She was the center of my universe. I simply couldn't imagine how I was going to go on without her in my life.

Then something happened. I went out behind our house and started walking. I am not sure how long I walked, but it would be the most impactful time I had ever spent alone. I realized on that walk that the best way to mourn my mom was to take her with me wherever I went. I needed to honor her and every single one of her sacrifices to keep me in skating. With that one decision, everything changed. I wasn't late for practice anymore. I worked harder than I ever thought I could, and the results of that decision changed the course of my life. I wasn't going to be the "loser" anymore.

The very next competitive season, I ended up winning third place at the US National Championships and placed eleventh in the World Championships. Two years later, I won a berth on the 1980 US Olympic Team. Placing fifth in Lake Placid set up a winning streak I never saw coming. From October 1980 to March 1984, I was able to go undefeated, winning four US Championships, four World Championships, and an Olympic gold medal.

All powered by the strength, commitment, and love of my mother.

I heard something during a press conference in Lake Placid during the 1980 Olympics that made a huge impression on me.

Eric Heiden won every single race and all five Olympic gold medals—a feat that may never be achieved again. After his last race, he announced that he would do only one product endorsement. People were dumbfounded. Most Olympic athletes would leverage their success into incredible wealth. Eric shared that he accepted that endorsement deal only to pay for his medical education. (He is now a very successful orthopedic surgeon in Utah.) He added, "It's not the events in your life that determine your character, it's how you respond to them." Flash-Boom-Bang! Those perfect words came at the perfect time.

I was given a perspective that allowed me to rise above anything the next few years would throw at me.

Following the success of those Games, it soon became apparent that it was time for me to go to work.

My first job was the Ice Capades. My goal was to be the best employee they had ever hired. After two years of skating at the highest level and never missing a show or press opportunity, I was told that the new owner wanted to present only women. Any starring male was now expendable. I was devastated but knew that the work I had done with them gave me a mountain of experience and the momentum to step into whatever was next.

After my dismissal from the Ice Capades, I had a meeting with my manager, Bob Kain of IMG. He had an idea to start a new tour and asked if I would be interested. I told him to check my empty calendar, and we both laughed.

Eleven tours later, when I was fifty cities into a seventy-two-city commitment, the pain I had endured in my abdomen throughout every performance that year finally proved too much to bear. I went to the emergency room, and it was there that I was diagnosed with cancer—the same disease that had taken my mother. The fear was extraordinary. I saw myself suffering, diminishing, and dying. And the worst part was the thought that I would never skate again. Then something happened that I didn't see coming. That fear was instantly replaced by feelings of bravery, a clarity of mission, and a true sense that I could determine the outcome of this frightening challenge.

After four months of intense chemotherapy, followed by surgery, I was declared cancer-free. Back to life. Back to skating. But something was different now. I knew I needed to see this as a second chance at life. A life I hadn't foreseen.

On the third-year anniversary of my cancer diagnosis, I met a woman backstage at the Stars on Ice performance in Memphis. There was something about Tracie that seemed different, and honestly amazing. It was then that I decided I was ready to fully get back into life. Little did I know that a few months later we would go on our first date. We have been together ever since.

A little more than a year after the birth of our first child, I noticed that I wasn't feeling normal. I went back to the Cleveland Clinic to get checked, and it was there that I was diagnosed with some sort of a brain tumor. Telling my wife was one of the most difficult things I have ever had to do. Tracie didn't respond to the news the way I anticipated. She took both of my hands and started to pray. It was the most powerful moment in my life, and I knew from that point forward where I would take every challenge.

After a solid week of praying, we realized there was no way to treat a brain tumor unless we knew what kind it was. A biopsy needed to be performed. In meeting with the surgeon, he was required to tell me all the horrible things that could happen during this brain surgery. He told me I could lose memory, motor ability, or speech, and that if they hit an artery, I could have a stroke that could cause paralysis.

I woke up from the surgery and looked at the clock in the recovery room. It read 10:20 a.m. I knew who I was, where I was, and why I was there. I wiggled my toes and whispered "test." I could speak! Hallelujah!

The doctor came into the room with a huge smile on her face, followed by my wife. They now knew what kind of tumor it was and that there were a few ways to treat it. What came next was mind-blowing. As Tracie was reading information about my brain tumor, she looked up and shared that people are *born* with craniopharyngioma brain tumors. They usually reveal themselves through a noticeable lack of growth and development in young children. It was the reason I went through everything I did during those four years in and out of hospitals as a kid. The realization that I hadn't been doomed to live in the shadow of a life-threatening illness, but that I was blessed by this tumor, was one of the most liberating moments of my life. And it totally ignited my faith—a resource of strength in the storm.

Having a relationship with Jesus has been the best way for me to rise above challenges. To learn His teachings, and to step forward into a new life based in God's wisdom, has helped me in countless ways—ways I never anticipated. I can now step into each struggle with power and with a true understanding that this life is meant for these periods of suffering. Romans 5 speaks of suffering producing perseverance, perseverance producing character, and character bringing hope. I believe that because I've lived it. Isn't it marvelous to see tenacity being honored in the Bible?!

Six years later, the brain tumor would grow back. This time it was treated with surgery. The surgery didn't go as planned, so I had eight more surgeries. After the last surgery, I woke up in my hotel room expecting to go home that day, but I was totally blind in my right eye. Straight to the emergency room I went. I was given clot-busting drugs and blood thinners, and the doctors were able to save about 60 percent of my sight in that eye.

I learned a lot from that period. Before the procedure where the doctor obliterated the brain aneurysm that was putting me at risk, I was praying in my room at around three in the morning. A nurse walked in and asked who I was talking to. I told her that I was praying. She asked who I prayed to, and I said, "God." Then she asked how I prayed. I shared with her how fortunate I felt in my life and that when I prayed it was out of complete gratitude. She then asked who God was to me. I told her, "I guess He is my Father," What happened next was totally unexpected. She asked if I had any kids, and I proudly said, "Yes, I have two sons." She then said, "If one of your sons was sick, or scared, or at risk, wouldn't you want them to come to you?" I could only say, "Absolutely." I completely understood where she was going with this, and she taught me how to pray differently. I now boldly ask for whatever I desperately need from the only one who can solve my greatest problems.

Six years later (do you see a pattern forming?), I was diagnosed with another recurrence of the brain tumor. This time surgery would be more complicated and, most likely, not the best solution. There was now a medical option that could target the tumor cells, but that option came with a laundry list of side effects. The strange thing about those options was that while the doctors were telling me the best way to treat this tumor, the only thought I had in my mind was, *Get strong.* That voice in my head wouldn't stop repeating this, so when they asked what I wanted to do, I just told them I wanted to go home and "get strong." The next few appointments would be miraculous. The first couple of scans showed no growth, and after that, to my amazement (and theirs), the tumor actually shrank. Then, in the subsequent scans it shrank more. It was a true miracle, and I still haven't treated it to this day, almost five years later.

I've learned that the most important thing to know about tenacity is that it's a muscle. The more you endure, the stronger that muscle gets. What would knock me down in the past barely bothers me now. Brain tumor number one ignited my faith. Brain tumor number two felt like a kick in the gut. Brain tumor number three was completely different than the other two. I 100 percent feel that I am in *His* hands, and He will do what is best for me regardless of what I would choose.

Being tenacious is truly about "getting strong," and I totally believe we are hardwired to thrive in our suffering. We were built for it!

The key is to lean into our affliction and let it do its work.

So be tenacious. Get strong. Learn. Grow. And allow the tough times to help you build the muscles you need to be more resilient than you ever thought possible.

And pray. It helps more than anything else.

Wow! How lucky are we that Scott Hamilton shared his tenacious story? Scott, you are the best! Thank you.

Scott's path has been riddled with setbacks and potential excuses for why he could have settled for less. Sure, there were times when he quit, barely tried, had doubts, and even failed. Scott is a legend, a household name now, because no matter what, he never quit for long. Scott Hamilton is the epitome of tenacity!

What about you? What reasons might keep you from trying? What if you just tried anyway and never stopped trying? That's what Scott Hamilton did, and it made all the difference in the world.

I'd like to note that to me, Scott is successful in every way. Beyond the career you know about, Scott is a happy, wonderful, giving soul.

He is a great father and husband. He coaches and does a ton of charity work. He is a light to all around him, and I count myself so lucky to be his friend. Another way that Scott gives back is by sharing his story. He has released three wonderfully inspiring books: *Landing It* (1999), *The Great Eight* (2008), and, most recently, *Finish First* (2018). I highly suggest that you read all three!

Meanwhile, back in my story, I had just barely graduated, narrowly dodging ultimate failure.

Once again I heard my name called. This time I stood and marched forward, tall and proud. Wearing a bright blue gown and a funny, tassel-topped square hat, my outfit lacked only one accessory, and here it was: My principal smiled as he handed me my diploma. Was he happy for me? Or perhaps relieved to be rid of me? A bit of both, I suspect. And that's OK.

I felt exactly the same way.

(A ridiculous pic of Scott Hamilton dressed up as a rock star, an iconic picture of him skating, and a pic of me graduating against all odds!)

*All photos and supplemental material can be found on TENACIOUSBOOK.COM

CHAPTER 2

Hard Wiring

> Until you make the unconscious conscious, it will direct your life and you will call it fate.
>
> —Carl Jung

"You have a debilitating fear of failure," the doctor told me.

Then he drove this point home with what he said next. "Scott, what I am about to tell you is true, although it doesn't make logical sense." He paused, giving the moment its full gravity. "It would be easier for you to grab a red-hot stove, hang on, and mutilate yourself than to actually try . . ."

Somehow, as crazy as that sounded and as soul-crushing as it was to hear, deep down I knew that it was true—all of it.

Scuttling Your Success

I was allegedly "smart." Years earlier, an IQ test (for whatever they are worth) indicated this. As such, there was always an expectation from my family and myself that I would go to college.

Somehow, neither the fact that I had graduated, barely, at the bottom of my class nor the overwhelming evidence of my dysfunction lessened that expectation. I enrolled and was accepted at Hudson Valley Community College. Believe it or not, I had received a scholarship due to my SAT scores. Thanks to the fact that I was excellent at deductive reasoning and the SATs were multiple choice, I was going to college for free!

I spent the summer building up my resolve. I had achieved my goal of graduating high school, albeit dubiously, and with that nightmare behind me, I was enjoying my life. I was absolutely determined to power through any subsequent troubles like those I had just been through. I bolstered my will and was set to triumph. By fall, I was fired up. I would prove to my parents that I could do well in school!

College was exciting. I felt smart as I walked across the open grounds of the campus. This place was huge compared to my high school, and there were so many pretty girls—college might actually be great!

My favorite class was creative writing, and I really liked my professor. He announced that he was going to anonymously read the best paper aloud every week. I liked writing when I could choose the subject because it didn't feel like homework. It was more like telling a story to a friend about some cool adventure. I set out to complete the task at hand, and, to my great pride, the teacher chose my paper to read aloud during each of the first few weeks. Mind you, the homework in my other classes was killing me. Once again I was struggling, fighting through my persistent fear of failure, but in writing class I was on top of the world.

Then it happened, something that should have been nothing. My creative writing teacher sat down and started reading the chosen paper for the week, and for the first time it wasn't mine. I was surprisingly disappointed. At the end of class he handed me my paper with a

B+ instead of the A I had grown accustomed to. For reasons that defy sensibility, that was the last assignment I completed in college.

I stopped doing all of my homework, and my attendance dropped. The grading system in college was structured such that no matter how well you did on the final, you couldn't pass without doing the work. I received zero credits my first semester. This was devastating. In the beginning, I tried harder than I ever had, but unlike in high school, I completely failed.

I think it's important to remind you that my struggle with school, where I failed repeatedly and painfully, brought about my first real attempt at being tenacious. I was finally trying, but I just couldn't make myself *consistently* try. I signed up for the next semester, telling myself I would find a way to do better. I tried to hype myself up, but sadly my confidence was broken. By now, I didn't really believe in myself.

Around this same time something else came into play. There was a beautiful young girl named Sandy who had been a friend for years; our families knew each other. Sandy's mom was great—she was a lunch monitor at my high school. Sandy and I had just gone out on a wonderful date earlier that week and discussed going on another. Sandy didn't know it, but I'd had a crush on her for quite a while. I couldn't believe that this beautiful girl was interested in me!

A few of us were at a friend's house when the phone rang; my friend answered, and I could tell that she was getting horrible news. She hung up, walked into the living room, and told us that Sandy and her friend Kelli were driving around a corner too fast, lost control of their vehicle, and collided head-on with a commercial truck. They were both fighting for their lives, and it didn't look hopeful. I remember crying so hard and feeling so very lost, but the rest of that day was a blur to me. Unable to accept that she could leave us, and so afraid that she would, I decided that she and Kelli would not die.

Sadly, this was not the case. Neither girl survived. I think we all feel invincible as kids, but in that awful moment when we experience the death of someone our age, we lose not only a friend but also the illusion of our own immortality. I was unable to reconcile the feeling of injustice, and it shook me to my core. Sandy and Kelli were so young and full of life. I had been looking forward to seeing Sandy again. Then suddenly, she was gone. I was a mess, and my poor cousin Rob was worse; he and Kelli had been dating for a while. Sandy's death, stacked on top of my failure at college, caused me to fall into a deep, deep depression.

I started the next semester ill-equipped for the challenge, and, once again, I was failing. I could say that I didn't care about succeeding or making my parents proud, but that wasn't true. I did care. I had always envisioned going to college, and I had always thought of myself as a good and capable guy. All of that was evaporating because I couldn't seem to stop myself from flunking. For the first time, I was truly seeing myself as a failure, and this was more than I could bear. I crashed. Hello, rock bottom.

Back in the Rubble

I had failed, and it leveled me. We have all heard the saying that "failure is just a step on the path to success," and indeed, it is, but have you come to believe that yet? If not, it's important that you learn to believe it. It took me quite a while to do so, but I promise that embracing failure has turned my life around. One of my favorite icons, Johnny Cash, once famously said, "You build on failure. You use it as a stepping stone. Close the door on the past. You don't try to forget the mistakes, but you don't dwell on them. You don't let it have any of your energy, or any of your time, or any of your space."

Hell yes, Johnny!

But I can tell you that back at this point in my life, I believed the exact opposite. Failure to me was a brick wall—a dead end. It was clear to me that I could not and never would pass college, and therefore my life from that point forward would be something less. My dreams would be smaller. *I* would be smaller. I would be a failure. I was so sure I had hit a wall that failure became just that: an impenetrable barrier.

I never went back to school.

Repeating that quote attributed to Henry Ford yet again, "Whether you think you can, or you think you can't—you're right." I wasn't ready to believe in me.

The author J.K. Rowling is a great example of what can happen when you fail (and fail, and fail) yet keep going. In 1995, twelve major publishers rejected *Harry Potter and the Philosopher's Stone.* Imagine being rejected by so many publishers and still moving forward. To her remarkable credit, she faced that rejection twelve times yet kept trying. What does she have to say about failure?

> Failure is so important. We speak about success all the time. It is the ability to resist failure or use failure that often leads to greater success. I've met people who don't want to try for fear of failing.

Where did Rowling's tenacity get her? In 1997, Bloomsbury, a small publisher of children's books, released that first Harry Potter book, printing only a thousand copies. Later renamed *Harry Potter and the Sorcerer's Stone*, it went on to win the Nestle Smarties Book Prize and the British Book Award for Children's Book of the Year. The attention these awards garnered opened the floodgates, and to date, Rowling's Harry Potter series has sold more than four hundred million books. Four hundred *million*! For her, failure wasn't a wall. Unlike me, she didn't let it stop her.

So, would you rather be like me back in those days, or like J.K. Rowling? It's a no-brainer, right? But are you sure? She faced a lot of failure, a lot of pain. Perhaps you're wondering what would have happened if she wasn't up for that kind of challenge. But I have a better question: Where can your life take you if you simply start trying? If you inevitably fail (as you will) and you still keep on trying? This is being tenacious. And I bet you will be happily surprised by where it leads you when you put it into practice in your life.

I have been pretty hard on myself in this chapter, but this is a book about not giving up, and I gave up! If I may, at this point, I'd like to cut myself a little slack. I did fail. I did give up. But was college really my dream? Or was it just an expectation? I did not have the desire to go back to school and face that defeat again, but is it possible that I was chasing the wrong dream simply to satisfy others? What would it have looked like if I had truly loved what I was doing?

To learn from my experience, I suggest that you find the right dream, the right cause, the right passion, then dive in and face whatever failure may come. If you discover that you are not chasing the right dream, and you are sure your conclusion isn't a cop-out, then you have my permission to let go of that pursuit in favor of finding a real passion.

Psyched

I think we can all agree that, passionate or not, I was a mess at the time. I needed help figuring out why I was incapable of trying. I started seeing a psychologist. Every two weeks, I would trudge into his office, facing my fears, hoping for a better me. It was tough work. We tore away at my dysfunction's emotional armor, leaving me broken and exposed. That's a dramatic description, but they were dramatic sessions.

The good doctor showed great care in trying to help me, but sometimes I felt like he was completely confused about what we were trying to achieve. Then, just when I was about to give up, he would make a connection that pulled his motives into brilliant perspective. He helped me face my failures even though the work was often painful. Sometimes, when you are working on yourself like that, you need to tear yourself down before you can build yourself up.

One day, our efforts crescendoed into a simple but stunning conclusion. He presented his observation as really important. I was all ears and ready to accept whatever it was he was thinking.

Please forgive my redundancy as I repeat what I foreshadowed at the beginning of this chapter. The doctor's diagnosis was one of the more impactful moments in my life.

"Scott, you have a debilitating fear of failure." He continued to explain that in the most challenging areas of my life I had not been allowing myself to try—that when I apply myself, the fear of failure kicks in even more. The fear manifests into a swarm of emotions that keeps me from properly functioning, and I have an anxiety attack. I fail, ironically, because I am so afraid to fail. I sat still and listened to him, absorbing every bit of what he had to say. He explained that this sort of illogical phobia was not uncommon—that it was, in fact, quite common and very, very real.

Finally, he drove it home with "Scott, what I am about to tell you is true, although it doesn't make logical sense . . . It would be easier for you to grab a red-hot stove, hang on, and mutilate yourself than to actually try."

That truth hung heavily in the air for a beat or two. Then I burst into tears and could not stop crying. The breakthrough was overwhelming. If you have ever seen some actor on a TV show pretending to have a psychological breakthrough, you might think they were overacting. Perhaps not. When it happened to me in real life, I was truly hysterical. I cried so hard for so very long that my stomach hurt, and I could hardly speak. The funny thing is that these were not tears of pain. Sure, there was some sadness. But these were tears of relief!

I finally saw *how* I was broken. It was as if I suddenly understood the greatest mystery of my life. The conclusion was sobering, but the understanding brought hope. I knew what was wrong with me, and maybe—just maybe—I could fix it. Thank you, doctor.

There is real power in understanding ourselves. After all, how can you hope to fix what you don't know is broken? Have you ever had a moment when you were shocked to discover the source of one of your shortcomings? Perhaps you learned that you are afraid of heights as you climbed your first tree. But, in this instance, I am talking more about realizing a deeper truth about yourself—one that has significantly held you back. A hidden fear or doubt that may be hindering your love life, your career aspirations, or, as in my case, your ability to even try. I would strongly suggest that you seek out the truth that lies beneath your behaviors and maybe even get help as I did. There is no shame in seeking guidance. I am proud that I did.

NHL first-round draft pick and ten-year league veteran Colin Wilson knows a little something about that moment when your inner enemy is revealed, and he has generously agreed to share his powerful story with us.

COLIN WILSON
ON BEING TENACIOUS

I am so grateful to be a part of Scotty's book. When he said it was about tenacity, I was all in.

My story begins with my forefathers. I was a third-generation hockey player, so despite the tremendous odds against it, there was this expectation that I would get into the NHL, and that was great by me. All I ever wanted to do was play. Some of my best memories were of hitting the ice at a hockey pond my dad built. The temperature might have been -20 degrees Celsius in

Winnipeg, but I loved it. To this day, whenever the ice-cold air hits my face, I pause and smile. The frosty air takes me back to that frozen pond, working on my game.

Just thinking about it now, I can hear the sound of playing "sticks in the middle." My buddies and I would pile all of our sticks in the center of the pond, then one guy would pull his tuk (hat) over his eyes and blindly divide the sticks left and right. That's how we would randomly pick teams. I can hear the sound of those sticks rattling across the ice right now. They would get so cold they'd become rock solid—so rigid you could hear it. The memory of that sound brings me right back. There was something so beautiful, so poetic about it all—your breath in the air, the sounds, the sights. It was always so dark in Winnipeg in the winter, so my dad put lights up around the pond. It was so cool.

So, about being tenacious: It's definitely something that has carried me through. There is no way I would have made it to the NHL, much less survived there for over a decade, without it. That said, Scotty asked me to speak specifically about what hidden demon might have held me back. For me, there was a big one: OCD, obsessive compulsive disorder. At first, I was pretty oblivious. Looking back, there were signs, so I guess it has always been with me. Still, when I was younger I never thought much of those odd signs. Riding in the car I would obsessively count trees as we drove. I remember one day at age nine, I started seeing my nose, and once I saw it I couldn't unsee it. Both of our eyes have a clear view of our nose, but our brains choose to block it out. My brain, however, stopped doing that. I actually went to the eye doctor because I thought something was wrong with my vision. That was the first sign of catastrophizing, or hyperfocusing, which is one of the symptoms of OCD. Still, I was assured that my eyes were fine, and I was sent on my way.

At times, my hyperfocus made it impossible to ignore things that shouldn't get attention. There is the example of my nose, but it manifested in other ways too. If something hurt, a normal reaction would be to register that discomfort and move on. You shouldn't be particularly aware of the pain again unless you aggravate it. Not me. At times I would injure myself and the presence of that pain remained in my awareness. If, for example, I had a sore shoulder, it would relentlessly demand my attention, distracting me from playing and stealing some of my focus. In a physical game like hockey, you can imagine how hard this might be. You always have some pain. If I noticed pain on any level from then on, it was always there. And if I told myself to make it go away, that attention would only heighten my awareness of it.

I think normal people's view of their reality includes a wider view of the world than mine. I see things as if through a magnifying glass trained on one little detail at a time. This is problematic, but it can also be fantastic when you have to get something done. It certainly has helped me achieve the skills necessary to play at the NHL level. I am incredibly grateful for my hyperfocus because it helped deliver and shape those skills. Still, it was a double-edged sword, and the darker side of it weighed heavily on me. During my first year in the minors with the Milwaukee Admirals, I was obsessing over my body. I was unwilling to take a full stride because I was afraid I would tweak something. The Nashville Predators (Milwaukee's parent club) staff figured it out, and they flew my parents in for a dinner. It was the general manager (GM), the assistant GM, the team psychologist, my parents, and me. They confronted us with their conclusion, recounting, among other things, my preflight ritual. Before flying I had to clean up the area, I had to touch the outside of the plane, and I had to talk to the pilot. That, coupled with my performance on the ice, led them to their conclusion. "Colin, you have obsessive compulsive disorder."

This is the part where someone else might tell you they were grateful for this thoughtful diagnosis. I was not. I immediately went into denial. I didn't want to listen. I was doing pretty well. I knew only one way to think—one way to be me—and that way was making my dreams come true. Who were they to tell me that was wrong? They prescribed meds, and I took them for about a week and a half before I decided that I just didn't like them. I decided I was good and they were incorrect. I will say that the diagnosis must have registered on some level, because I do remember doing certain things and thinking, *Oh, that must be my OCD.*

I did pretty well for a couple of years, but I remember my first year in the NHL, I pulled my groin. This was probably the traumatic event that triggered my full-on OCD. At the end of practice we were stretching, and I was so hyperfocused on my groin that it was excruciating. I recall turning my head away, fighting back tears. I mean, we are hockey players—we don't cry while stretching. It was such a crushing feeling.

There were other things, but before I go deeper, I'd like to be clear about something. I'm sharing these painful truths because I feel like they might help you. We all have what Scott called our inner demons, but one of the best tools that we have in fighting them is understanding. Please don't think that I am glorifying my path. As you continue to read, it gets a lot less glorious. Likewise, please don't feel sorry for me. I have done and continue to do amazing things. I am sharing this struggle so as you do amazing things, you will be better equipped to fight your inner demons too. If I can share my story and help you understand yourself a little better, then mission accomplished. I know all too well that back then I didn't understand what was happening to me. That lack of understanding—that loss of control—pushed me into some dark places.

Another major struggle was my skates. I never thought about them, really, until I got a pair that felt different, and that was it. From that moment on I started obsessing about skates. Over the next two years I tried every kind there were. They all felt wrong. I would obsess over how I tied them. I would unlace them, then re-lace them repeatedly, desperately trying to make them feel right. I did this as the locker room looked on, for more than a half hour at times, until my hands bled and the coach implored me to stop because it was game time.

It's an awful feeling to look down at your bloody, painful fingers and still be helplessly compelled to keep trying, even though your hands are killing you, giving you yet another thing to hyperfocus on. I would finally yield to the coach and trudge out to play this incredibly fast and dangerous sport, still hyperaware and still feeling like I was trying to skate on stilts. Compounding this was the sweat—the salty sting of it on my cut-up hands screamed for my attention. Then, when the puck landed on my stick, I would become hyperaware that fifteen thousand people (or more) were watching me. I would get so overwhelmed at times, I would not even realize that I had lost the puck and was still skating toward the goal without it. Skating back to the bench and seeing the look on my teammates' faces after a shift like that was painful.

All of this obsession and anxiety took a toll, and I started having real trouble sleeping. That is when things really went off the rails. For the anxiety, I started taking Xanax—a highly addictive pill that makes you feel good. And to help me sleep, I took Seroquel, which is basically a horse tranquilizer. I was also drinking, and worse, at times, I was smoking marijuana and taking cocaine as a coping mechanism. The drugs and alcohol made me feel better in the moment—what I imagined normal must feel like. But when the high would end, it would hit me square in the chest, way worse than any hangover. That description doesn't even come close. Ultimately, the anxiety, obsessing, pills, and drugs all came to a head, and after years of struggle, I finally hit rock bottom.

The skate thing had gone on for too long. I had lost so much sleep that my nervous system was jacked. That's when everything blew up. I remember in 2017, when we won the Western Conference series to advance to the championship, I just wanted to cry. Think about that: I was going to the Stanley Cup Final—every hockey player's dream—but for me it all hurt so bad that in that moment I just wanted to give up.

So why am I taking you here, to this dark, dark place? Two reasons. One, I never gave up. With all of that trauma and OCD, another guy might have collapsed. Because I didn't collapse, I achieved amazing things—things I am so very proud of. Not every day was dark, and the days when the OCD wasn't front and center in my life, it was literally the life I dreamed of. This is a story about being tenacious that I am truly proud of.

That said, the second and most important reason I am sharing my darkest times with you is to offer some advice. Even though I had the stubborn tenacity to power through my OCD, ignoring it and carrying that weight wasn't necessarily the best course of action. I now know that I should have listened to my GMs and accepted their help. My advice to you is to recognize your inner demons early and address them head-on. Don't do what I did. Instead of dragging that burden around like an anchor, do the even harder work of reeling that anchor in. It will probably be twice as hard at first—maybe ten times as hard—but imagine

> how it will feel to live your life without it holding you back. Knowing what I know now, if I could go back to that day when the Predators' management team told me about my OCD, I would tell myself to accept that diagnosis and put as much effort into working on that demon as I did into being great despite it.
>
> The beautiful thing is that's exactly what I am doing now. I not only am personally working on my OCD but am working toward my degree in psychology as well. My goal is twofold: to better understand myself and to couple this knowledge with my experience of OCD to really help other people.

I think what Colin is doing is just so beautiful. I love that he is turning his struggle into yet another gift he shares with others. It is the ultimate silver lining.

Colin has lived an amazing life, and he has spent it doing what he loves. To his great credit, he played hockey at the highest level for over a decade against incredible odds. And, as you now know, he did it at times through gut-wrenching internal struggles. Colin's is indeed a great story of tenacity. But as he pointed out, the lesson here is to find and face your demon. That's what he is doing right now as he gets his psychology degree. He has been blessed to find a second pursuit he loves, helping people. It's an awesome next chapter in his story, and I am so proud to call him a friend.

Authors note: It's been a few years since Colin wrote this. He is now six years sober! He received his psychology degree and uses it and his experiences to help others through AA and by sharing his story here and elsewhere. Way to go, pal!

OK, so back to my struggle. With some help from the psychologist, I found my demon. I finally knew what was wrong with me. But what was I to do? Go back to school? You know by now that school wasn't really my dream. How could I expect to overcome my fear without some real motivation?

Luckily, the good doctor, my therapist, supplied me with plenty of fuel for thought. I wanted to be better. I was tired of failing. I was scared I wouldn't be able to overcome my dysfunction and that my life would be something way less than I'd expected and far less than I had dreamed. I had all this pent-up frustration, yet no direction. Could I be more? I really wanted to believe I could . . .

(Action shots of Colin, and a team picture of the Nashville Predators with me front and center in a ridiculous custom suit!)

*All photos and supplemental material can be found on TENACIOUSBOOK.COM

CHAPTER 3

Don't Stop Believing

The future belongs to those who believe in the beauty of their dreams.

—Eleanor Roosevelt

In addition to attending college, at this point I was holding down three jobs. One of them was waiting tables at a Howard Johnson's. For those of you who haven't had the pleasure, HoJo's is a mid-level chain of restaurants and hotels that sprouted up along highways. This one was located off Interstate 90, the main route from upstate New York to Boston. Being a waiter at Howard Johnson's wasn't my ideal job, but I needed the money, so I endured. I stood just inside the entrance, waiting for my first customers to arrive on what would be another long, tedious day.

I can still feel the soles of my Docksiders clinging to the floor, the maple syrup from breakfast proving more resilient than our efforts to clean. My cheap khaki pants already felt muggy on my legs, my once-white polo was no longer bright, and my green apron was frayed. Pinned to it (a bit askew) was my name tag, SCOTT. I sighed. Was this really me? Was this my life? Was this all I would be? All that my dysfunction would allow?

I wasn't particularly good at waiting tables. My short-term memory was fickle, making the job stressful. So many times, I would stand facing the cooks in the kitchen, positive I had forgotten something. All too often I was right, letting a customer down. I had nightmares about being overwhelmed while serving too many tables. (These dreams are actually common among servers.) I can still feel myself nervously fumbling with the extra jelly containers in my apron pocket, forcing a smile, waiting for an indecisive customer while impossibly falling behind. (Yes, the fondled jelly containers would ride in our aprons for hours to save us a trip to the kitchen. Yes, they might have previously been on someone else's dirty plate. And yes, that is gross. If you dined with me, I'm sorry; we relied on shortcuts to keep up.)

I dreaded working my shifts. I had all of this pent-up energy and desire. I am even tempted to say I had ambition. But ambition for what? I knew I wanted to be more. I knew I was tired of failing—tired of being afraid. I had all the fuel but no spark. What I didn't realize then is that I wasn't excited enough about anything to inspire the kind of hard work necessary to rise above my circumstances or shortcomings.

Are you failing to achieve something right now? Do you feel stuck like I did then? Ask yourself if you are working toward a future you really want or just biding time. This would have been a great question to ask nineteen-year-old me, flunking college and standing there stuck in syrup, going nowhere fast. "Hey kid, you're miserable. Ever thought of doing something else?" Funnily enough, I wonder if I would have defended my poor choices. I probably would have.

It would be wonderful if we could go back in time, but absent that possibility, we can do something almost as good. We can step away from *this* moment and take a good look at ourselves right now. What would "future you" wish you'd started doing by now? Is there a passion you could pursue today? Is it something exciting or scary? What if instead of anticipating the regrets of tomorrow, you dared to embrace your dreams today?

What I can see now is that real tenacity is best when it is sparked by a dream—an exciting vision of what you want to accomplish. Yes, I wanted to get a college degree, but it wasn't my dream, nor a step toward one. Often, responsibilities like school and work are great steps on the path to fulfilling your aspirations. But I wasn't on that path. I didn't have an aspiration other than to succeed. Instead, I was letting failure define me. I was allowing it to crush my soul. Does this sound familiar? If so, take a hard look at where your energy is going. Are you beating yourself up for not achieving something you don't even want?

Right now you might be thinking, *You don't understand, Scott. My choices are limited. I have to work at (fill in the blank).* And maybe you do. But maybe you don't. For example, did I truly have to succeed at college? At the time, I felt I absolutely had to. Succeeding academically is a brilliant idea, but I wasn't succeeding and it was killing me. Was school really getting my best efforts? Or could I have found something else I *truly* loved? I can tell you I didn't *love* school, and I certainly didn't love standing there at HoJo's that morning.

As a Muzak version of Journey's "Don't Stop Believing" played faintly from the restaurant's overhead speakers, I laughed to myself. "Don't stop believing . . . in what?" I lifted my left foot momentarily, freeing it from the grip of the sticky floor, then placed it back down where it would remain stuck for a while. It felt like a metaphor for my life. It had been only a few months since Sandy passed. I was still processing the diagnosis from my psychologist, which had rocked my world, and of course I was flunking out of college. I was deeply depressed and lost.

Just then, something caught my eye. It was a glint of shiny steel outside the restaurant window. An amazing-looking bus had just pulled into the lot. It had a massive space shuttle painted on the side of it. I have always been a space nut. Did the people inside work for NASA?

Before I get much further in this chapter, realize this all happened forty years ago! Please forgive anything I might not remember exactly right; it's not for a lack of trying. I managed to track down many of the people within these stories, but some I couldn't find, and still others I was sad to discover were no longer with us. Doing my best to get it right has had its rewards; I have loved connecting with those I did find!

The Space Shuttle

I rushed over to the hostess and asked her to please seat the bus passengers in my section, and she agreed. As I watched them exit the vehicle, my anticipation quickly fell to disappointment. They were all dressed in black, and several of them had long hair. They did not look like they worked for NASA.

I took their drink orders, then asked, "Why the bus?"

One of them spoke up in the thickest of Irish accents. "We work for the band U2."

Holy cow! I was taken aback, but coolly replied, "Oh, OK." Then I walked to the kitchen to collect myself, my mind buzzing.

Why was my mind buzzing? Let me give you some perspective. This was during the peak of U2's explosive popularity. This was 1987, their album *The Joshua Tree* had just been released, and it was phenomenal. Suddenly, U2 was the biggest band in the world and, in my opinion, the most exciting thing to hit rock and roll since the Beatles. I played the album incessantly. It was the soundtrack to my life, but, more than that, the music was a comfort, the songs almost a place where I could hide from my hurtful reality. These guys worked for U2? Still incredulous, I went back out to the table with their drinks. I had a lot of questions.

"Hi, how can you guys possibly work for U2? How is that even a thing? I thought you'd have to be Bono's cousin or something to get a job like that."

The guy who seemed to be in charge (let's call him Liam, as sadly, he was one of the people I just couldn't reach) lit up with a mischievous grin.

"We put on the show. Seven of us are the very best at what we do." He paused and then gestured to the eighth man, playfully continuing, "And this is AJ, Bono's cousin."

The table cracked up as AJ smiled broadly. With the ice broken, my questions must have seemed endless. The picture coming together in my mind was wild. These guys worked for U2, my favorite band ever, and this was actually something you could do with your life. That was beyond fascinating to me. Traveling around the world with Bono, the Edge, and the boys, getting paid to go to shows? Wow!

They were wonderfully kind, and I found myself having a really great time with them. Months of depressed and bottled-up feelings seemed to evaporate. We were all having a blast, and at times I had them laughing so hard that they couldn't eat. Liam kept saying, "We can't give you tickets." I honestly wasn't looking for tickets, or anything, so as a part of the fun, I feigned insult and countered that I was going to throw him out of the restaurant. This ruse escalated over the next hour.

By the end of the meal, they actually insisted that I come to the next show. It was in Worcester, Massachusetts, a few hours' drive away. I hesitated to say yes—I didn't want them to think I was pretending to have fun with them just to get tickets. My pride wanted me to say no, but I was too intrigued.

"OK, I guess so. I mean yes, *please!*"

Liam laughed and told me they would leave tickets for me at the will-call window in Worcester. Great! I hadn't been to many shows, but I wanted to find out more about what these guys did. Honestly, even though U2 was my favorite band, I was more fascinated by the crew than by the opportunity to see the show.

My great friends and roommates, Rob Wright and Matt Guilbault, hopped in the car with me and we headed toward Massachusetts. On the three-hour drive to the show, they had fun teasing me, saying that the people I waited on almost certainly didn't work for U2. They probably all worked for AC/DC and were laughing their asses off thinking about the three of us driving out to a U2 show, one where we wouldn't have tickets waiting. I laughed along with their heckling, confident, however, that the crew was being honest. We arrived, went to the ticket window, and were not disappointed. They had indeed left three free tickets for us!

As we waited outside for doors to open, a long black limo pulled up. The fans went wild as Bono himself stepped out of the car. Security was desperate to keep people back, but Bono walked right up to the mosh. What a presence he has. In awe I watched him work the crowd. He was cool, calm, and collected—smiling the whole time. He conveyed joy and gratitude. I was a bit shy, but Rob ended up close enough to talk to him!

The doors opened and, with tickets in hand, we filed through security like cattle. Our seats were amazing. We were on the floor, close to the stage. I struck up a conversation with our seat neighbors, two beautiful young ladies who were infatuated with the band.

They were buzzing with excitement. Heck, everyone was. You could feel this was something special—the hottest band in the world at the moment their fame was igniting.

Honestly, I wasn't a concert fan. To be completely truthful, I mostly went to concerts in the hope of meeting cute ladies. You know, I was a teenager. Concerts were cool; ladies were cooler. This felt different, though. I was enthralled with *The Joshua Tree*. I stood there vibrating with anticipation.

The lights dropped, and the hair on my arms stood up when the opening keyboard notes from "Where the Streets Have No Name" poured out of the massive PA. Here we go!

Bono was the epicenter. His charms were so irresistible, he cast a spell over everyone. The feedback loop between Bono and us in the crowd was insane. We fed off each other, building to a frenzy. It felt like all thirteen thousand of us were on the same roller coaster ride—up, then down, anticipation, then incredible release! Bono led us in a way that I had never been led before. He seduced us all. I know, the description is over the top. I'm reaching for the words—maybe you just had to be there.

That experience was a display of power and charisma unlike anything I had ever felt. But here's the icing on the cake: What did Bono do with that power? He spent that currency teaching us about injustice in the world. Twice Bono stopped to speak of an organization called Amnesty International. In the midst of a sold-out crowd in an absolute frenzy, Bono wedged in messages about human rights and how the audience could make a difference. The fans loved it. They basked in his enlightenment. In that moment, Bono became one of my very few heroes, and he remains one to this day.

At the end of the show, I managed to make my way to the lighting console to thank a few of the crew guys, and they asked if I wanted to come back tomorrow.

"*Yes!*" was my emphatic response. I made the three-hour trip home, more excited than I had been in a very long time.

Paradigm Shift

The next day, I called in sick to work and hopped back in the car, this time alone. The U2 guys had suggested that I come early, so I did and was able to park right by their bus with the space shuttle image on it. As I was getting out of the car, one of the crew was stepping off the bus. He smiled, waved me over, and took me backstage to get my ticket. As we walked, we ran right into Bono and the Edge. *Holy shit!* The Edge had a question about the show for my crew escort, who answered him and then introduced me.

"This is Scott, he's hilarious."

There I stood, face-to-face with Bono and the Edge.

Stunned, I was anything but hilarious. I was too awestruck and tongue-tied to speak.

Smiling and patient, Bono and the Edge took a beat, allowing me to at least say something funny . . . or not. When it was clear that I was currently incapable of humor, they chuckled. I guess you could say I made them laugh after all. They both had a great demeanor: cool, but approachable and real. The wild thing is, as awesome as it was to meet my heroes, I was even more intrigued by the industry I was discovering. As the crew member and I continued walking, I peppered our conversation with a bunch of questions about touring. He answered them all, and I was riveted.

He grabbed me a ticket and showed me back outside where I should wait. They had work to do, of course. I passed the time patiently, but when the doors opened I headed straight for the sound and lighting consoles. I was so curious! I was in awe of the technology, and every answer they offered brought two more questions. It was amazing to learn about all that it took to put a show like this together.

I was especially interested in the lighting console. I was watching the opening act, Lone Justice, when their lighting director noticed my fascination. He gestured for me to come close and demonstrated to the beat.

"This button, this button, this button.

"This . . . is . . . the chorus.

"Do . . . you . . . see?

"This button, this button, this button."

I nervously nodded yes. Was he going to let me run the lights? During the verse, the lights were static. He slid his chair aside and asked me if I was ready to try. I nodded and stepped up, remembering the progression he'd shown me. He gestured as the chorus arrived, and I started pushing the buttons on the beat. I was running the lights! I had the world's biggest remote control! Each button push ignited different banks of lights, flooding the stage more than one hundred feet away with brilliant colors. This was incredible to me. The chorus ended and I was grinning from ear to ear. For a moment I was running the show!

After Lone Justice, a few of the other crew guys came out front to the consoles. One of them had just been to China with Stevie Wonder! Holy cow! Back then, no one went to China. The U2 crew were full of fascinating stories from around the world. I relished the idea of traveling, and these guys got paid to do it! It was enthralling.

Finally out of questions, I stood in the middle of the arena processing this exciting lifestyle. Then it happened . . . arguably the biggest moment in my entire life. The lights went out and the crowd went wild, really wild. There was no safety lighting back then—it was pitch black. Thousands of people screaming together produced the most incredible sound. I stood there in the dark, overwhelmed by the roar, and it hit me:

THIS IS WHAT YOU ARE GOING TO DO WITH YOUR LIFE! You love music, technology, people, and travel—this is what you are going to do with your life!

These people roamed the world, implementing incredible technology, making the music happen. The product they produced was the roar of the crowd. The sound of joy. They made people happy for a living! Not just happy, but so happy that they screamed!

Amazing! And the icing on the cake? Bono was trying to make the world a better place. *Count me in!* Right then, right there, I had a paradigm shift, and I have been a different man ever since. For the first time in my life, I truly knew what I wanted to do. It was the most powerful, positive feeling I had ever had, and it remains the most powerful moment to this day!

But then a serious realization followed right on its heels, and my heart sank. I was going to have to try. And we all know what happens when I try. *Not anymore.* There in the dark, I swore that I would start trying, and never stop trying, no matter how many times I failed or how much it hurt. I'd persist until I was living this dream.

I made myself this somber promise, and at that moment, true, lasting tenacity was sparked within me. I have often wondered if I would have made such a commitment to myself had I not been at rock bottom. There is a power in having nothing to lose. I am certainly not recommending that you drive your life to your lowest low as your next step. No, what I want to share is that even if you feel you have nothing to lose, don't stop believing.

I spent the rest of that amazing U2 show reinforcing my commitment to myself, believing in me, daring to dream. Hell yes, traveling with music would be incredible. Hell yes, I was going to do it no matter what. For the first time in my life I had a dream that was mine.

My tenacity had been sparked!

Before telling you where that ultimately led me, let's check in with our next guest. Earlier in the chapter, I was standing in syrup as the song "Don't Stop Believin'" came over the radio. Journey member Jonathan Cain had written beautiful words, but in that moment the song begged a personal question for me: *Believin' in what?* I was on the precipice of discovering my dream, but I didn't know what it was yet.

Since Jonathan had such a presence on that day through his song, it seems fitting that he have a presence in the pages of this book as well. It is with great pride that I introduce Jonathan Cain. Jonathan, would you be kind enough to share with us the tenacious story behind the making of the song "Don't Stop Believin'"?

JONATHAN CAIN
ON BEING TENACIOUS

Thanks, Scott, you are so right that being tenacious makes all the difference. It has for me!

All I ever wanted to do was make music; I dreamed of being a rock star. My dream came true when I found myself in the band The Babies with John Waite. Sadly, I found that the dream was not all it was cracked up to be. The Babies were bankrupt for years and, as such, barely paid me—if they did at all! Despite enduring a grueling tour schedule, I was unable to provide for my family. The strain of the schedule and the lack of funds were tearing me apart. Then, on top of it all, my dog was in a tragic accident. I found myself unable to afford the nine hundred dollars needed to care for my pup. I swallowed my pride and called my dad, asking for a loan, but then I snapped. I asked him if I was just dreaming. Should I just come home to Chicago and get a real job? I had lived the rock and roll life in LA for ten years, and it wasn't kind. I had had enough, and I just wanted to quit.

My dad didn't say anything for a minute, and I waited. Then he said, "No, John, this is your vision. I'll give you the loan. You gotta stay put." He continued, "Stay the course, don't stop believing." I was like, "That was beautiful, Dad." Those last three words hit me, and I doodled them down in this little lyric book I kept.

My dad had always been my greatest champion, and he certainly was in this moment. Even though Dad didn't really have any money, he sent me the cash to take care of my dog and, more importantly, provide a little emotional fuel for my tenacity. I didn't quit, and as we all know, I was offered the incredible opportunity to join the band Journey. Shortly thereafter, we were working on the *Escape* album when Steve (Perry) called me.

"The record label wants another song," he said. I was kinda pissed—we had already poured our hearts into seventeen songs. How many did they need? Were none of them good enough? I tramped around the house aggravated for a few minutes, then sat down in a huff. In front of me was my little lyric notebook. I sighed and started thumbing through it. On the last page, my dad's words jumped out at me. I sang them in the melody that we all know, and instinctively added, "Hold on to that feeling."

I liked it. I grabbed the phone and called Steve. Instead of saying hello, I just sang the opening line. "Don't stop believin', hold on to that feeling."

Steve's reply? "Yes!!!"

The result? An anthem for tenacity that I firmly believe is the reason Journey made it into the Rock & Roll Hall of Fame. I'm proud to say that it became the most downloaded song of all time. Thanks, Dad!

So, at this point, I'd say to everyone reading this, "Don't stop believing! Be tenacious about believing in whatever dream matters to you, and don't stop chasing that dream!"

Thanks, Jonathan, it is such an honor to have you share this story. It gives your incredible song even more meaning. While I'm at it, thank you for your book, appropriately named *Don't Stop Believin'*. I enjoyed it so much that I read it twice!

Well, readers, as you can see, with a little love and support from his dad, Jonathan did not quit. Let's take a moment to give a huge shout-out to those who love and support us. The people who believe in us can make all the difference. In this case, Jonathan's dad encouraged him to keep believing, to keep working at his dream. How lucky was Jonathan to have a dream to chase? How lucky was I to have discovered my dream? How tenacious might you be if you found and let yourself pursue the right dream for you?

(Jonathan Cain, the bus emblazoned with the space shuttle that started it all, and my Howard Johnson's name tag. Yes, I still have it!)

*All photos and supplemental material can be found on TENACIOUSBOOK.COM

CHAPTER 4

When Sparks Fly

You're only given a little spark of madness; you mustn't lose it.

—Robin Williams

A spark—such a powerful thing! It has the potential to ignite a tremendous blaze or perhaps trigger the explosion that drives the pistons on a tour bus. A single flicker over some kindling could be lifesaving if you are exposed to the elements and nearly freezing to death. The last analogy feels the most on point for me back then. My failure was killing me, and my spirit was dying of exposure, when, suddenly, U2 lit a spark within me. For the first time in my life, I truly wanted something. I had discovered a passion. Much like the crowd at that U2 show, my heart was screaming for more.

I had tried my best for almost a year in college—a noble endeavor—but it brought me nothing. It made me feel small and incapable. Remember this: True tenacity is fueled by passion. If you want to unlock everything that tenacity can bring to your life, spark your passion. That was the missing ingredient. Suddenly, thanks to U2, I felt as if I could take over the world. Somehow, I knew in my heart that I was going to do this impossible thing.

What dream might be sparked for you? Where is your passion? Are you willing to ignite a new reality for yourself? Even if your dream seems unrealistic, bizarre, or unachievable, it's still possible. You could certainly argue that going from being stuck in the syrup at Howard Johnson's to touring with the greatest band in the world was crazy and improbable at best. It didn't even register with me that this was a seemingly impossible pursuit. What if you let yourself chase the big dreams? The scary ones? The bizarre ones? How exciting might your life be if you started thinking that fearlessly? How hard might you try to achieve something incredible versus something merely expected of you?

> The greater danger for most of us lies not in setting our aim too high and falling short; but in setting our aim too low and achieving our mark.
> —Michelangelo

I drove home that night rocked by the discovery of a way of life I found utterly thrilling and irresistibly attractive. And yet I was literally driving in the wrong direction. The U2 crew were living in what to me was a dream world, and I was headed back to my life—a place where things weren't going very well. I needed to make their reality my future. But how? Where would I even start? Doubt and fear began creeping back in. For a while they had the usual effect; I did nothing. But the spark of inspiration from that night had found some kindling. The dream was lit. I knew a choice had to be made. Either I would fan the flame or keep hiding behind my fear. Which was it going to be?

The T-Shirt

A few weeks after my revelation at the U2 show, I was sitting in my room back in downtown Troy, New York. I had been going through the motions in my life while trying to process all that had happened. Sandy had been killed, I was still flunking out of school, the breakthrough with my psychologist was still fresh, and the encounter with U2 had sparked such vivid dreams. I had been emotionally astray for years, and I still was, but now I was also exploding with inspiration.

The spark had connected with something combustible inside of me, leading to an explosion not unlike the one that drives the piston of a tour bus. But just as what happens within a big engine, a void followed the explosion—a vacuum where I built up more fuel hoping for the next spark. There I sat, in that vacuum, growing in desire, fighting doubt, and hoping for another explosion, another push of momentum.

I looked down at the bootleg T-shirt I had purchased in the parking lot at the U2 concert. I wore it often. As it lay dirty on my floor, I contemplated its link to my dream. I flipped the T-shirt over and looked at the tour dates on the back. This was before the Internet existed, so there was no such thing as googling the band's schedule. The tour was far away at the moment, Europe in fact, but they would be close soon! In fact, they were coming to the Nassau Coliseum on Long Island, only a few hours away. At that moment the next spark ignited. *Boom!* Since I was convinced that this is what I was going to do with my life, Nassau is where I needed to be. I was going to that show, and somehow it would lead me toward my dream.

I smiled. All at once I had a different feeling—the dread and fear now had company. I had hope. I had dreams of what my life could be. I was going to travel the world working with music. I made myself a promise in the dark at that concert; I vowed I would try, and never stop trying, until I made that dream a reality. I promised myself I would be tenacious!

For my buddy Scott Hamilton, the spark ignited when his skates hit the ice and he discovered that he could be good at something. For Colin Wilson, that spark was arguably with him from conception, inherited from his dad. For Jonathan Cain, that spark was music. I was curious about where my pal and country music superstar Dierks Bentley thought he got his spark. When we sat down to talk about it, I was thrilled that he claimed that he got the goosebumps from my story. That really meant a lot coming from a guy who doles out goosebumps by the thousands every show. I asked him two questions: Was tenacity an important ingredient in your amazing journey? And was there a moment when it was sparked? Here's what he had to say . . .

DIERKS BENTLEY
ON BEING TENACIOUS

It's funny, I had a slightly smaller crowd than a sold-out arena at my spark moment—arguably I had two spark moments. For me, the start of it all was meeting a new friend at his house when I was thirteen. I was blown away to see that he had an electric guitar, an amplifier, and some distortion pedals. I was like, *Whoa! I still remember the feeling. So you don't just listen to music, you actually make music?! Wow! Could I do that?*

Then I started playing guitar too. For some reason, what really stuck out to me was the thought that I can change my mood. By playing this instrument, I can dictate how I feel. I don't know why that stuck out to me—it's just . . . music. But I realized I could participate in it and it could have a direct influence on how I felt. I knew from right then I wanted to do something involving guitar. Arguably, it was my spark moment, except . . .

Four years later, when I was seventeen, a friend played me two songs that introduced me to country music: "Blues Man" by Hank Williams Jr. and "That's Country" by Marty Stuart. They changed me forever. When I heard the last note of "That's Country," I fell down into a chair and was like, *Wow!* In that moment I knew, without a doubt, exactly what I wanted to do. Everything just lined up. I mean, I've had that experience a couple of times in my life—when I met my wife would be one of them. But yeah, it was almost like a slot machine where the coin goes down, it hits all the levers, and *boom*, you just know! I knew! I'd found direction. I had my North Star.

That spark ignited my passion for country music. And with it, tenacity! Once you have that fire, it's just limitless how much you can do because it's your passion. I started off by just practicing at home—constantly working on learning country songs and on my own songs—and then cowriting with people. I had a voracious hunger to get better at my craft. I was hooked. I mean *hooked*. Like a fish with a barbed hook and no way to get it out—that kind of hooked.

I was also going to Lower Broadway in downtown Nashville, listening to other bands play and learning how they do it. BR549 or Wayne the Train Hancock and the Side Men were huge influences on me. I eventually put together my own band and got a gig at Springwater Supper Club & Lounge. That was my first real gig. I played there every Wednesday, often for nobody, for free Busch Light beer. But for me it wasn't about playing in front of people and getting recognized; it was about having a place to go work. I didn't care if anyone was there or not, you know. I just wanted to get better at what I was trying to do. And that led to another gig playing downtown where there wasn't a PA system, so I had to go put one together. It was a total pain in the ass. I'd have to load the PA in the back of my truck, drive to Second Avenue, park with the flashers on, and try to dump everything really quickly into the building, hopefully without getting a ticket. Then I'd hunt for a free place to park; there was no money to pay for parking. I'd play the gig for hours and then tear this stuff back down, get my truck, and reverse the whole process. We're talking about huge speakers on heavy stands, but . . . I loved them. Heck, I loved it all.

Looking back on that now, I'm like, *Wow, that was a lot of work*. The whole deal, every step along the way. But those were some of the best days of my life playing Lower Broad. All that stuff was just so fun.

Yeah, I'd see guys like Joe Nichols down there playing, and he'd get picked up and suddenly have a record deal. I wasn't really frustrated about that because I was just so happy to be doing what I was doing. And that continued for a long time. I turned down a lot of opening-act tours because I just liked doing my own thing with my band, playing the clubs and bars. I wasn't focused on stardom. I was happy.

That first gig downtown was the pinnacle of that certain goal. But then you settle in and there's the next step. OK, now we should get a gig with a bigger crowd. Then, how do we get in front of certain record label people? Can we get a publishing deal? Finally, you get a record deal, and you think that's the top of the mountain, until you realize, *Oh, now I'm starting all over again*. Because having a record deal doesn't mean anything. You have to get a song on the radio. It's just a never-ending mountain that you're climbing.

Without the passion that moment sparked, without tenacity, the climb wouldn't be possible. Heck, the reason I was able to succeed in the music business at all is because of tenacity. I'm certainly not the best singer in town. I never had any connections or "ins" to the music business. I didn't know anybody in Nashville when I moved here. I'm not a great guitar player—I play well enough to write songs. When it comes to songwriting, I don't have any special gift. I just have the determination to succeed. You can't be tenacious without having passion. You have to have borderline obsession—almost like a disease—and a desire to do whatever you're interested in pursuing. From the moment of that spark—the discovery of country music and the discovery of my passion—being tenacious has unavoidably become natural to me.

So my motivation for doing this was a love of country music. It had nothing to do with fame or celebrity. My spark moment wasn't watching an arena go wild for someone in the spotlight. It was just the music. Music has always been the reason. So, yes, I had a spark moment, and yes, it changed my life forever!

Let me see if I can put a bow on my view of tenacity—channel my best Marty Stuart, the king of a wrap-up. Man, he's so good—better than anyone I've ever heard.

Here goes. There's a quote I associate with the great producer Jerry Bradford. It's written on his tombstone here in Nashville, but it actually came from President Calvin Coolidge.

> Nothing in this world can take the place of persistence.
> Talent will not: nothing is more common than unsuccessful men with talent.
> Genius will not; unrewarded genius is almost a proverb.
> Education will not: the world is full of educated derelicts.
> Persistence and determination alone are omnipotent.

How do I remember that? I actually took that quote, printed it up, and put it on the cover of one of my songwriter notebooks. It

> stared back at me to remind me that it's all about consistency and determination, which I would say is the definition of tenacity. It just comes down to how relentlessly you're willing to work for it. And there's no shortcuts, you know. In this town, you may get a record deal earlier than somebody else, but at the end of the day, you're going to pay your dues. I think you can look back on the entire music business and all the artists who have succeeded, and on the surface, you may see a pretty face, or a good voice, or someone who had a hit song. But if you dug a little deeper under the surface—not very deep at all—you would find out how much work has gone into that career, probably from an early age.
>
> There's always a story. And the story always revolves around being tenacious.

I don't know about you all, but now *I've* got goosebumps. Many thanks to Dierks for sharing his spark with us. It's awesome. I'm so grateful for his insight *and* his music. As an aside, we played hockey together for years on the Nashville Iceholes. None of our teammates worked harder or were as tenacious on the ice than Dierks was.

As all you readers can see, while Dierks's story was wildly different from mine, he also experienced a moment when everything changed—when a spark ignited his dream and drove him to do incredible things. I love the story he recounted here, but I will protest a few things he said. Dierks's voice is so special; it has a great quality to it. That voice, coupled with the amazing heartfelt songs he writes . . . Man, I could listen to his music all day long, and sometimes I do!

Meanwhile, back to my story. I was still a mess. I had hardly done anything I was proud of. But for the first time in my life I'd found a passion. My dreams were lifting me up from my misery. I had hope. This is the power of the spark—of the game-changing moment when you let yourself hold an incredible dream in your heart. You want to be tenacious? Find a spark that lights your fire, that stokes your fervor. Look at the path it sent Dierks down. You can already see what this spark was doing for me—the hope it was breathing into my being.

Discovering and sparking these dreams is the secret sauce to attaining incredible joy and accomplishment. And great news: It's not one to a customer! Later in the book, you will see that I have embraced spark moments and dared to dream many times, in many ways. I relish pursuing different passions, fanning those flames, and letting them take me to amazing places. Navigating through icebergs in Antarctica, speaking onstage in front of over eighteen thousand people, astronaut training! As you read on, you will see what a tremendous impact sparking a true passion has made in my life as well as in my friends' lives.

Step back again and ask yourself: What would the future version of you wish you were doing right now? Where is your spark?

(Dierks and I are Iceholes! Fun hockey pics of he and I playing ice hockey for the Nashville Iceholes, the Mad Cows, and attending Predator games.)

*All photos and supplemental material can be found on TENACIOUSBOOK.COM

CHAPTER 5

First Steps

The most difficult thing is the decision to act, the rest is merely tenacity. The fears are paper tigers, you can do anything you decide to do.
—Amelia Earhart

The song "Bullet the Blue Sky" rumbled through the stadium, the Edge's long, drawn-out notes slashing through the air. Bono grabbed a handheld spotlight and turned it on the crowd. Its beam, as it swung around the stadium, generated a frenzy wherever it landed. Bono was looking at them! The girls shrieked with excitement; the guys pumped their fists in the air. Just then, the light landed on me, pausing for a moment. The hair stood up on my neck. It was exhilarating! What a cool way to make a living, bringing joy. I loved it. I wanted this life!

Worst Plan Ever

I felt like I was going to explode. This dream was so vivid, so important, I wondered, *If I fail at this, will I ever recover?* I desperately wanted to be on tour with U2 living my best life, but all I had known up to this point was failure. I was afraid to act. Ever been in that situation? Wanting something so badly it actually kept you from trying? Is there something you feel that way about right now as you read this? Oh boy, do I understand. But I urge you, don't let fear win!

Even though I was terrified, I spontaneously did something incredibly important. I decided to intercept the U2 tour on Long Island. That, my friends, is what you call a first step. And taking a first step is undoubtedly *the* most important thing you can do when chasing your dreams.

If you applied the wisdom of Nike back then and told me to "just do it"—just take that first step—I would have had a list of "yeah . . . buts" and reasons why that wouldn't work, at least not in *my* case. But coach me to *just do it* today, and I'd tell you that you couldn't be more right! Let me share with you what happened when I decided to act. Shy of a sensible plan, I allowed my personal desperation and ability to vividly dream dictate a set of choices that, by all reasonable accounts, stretched the plausible. Frankly, the sequence of events was nuts.

The Joshua Me

As U2 returned to the States, I hit the eject button on my life. To my dad's horror, I dropped out of college. I quit all three of my jobs and sold my beautiful Super Sport Camaro for money to live on. My idea was simple and naive: I was going to follow U2 around, living in my Subaru BRAT. I would sneak into the venue every night and somehow trick them into letting me work for free while figuring out how to get myself on the crew for real. Great plan (sarcasm)—what could possibly go wrong?

My dad was adamant that I was ruining my life. Was I? My mom was supportive, but she was worried sick about my safety. This was way before cell phones. For her to know that I was alive, I was going to have to call home on pay phones *if* they were available.

The Subaru BRAT, my home for the quest, was quite a machine. Part economy car and part tiny pickup truck. Mine had a cap over its short bed, which would serve as my sleeping quarters so long as I stayed curled up. There was no room to stretch out. I packed several layers of blankets for cold nights, as there would be no heat or AC back there. My parents shuddered as I drove out of their lives.

My Subaru and I were buzzing south, its little four-cylinder engine pushing steadfast against the wind. Taking that first step, I was chasing a dream! Even as I reviewed my plan on the drive, it sucked. Ready to be unimpressed? I was to sneak in every day so the crew wasn't responsible for me being there—something I was sure they couldn't allow. Then, once inside, I would count on their understanding and good nature to not turn me over to the police. I would work alongside the local stagehands as free labor. If somehow I was successful, this process would give me valuable insight and work experience. Ideally, I would be bolstering relationships with people who might hire me in the future. Heck, I was going to be so great that they were going to eventually offer me a job on the *Joshua Tree* tour.

What a plan . . .

What a terrible plan.

The song "With or Without You" blared from my speakers. I had been told as a child that I couldn't sing, but I never let that stop me when I was alone in the car. My voice cracked as I strained to hit Bono's high notes.

🎜 "I can't live, with or without you . . ."

The words had real meaning for me. That was the magic of so many U2 songs—you weren't sure what they were about, so you made them your own. A country song tells you a story, and the best ones feel like yours. A U2 song conveys emotion beautifully, but the story is usually vague. You naturally see a part of you in it. While I wasn't invited to live the music life, I was desperate to get in, to find some direction or meaning. I couldn't live with or without it. I poured my heart into that song as I sang, and Bono sang right along.

The freedom of the drive felt great. The hope and excitement of taking that first step welled within me. It's funny, but the fear of failure was actually less pronounced once I started moving. Somehow failing wasn't as scary to me after I entered the game. At the top of the chapter, I mentioned Amelia Earhart calling her fears "paper tigers." I was starting to understand. Perhaps I was ready to fail. But this time, I wasn't ready to forgo trying.

I needed to find Nassau Coliseum on Long Island. That would be simple today, but back then, things like locating a building could be really difficult. The 1987 version of the Internet and Google were the Yellow Pages—a printed phone book! This was also before GPS was a thing, so I had to have a massive Rand McNally *Road Atlas* of the US with me. The process was not easy. As I navigated my way to each city, I would hit a truck stop, find a payphone, and use the local Yellow Pages to get the venue address. I would then look up the street in the back of the atlas and figure out where it was in relation to where I was. In order to get to that street, I would find some scrap paper and write down the directions, which I would lay in the passenger seat for reference. It was often hard to spot street signs. I can't tell you how many times I missed a turn and got lost. Ugh, I would have to do this every day!

So I set out to find the arena on Long Island. Several hours and a few exasperating wrong turns later, I finally saw the Nassau Coliseum. Even better, as I pulled up I saw one of the tour buses at the Marriott across the street! I grabbed a parking spot under a tree and settled in for the night. It was freezing cold. I went to bed in my clothes under three layers of blankets and was still shivering. I had a GE cassette boom box in the back, so I hit play on some U2 and dreamed of the future. I was tired, but sleep didn't come easily. My plan was so bad, I wondered if I'd ruin everything tomorrow. Would I break my dreams?

🎵 "One Tree Hill" played as I drifted off . . .

"You run like a river runs to the sea."

T-Day

I awoke early in the back of the cramped Subaru. I had survived the frigid night, but now the sun was baking hot, and I was a sweaty mess under all those blankets. I twisted myself around and got to where I could open the back gate and let some air in. At six two, I couldn't straighten my legs in my makeshift bed on wheels—not even close. I crawled out of the BRAT barely able to stand.

I gathered supplies in a bag and headed into the hotel. After a little exploring, I found a deserted bathroom adjacent to a currently unoccupied meeting room. Using paper towels and the sink, I gave myself something resembling a shower, or at least that's what I told myself. In the handicap stall I put on fresh clothes and deodorant, then headed into the hotel lobby. I was going to wait there until Liam (the man in charge whom I had met at Howard Johnson's) appeared. Then I would spring my plan on him.

Why was I waiting for Liam? Remember, the idea was to sneak in, work for free, and see if I could figure out how to get an actual job with U2. This required some dishonesty, and, truth be told, trespassing. I could live with sneaking past local security. However, I could not be dishonest with my friends on the crew, not if they were ever going to trust me. So, here was the next level of my half-baked plan. I would confide in Liam that I was sneaking past security and somehow make him OK with that. In hindsight, I have no idea why I thought this could work.

I waited alone in the lobby for what seemed like forever . . .

Finally, many hours later, a group of black-clad, rockish-looking people walked in. I could feel my heartbeat. There was Liam! I positioned myself where he would see me after he got his room key. Liam looked up, surprised.

"What are you doing here?" he asked, smiling, but confused.

(Note to the reader: I suggest reading my dialogue below as run-on sentences. I was definitely doing a nervous fast talk with Liam.)

"Hi," I responded cheerfully. "Quick version: I am trying to make some major life decisions, and I could really use your help. I know that you just got off an international flight, and you must be exhausted, so I understand that you probably won't want to talk to me now. But I also know that you are in town for three more days, so I will patiently wait here in hopes that you can give me fifteen minutes at some point. If you can, I would really appreciate it."

Liam didn't seem very surprised by my request—with one exception.

"You will be here waiting?" he asked.

"Yes," I replied.

"For three days?"

"Yes." I nodded my head.

"Where?" he asked.

"Right over there in that chair unless they make me leave. Then outside, I guess."

Liam smiled. "I did just get off of a flight, and I do want to clean up. I'm going to take a shower and then I will come back down."

"Awesome," I beamed.

Liam came back down surprisingly quickly. He smiled and asked, "What can I help you with?"

"Everything," was my honest reply.

Liam smiled as I continued, once again talking really fast. "Ever since meeting you guys and seeing what you do, I have been consumed.

All of you were so nice and kind to me, and everything about what you do for a living appeals to me. Great people, traveling around the world, working with amazing technology, making music happen. I'm hooked." (Liam laughed.)

"For the first time in my life, I think I know what I want to do, but I *need* to be sure. I dropped out of school, quit my three jobs, and hit the road on a mission. I plan on making my way inside the arena every day to work for free as a stagehand." (Now Liam's smile became strained.)

"I need to do this to be sure that this industry is all I hope it is. This will take a couple of weeks to figure out, then I will get out of your hair. The reason I am telling you all of this is that while I am fine with sneaking past local security, I would never want to be dishonest or sneaky with you. That wouldn't be a very good way to repay your kindness."

Liam's strained smile was fading, and his head was tilted as if in disbelief. I continued quickly before he could speak. "I know that you can't give me permission to do this. I am only telling you so that I won't be sneaky with you. I will get past security and then just be another one of the stagehands. A couple of weeks, tops."

I took a deep breath and waited.

Liam looked at me and started to smile again, now apologetically. "Well, we do have security. You won't be able to get in."

"Maybe, but I plan on getting in. I just wanted you to know that I was doing it and that I respected and appreciated you enough to tell you. Also, that I understand you could never approve my plan, and I can see all of the reasons why. Nonetheless, I'll be there working, just another stagehand."

Liam shook his head. "You will never be able to get past security. Let me give you some real advice on how to legitimately get in the industry."

"That's a wonderful offer," I said. "I would love to hear that advice. So you are saying that I won't be able to get in, and that when I fail you are willing to sit with me and give me some great advice? I look forward to it!" And then I changed the subject.

Liam looked confused while waiting for me to stop talking about this new, unrelated topic. The break finally came, and he asked a bit impatiently, "Are you ready to talk about the industry?"

"Oh, not yet," I replied matter-of-factly. "You said that I would try to get in, then not be able to get in, and that you would then be willing to have a talk with me. While I look forward to our talk, I don't want to do this out of order. I will try to get in, probably fail, as you suspect, and then we'll have the talk. Thank you in advance again for that eventual talk."

Once more I quickly changed the topic. Liam looked bewildered by my completely illogical tack on all of this. Who could blame him? I knew that I could get advice from any of the guys—they were already supplying that. What I wanted was hands-on experience and a chance to earn my way in. I wasn't going to settle. I was nervous as hell and so afraid of losing my dream, this was the one lifeline I was holding on to. I knew that he would say no. I was expecting that. All I had to do was find a way to get inside the venue without him thinking that I was disrespecting him. I was just trying to achieve that with this conversation, not actually get permission. He thought I was crazy, naive, probably a fool. Nonetheless, grinning and full of positive energy, I had expressed my plan and, simultaneously, my deep respect for him. Mission step accomplished, really.

Liam gave it one more shot, shaking his head with a tense smile. "You won't be able to get in."

"You are probably right, and I hope when that happens you will still be willing to have that talk with me."

Liam smiled another tense smile and seemed to indicate that he would. I thanked him and told him that I would see him soon. I walked away with Liam no doubt thinking I was nuts. He wasn't wrong. But I let out a huge sigh of relief. The worst plan ever was coming together. If I somehow got past security and Liam saw me inside, it wouldn't be like I hadn't warned him. I had made my intentions clear. *Who knows*, I thought, *he might even be impressed.* At the least, I was pretty sure he wouldn't have me arrested.

Sometimes the craziest plans are worth a shot. There is a legendary story about a young, unknown, and desperate Kris Kristofferson commandeering and landing an army helicopter in Johnny Cash's yard to deliver demo tapes of his music. Kris had been a helicopter pilot in the Vietnam War. At the time of this feat, he was part-time with the National Guard. Needless to say, they did *not* give him permission to take a chopper over to the Cash home. Johnny's version of the story was that Kris landed, hopped out, and sauntered up to Johnny with a beer in one hand and a demo tape in the other. Instead of shooting him with the rifle he brandished, Johnny decided to listen to the demo, and the rest is history. Pretty amazing first step, Kris.

The Sneaker

That night it was freezing again, but I slept a little. I awoke sweating just as I had the day before, so I opened the hatch for air and flopped back down inside with my legs stretched out over the tailgate to review the plan. Yesterday was a great step—a huge win—but today was show day, and it was certain to be even scarier.

I surmised that the best time to sneak into the arena would be near the end of the show. Security would be expecting local stagehands to arrive to help tear down and clear the stage, and I would try to blend in with their arrival. When I had first visited the tour weeks ago, I noticed that several of the guys wore multiple passes around their necks. The *Joshua Tree* credential was very distinguishable, but along with the tour pass the crew laminated things they needed to remember, such as the order that equipment was loaded in the truck. Thus, before leaving home, I made a couple of laminates that had type on one side and were blank on the other. My plan was to fall in with some stagehands and walk past security, smiling naturally and nonchalantly. If they stopped me, I would look down and panic, pretending to realize just then that my credential was missing. I would say something like, "Shit! Is it on the bus?" Feigning that I was upset because I had possibly lost my pass and might be in trouble, I would hurry off the way that I'd come in.

Waiting all day was hard. The parking lot filled with excited fans and then emptied as they went into the show. I stood alone outside. I could glean what song was playing from the low rumble that escaped the building, the sound calling out to me. I imagined the energy inside.

Those somber feelings were replaced by a spike of nerves as I saw the stagehands arriving. It was time. There was just one tweak to the plan: They didn't smile; they mostly looked like they didn't want to be there. My heart was pounding as I tried not to imagine being arrested for sneaking in. I moved close to the backstage ramp and timed my descent. I fell in at the rear of a group of stagehands, doing my very best to look completely disinterested. Whatever you do, Scott, don't look at the security guy—keep walking, eyes forward. That ramp felt like it was a mile long, but I found myself passing security, walking through the loading dock and into the coliseum! It had worked! I was in!

Once inside, I quickly found an out-of-the-way place to stand. I leaned against the wall trying to look bored. The show ended, and I caught a glimpse of the band down the hall. Cool, but not why I was here. Backstage quickly became busy, and I went out into the arena bowl. Now what? There was a lot of stuff below and next to the stage. A maze of wires ran underneath. Hmmm, under the stage seemed like a great place to work if you wanted to minimize being seen. I noticed that one of the crew guys I knew from the restaurant was working under there. OK, here I go. I walked up to him.

"Hi."

He smiled. "Hey, what are you doing here?"

My reply was surprisingly smooth for such a stretch of the truth. "I have an arrangement with management. I am going to shadow somebody for a couple of weeks. I thought it would be great if it was you. I'll be like any other stagehand, except you'll have me again tomorrow, so I will remember a lot of it. In no time, I'll have it all down and help you get your job done twice as fast."

He seemed skeptical. "Who said this was OK?" he asked.

I looked disappointed. "Liam," I replied. "But if you would rather not work with me, I can find someone else. It's no big deal; I'm just another stagehand."

He pondered for a moment and then shrugged. "I guess you can work with me. Um, here, we need all of these connectors disconnected from this rack, then we need the cables coiled up."

Holy crap! This was working! I had no idea what I was doing, but I started coiling the cables. He stopped me, shaking his head, then showed me the right way. I tried very hard not to mess up the same thing twice. There was a redundancy to this kind of work, so I was able to contribute without too much guidance. *How is it possible that a plan this bad is working?*

After loading out the gear, I excitedly headed back to the BRAT, got a change of clothes, and returned to the hotel bathroom to clean up. I looked at my grimy face reflected in the mirror and grinned. I had snuck backstage at U2's show without getting arrested, and once inside I'd been able to work the load-out and learn something in the process. I had been all but sure that I would fail, willing to learn from that experience. Magically, my first step was paying off!

What first step are you afraid of? What if you took that first step? Look what happened to me! My entrepreneurial hero Richard Branson says in his book *The Virgin Way*, "Luck is what happens when preparation meets opportunity." I had prepared a plan (albeit a crazy one), and those first bold steps created the opportunity I needed. Boom! What can *you* do to make some luck for yourself? Take that first step!

As I stood there staring at myself in the bathroom mirror, I had a thought. *If I hurried, I could follow the buses and trucks and not have to deal with the struggle of finding the venue tomorrow.* Thirty minutes later, the Subaru BRAT and I were humming down the highway with the convoy, a flea on the back of the *Joshua Tree* circus. Next stop, Philadelphia! I was exhausted, but the adrenaline of the day's events carried me through the night.

"Where the Streets Have No Name" cranked out of the stereo.

🎵 "Oh, when I go there."

It was already getting hard to keep my eyes open. It had been a tension-filled day, an exciting but physically taxing load-out, and now I was driving all night. I kept eyeing the gas gauge as it dipped painfully low. Darn it, if I pulled over to refuel, I'd lose the buses. That meant I'd have to struggle to find the arena in Philadelphia on my own. I stressed over that gas gauge for what seemed like a hundred miles that night. Just as I was giving up, salvation came as the bus in front of me put on his blinker. They were stopping for fuel too! I filled up the BRAT, used the restroom quickly, and loaded up on snacks and Mountain Dew. As we pulled into Philadelphia, I parked and crawled into the back, exhausted but smiling.

Rocky Town

When I awoke in Philadelphia, the sun was again heating up my greenhouse on wheels. I unfolded myself, hopped out of the BRAT, and stretched my cramping legs. I took a walk and was pleasantly surprised to come across the steps that Rocky Balboa ran up in that iconic scene in the movie *Rocky*. After the victories I'd enjoyed the day before, inspiration hit me. I started humming the *Rocky* theme song, "Gonna Fly Now," and ran up the steps full speed. When I reached the top, I threw my arms up just like Stallone had. I was a champion! Granted, a champion who lives in his car, hoping for another chance to work for free.

> It ain't about how hard you hit,
> it's about how hard you can get hit
> and keep moving forward.
> —Rocky Balboa

With each step I was exposing myself, ready for reality to punch me in the face. Surprisingly, life wasn't being as tough as I had feared. Do you think it's possible that you, too, are overestimating whatever fear may be holding you back? Take the step. If you get hit, be like Rocky and keep moving forward.

That night, I got brave and decided to sneak in early to see the show and, hopefully, talk to the guys. This was ill-advised, as preshow security was in full force. They did ask me for my pass, but I kept walking, seemingly disinterested, holding up my collection of fake white laminates and mumbling, "Pay attention."

It worked! They let me go without insisting on seeing my pass.

The show was magic—fuel for my tank.

Bono gestured with the mic and let the crowd take over during "Sunday Bloody Sunday." "How long, how long must we sing this song?" I sang along at the top of my lungs, hoping that I could sing this song for the rest of my life. As the lyric goes, "Tonight, we can be as one." Something came over me as I sang those words. Only a few days into my odyssey, I knew I wanted to be as one with live music forever.

The concert came to an end and once again I snuck past security. I had this down!

Giant Sounds

The next stop was Giants Stadium in New Jersey. Out by the buses, Bono's cousin AJ rolled up in a golf cart and told me to hop in. We tore away and started working our way up the spiral ramp to the top of the stadium. AJ, whom I'd met at the restaurant, as you may recall, asked what I was doing there. "Working," I replied. Somehow, that was good enough for him. I asked him where we were going. AJ smiled, replying with equal brevity.

"To the top."

"Why?" I asked.

"To go back down," he declared, a mischievous look in his eyes.

Once at the top of the stadium, we drove around a bit. It was like nothing I had ever seen. The previous shows were at arenas. They were huge, but under twenty thousand seats. This, however, was a stadium—more than three times the others' capacity. It was the biggest place this farm boy had ever been in. It was hard to imagine that this huge bowl would fill with fans in just a few hours. The drum tech was hitting the kick drum, and the echo bouncing around in this cavern was thunderous.

It's a sound I have since grown to know well, but, back then, a stadium sound system struck awe in me. AJ turned the cart around. While the limiter kept us at a reasonable speed on the way up, it did no such thing on the way down. In short order, we were racing like a bat out of hell, tires squealing as we tried to make the corners. AJ was scaring the crap out of me! The more scared I got, the more he howled with laughter. He was a maniac, coming impossibly close to the concrete columns on each floor, swerving at the last moment! AJ was having a blast. I was not. I might have loved it too . . . if I were driving!

AJ parked the cart, and we talked about Ireland for a bit. He surprised me by saying he missed it, wishing he was home. Of course that made sense, but to a kid who wanted so desperately to be a part of the tour, it was hard to imagine wanting to be anywhere but where we were, on the road. His homeland seemed magical. He described it as a whole country of pubs, full of best friends you just hadn't had time to meet yet. I had never left the US; I wanted to be in one of those pubs with some new best friends. I promised myself that someday I would make it to Ireland. But not yet.

That night the sound poured out of the open stadium unhindered, so I had no trouble knowing when it was time to think about sneaking back in. As the Edge struck the keyboard for the opening notes of "New Year's Day," I collected myself, uneventfully made my way in, and went straight to work. Man, even empty, the massive space had an electric energy—an echo of the frenzy that was there just an hour before.

I was under the stage coiling a cable when my crew guy spoke up. "Liam is looking at you."

I kept coiling while trying to hide my concern. "Oh," I replied dryly, my heart jumping into my throat.

"You said this was cool, right?" asked my friend on the crew.

"Yup, he's probably watching me to see how I'm doing," I offered, trying to think fast.

"He doesn't look like he's OK," he remarked.

"Alright, I'll go check in." I dropped the cable and walked over to Liam, thankfully just out of earshot of my adopted crew member.

"Hi," I offered, forcing a huge grin.

"What are you doing?" he asked, a concerned look on his face.

"Learning!" I replied enthusiastically. (I once again started talking really fast.) "I have been picking up a ton. I know that you said I wouldn't be able to get in, but somehow security hasn't stopped me yet. I'm sure they will soon, and when that happens, I hope you'll still be willing to have that talk with me. And thank you for that in advance. In the meantime I've been observing and doing a lot and I'm loving it!"

Now Liam looked *really* concerned. "Wait," he asked, "they haven't stopped you yet? Have you been doing this every day?"

"Well," I replied a bit sheepishly. "I'm not sure. The cities have all started to blend in together." He didn't know what to say, so I continued. "Look, thank you again for our eventual talk. I would say that I can't wait to have it, but I think we need to wait, as I still have a bunch of work to do tonight. It's fine, just think of me as another stagehand. Thank you in advance, and I'll see you soon."

I smiled and walked back under the stage, where I began coiling the cable again.

My crew buddy spoke again. "He's still looking at you."

"Uh huh," I replied casually. I glanced up at Liam and waved. He gave me one last quizzical look and turned to walk away, shaking his head. I grinned. He didn't tell me to stop! I'm working for U2!

Exit Stage Left

Fast-forward one remarkable month, and I had become a fixture on the tour. There was plenty of struggle, though. I got caught sneaking in a few times and was nearly arrested! I talked my way out of it, and when my heart stopped pounding through my chest I walked to a different entrance and snuck in that way. There was a solid week when it rained. The relentless work in the downpour, with no sleep and nowhere to dry off afterward, developed into bronchitis, which quickly turned into walking pneumonia. This was no joke for an asthmatic. Near death, I was forced to miss the Madison Square Garden and Montreal shows. But against doctor's orders, I rolled to Toronto in time to load out in the rain yet again.

My struggle didn't go unnoticed—I was becoming something of a tour mascot. I flexed that currency and turned up my efforts in Cleveland, Syracuse, and Buffalo, asking more questions, trying hard to become needed and valuable. I felt like it was working!

I felt at home loading the gear out. Loading out after the Rochester show, I rounded the corner pushing a heavy case full of cable to the exit. I knew what I was doing. My confidence was high . . .

And then it happened. One of the crew spotted me. Looking nervous, he said, "Let go of the case and head out the closest door. We'll see you in Pittsburgh."

Surprised, I said, "What's up?"

He shook his head. "It's not good. Go out the closest door and come to my bus in the morning."

Stunned, I let go of the case and walked to the exit. A moment before I was living my dream. Now I was suddenly outside, pressed in with the mosh of fans still leaving the show. I racked my brain but couldn't think of anything I had done wrong. I decided to drive straight to Pittsburgh, which was a mistake, as I was jammed in concert traffic for more than an hour. I was separated from the tour and my dreams, no longer connected, no longer a part of it all. The first several words of "Where the Streets Have No Name" rang in my ears. I wanted, as Bono sang, to "tear down the walls that hold me inside."

I hit stop on the cassette; I needed to think.

It was a long night of driving in silence, searching for understanding. As I entered Pittsburgh from Rochester in the predawn, I traveled through a short tunnel and emerged into a spectacular sight. The tunnel mouth opened up from a sheer hillside and I found myself on a bridge high above the city with an incredible view. The stark contrast between the dull gray tunnel and the panoramic cityscape offered a breathtaking moment. It was like being shot out of a cannon—one minute you can't see a thing, and the next you are flying through the sky! The sun was just rising, and the warm glow on the city from the bridge a thousand feet above was surreal. It moved me, even in my dismal state.

Was this the last magical experience I would have on this journey? What happened that compelled the crew member to tell me to exit at the closest door? After parking, I tried to catch a few hours of sleep in my cave on wheels. Yesterday it was home; today it felt claustrophobic. I tossed sleeplessly, eventually hearing the rumble of the arriving buses. The crew would be awake soon, and I would finally get some answers.

I saw the lights come up inside the bus, so I got out of the Subaru and leaned on the fender. When the bus door opened, one of the guys motioned for me to come aboard. The guys were all looking at me with somber expressions. One of them finally spoke.

"Apparently, somebody was bragging about you and mentioned how you were following the tour around driving your own car and working for free. There was some other union-related dispute, and the union steward decided in frustration to tell management that he was going to fine the band $5,000 for having non-union labor on tour."

My heart sank—$5,000? That was a fortune to me. Seeing my discomfort, he continued, "We don't think anything will come of it financially, but because of this, U2's upper management is now aware of you. Management pointed out that letting you do this was crazy. If you got hurt loading out, or fell asleep at the wheel, the band would be responsible. In short, I'm sorry, Scott, we can't let you help anymore. I wish we knew last night so we could stop you from driving all the way to Pittsburgh, but we didn't get all of the details until after you left."

They all sat silently, waiting for me to process this news. Resigned to my fate, the only feeling I had was guilt.

"Guys, don't be sorry. It's me who should be apologizing to you. At the start of this whole thing, I told Liam I was just going to work for a couple of weeks tops. Then, I got greedy and stuck around. I loved being a part of it. At first I knew I didn't belong here, but you guys were so great to me that I started to believe there was a chance I could actually get on the tour." I scanned the room, praying for an opening. Their looks of pity told me this was not an option now. I sighed, nodded my acceptance, and continued, "My greed ended up getting you guys in trouble; I feel awful."

Their reply was heartfelt and kind. I believe it was John Ross who spoke up. "We aren't really in trouble. I think management sees that you were a unique situation. Plus, I think we all agree that you were pretty sneaky." Everyone laughed when he said that. "But it has to end. It won't be cool for you to work anymore." He was making sure I really got the message.

"Yeah, I totally get that, guys."

"What do you want to do in the business?" asked Lawrence Anderson.

"I think I want to do video," I replied. They all seemed surprised by my answer. None of them did video. This was one of the first tours to have video screens.

I explained, "I've had a lot of time and miles to chew on it, and my thought is that I'm brand-new to the industry, and video is brand-new too. If I do lighting or sound or power, I will be the new guy starting at the bottom of a really tall ladder. If I do video, I will be surrounded by new people since it's so new to the industry. I think it's my best bet for success."

They all raised their eyebrows and nodded.

"OK," Lawrence said. "Give me a couple of weeks, and I will look into a good path for you. Give me your number and I'll call."

Was this it? Were we back to advice like Liam had offered initially? I had climbed so high, done so much . . . and now I had fallen from the sky all the way back down to earth, with only the original offer of advice to show for my efforts.

"That would be great. I really appreciate that," I said. God, I hoped he would call.

"I'll call," Lawrence said, catching the look on my face.

One of the guys added, "You'll make it happen. Considering what you did here, you will *definitely* make it happen. We'll be seeing you at gigs before you know it."

It was hard for me to take solace in his words; the reality of my failure was just starting to settle in. I sighed again. It was time for them to go to work, and what else was there to say? I thanked them one last time and paused a moment to take in the feeling of being there on the bus with the crew. Then I got up, walked down the bus stairs, and climbed back into the BRAT. I fired up the engine, taking one last long look at the shiny silver bus, its space shuttle image glowing in the morning sun. I looked at the map, put the BRAT in drive, and started to cry.

After all of that, I was not going on tour with U2; I had failed.

Weeks later, back in Troy, New York, the Subaru BRAT sat sadly still out on the street, its great odyssey having run its course. Inside my flat I was lying in my dark bedroom. I had been fighting a sort of a postpartum depression . . . and losing. It had been weeks since that painful conversation in Pittsburgh. I was trying to work out what my next move would be if I never heard from Lawrence. All I could do was try to recover and lick my wounds. But I was so beat up.

Then the phone rang. I answered dryly, "Hello."

A familiar voice asked, "Hey, is Scott there?"

My heart jumped. "Yes!"

"It's me, Lawrence. I have a plan!"

"Yes!" was my reply—yes to whatever the plan is!

To the Moon and Back

I am fiercely proud to introduce this next contributor to the book. To my mind she is the biggest star of them all. She is beloved by everyone who meets her and has influenced my life in the most incredible ways. Heck, she gave me life! Ladies and gentlemen, meet my mom!

SCOTT'S MOM, JEAN
ON BEING TENACIOUS

Do you know how hard it was to watch you drive away in that BRAT? But I knew that you had to do it. I am so proud of you.

Now you are going to make me talk about myself, huh? That's not really what I do. Well, I really want to read the book, so I guess I'd better help you finish it. Here goes!

I was born in the Great Depression, but I don't remember it. I know my mom and dad did. Daddy drove a big old Mack truck for an asphalt company and Momma quit waitressing to raise us three girls. We got by, and to me it was great. We didn't grow up rich, but I never felt poor. I was the middle of three sisters, so I got my older sister, Joan's, clothes when she outgrew them. That was OK because I kind of idolized her; I thought she was the greatest. I also remember there was another family who would give us their hand-me-downs. That was exciting; they gave us some really nice things.

Daddy would drive all summer and in the winter work in the shop. Of all the guys they had, he was one of only two they kept on during the winter to repair and work on everything. Daddy was a good man, a good worker, and his boss thought a lot of him. Momma worked hard at making sure everything was always right in our household, both for the family and the frequent guests we had. Our door was always open, and we always had company. Even though we didn't have money, she found a way to be a great host. Momma and Daddy were both first-class people.

I put myself through business school and got hired to be the secretary in the metallurgy department of RPI (Rensselaer Polytechnic Institute School of Engineering). I worked there under three professors: Dr. Ferguson, Dr. Nippes, and Dr. Savage. Dr. Hugo Ferguson decided to take one of his ideas and make a business out of it. He left RPI to do so, and I agreed to join him. He made me vice president, as no one else wanted the duties. That was daunting, but the title was fun and I stepped up. You do what you need to do. The company grew and evolved, and I evolved with it. We eventually employed over fifty people. It was hard work, but I enjoyed it—especially looking after all of the employees, making sure they were paid, appreciated, and happy. For most of that time I didn't make much money. As a woman with just a two-year business degree, I guess I didn't feel that I needed more. I was never worried about that. Plus my husband (Scott's father) made a decent salary, so we were OK.

But then I filed for divorce, and the $3,200 (or thereabouts) a year I was making didn't really suffice. Scott's father told me that he would take custody of him if I didn't give him everything. I think he might have been trying to punish us for leaving—or even keep us from leaving, perhaps. But I knew we needed to leave, and Scott was all that mattered to me anyway, so I told my soon-to-be ex-husband to take it all. He kept the house, the cabin, the new sports car, the boat, the motor home, and the apartment building. I got the old station wagon and Scott. That was great by me. I knew we'd find a way—and we did.

We bought a run-down house on the mountain. The side door was open and a family of raccoons was living in it. There was a dead raccoon in the living room. I remember my dad cried when he first saw it. But you and me and Daddy and Momma rolled up our sleeves and went to work remodeling it. Oh, the dust from that ancient plaster. We replaced every wall and every window over the next few years and made it into a beautiful home. I remember that we would sleep down by the wood stove in the living room to stay warm in the winter. We stapled plastic sheets to the beams to hold the heat in so we could use the least amount of wood. We'd alternate sleeping on the couch or the rollaway bed so my back wouldn't hurt. It was like camping—it was less than ideal, but we were working toward making it better.

Oh! And as soon as we fixed it up, the home's previous tenant claimed they owned the place instead of the man who sold it to us. They sued to take it away, and eventually the court found they had no claim. But it was scary; we had everything in that house. And those same people had abandoned the house with their stuff inside. They dropped an empty tractor trailer in our yard expecting us to move all of their things out. We needed to get in the house, so we did it. Then they wouldn't come and get the trailer! That forty-five-foot trailer sat full of their stuff in our yard for over a year before a friend of ours with a semi finally asked us if he could help us get rid of it. He delivered it to them, but instead of parking it in the driveway, he parked it on their front lawn right in front of their windows! It's funny now, but at the time I was so afraid that they would be mad and cause problems for us.

To hear all of this you might think *poor us*, but the funny thing is that we were happy. We loved our time together. We did whatever it took. All the while, we kept our spirits up and had a great time doing it. We made it through. The only regret I have was that all of the hours I worked to pay for the house, and all of that work I did on the house itself, took me away from Scott so much. I knew, though, that he was happy with Momma and Daddy or his friends when I was at work. But still, it weighed on me.

As time went on, Hugo Ferguson's son David graduated from RPI with an engineering degree and an MBA. As he was getting older, Hugo transitioned into more of a CEO role, making David president. David, the kid who used to sleep in a bassinet at my feet and wake up to watch me type! He looked at my compensation and suggested that they give me 10 percent of the company and a healthy raise. This was a big deal, but he reasoned that I had been the one holding the company together, allowing Hugo to be the visionary. Hugo agreed. We weren't really profitable, so 10 percent wasn't as exciting as it might sound, but David brought a lot of business mindedness to the presidential chair, and suddenly we started doing all right. David and I were a great team; I loved working with him. I remember bringing home my year-end pay stub, including my bonus that year. When I showed it to Scott, we both started to cry. We weren't rich, but for the first time in years we weren't poor! No more plastic on the ceiling—we could turn up the heat!

It was never about the money; you just do what you have to do. It's nice to not have to worry, though, and I will say that I loved spending extra on everyone's Christmas gifts! So I guess money is OK. But I was lucky that I loved my job—I loved the challenge, and I loved the people. Heck, I worked there for fifty-five years! From age twenty until seventy-five. They told me after I left that they hired three people to replace me, and then a fourth a few months later. I don't know about that, but it's fun to imagine it's true.

You just do what you need to do. Do the right thing and good things will come. If they don't, at least you know you did the right thing. You did your part well. You did your best to make it better for everyone else, and that's its own reward.

Thanks, Mom. You have always been and always will be my hero. The relentless support and love you have poured into me is what fuels my dreams. I know you were a nervous wreck while I was living in my car, working all day, and driving all night chasing this dream, but you always backed me and encouraged me to pursue my goals. I love you to the moon and back!

My mom's brand of tenacity is my favorite; she is tenaciously giving. She has always possessed an indomitable spirit—a drive to make things better for everyone, coupled with the vision to see how that could be. There's bottomless generosity in every little thing she does, even today. She just naturally works to make things better for all those who cross paths with her. I am grateful for the tenacity that she bequeathed me, and I aspire to carry the torch of her giving spirit forward.

By the way, I had to coax her to share these details. She'd be just as happy to tell you, "You just do what you have to do" or "You just do what you need to and make it right" rather than get into the specifics. You'll notice that she didn't talk about the challenges of being a woman executive in the 1960s—of the prejudice and judgment or the inappropriate behavior she faced in the office in the early years (not by Hugo or David, mind you). She doesn't mention those things because she handled them, proved her value, and rose above them. She was a female vice president at a time when that just wasn't a thing. I'm immensely proud of her.

Because I know she never would, I feel compelled to shine a light on her tenacity in the early 1970s as well.

Not only was she a glass-ceiling-breaking female executive, she was paving that road at the same time she was making the brave move to divorce my dad—something that bore its own judgment in those days. She endured the scorn of our church community; one person told us we were going to hell. (Yes, I was told that at age six.)

Simultaneously, some investors had run one of Hugo's companies into the ground. As he tried to salvage it, he trusted my mom to take care of the main company. Then, as that dust was settling, Hugo was in a horrible plane crash. Mom carried the company for another year while he recovered. She did all of this as a single mom fending off my spiteful dad. It's overwhelming to think about her managing such stresses. But . . . if you ask her, she will tell you about all of the great times we had, and you know what? We did! That lady provided a safe place for me to grow up. I was never hungry, and while we were occasionally cold, I had tons and tons of love and support. I had a wonderful childhood overall—one that cultivated the dreams I have lived. Mom's tenacious spirit and her relentlessly loving and giving ways formed the foundation of the man I am today. I am so lucky to have her as not only my mom but also a best friend.

Author's Note:

I would like to express gratitude to David and Hugo Ferguson for supporting my mom as vice president. She did the work, but you gentlemen saw her talents over her gender in a time when that wasn't the norm. Thank you.

My *Joshua Tree* Odyssey Concludes

In my *Joshua Tree* Odyssey, I did the most important thing anyone can do on their journey: *I took the first step.* And then the next. I made myself a promise to never stop trying, and I walked the walk.

The broken kid who was afraid to fail laid it all out there. He tried relentlessly, ate crap for food, lived in his car, and was nearly arrested! He froze, sweated, and almost worked himself to death. He succeeded in many ways, though other times he failed. But most importantly, he woke up every day and set out to try. He took steps toward his future, even crazy ones. One step at a time, that's the point. You don't have to be a rocket scientist. I think my plan proved that I wasn't. You don't have to be the most talented person. I certainly wasn't that either. Yet I set out on a daunting mission and made amazing progress because I never stopped taking those little steps.

Ultimately, I failed to achieve what I wanted, but as Lawrence hinted, after all of that effort, all of that relentless pursuit, all of that tenacity, there was still the prospect of another path—one that never would have revealed itself otherwise. Lawrence had a plan . . . and this book is far from over. I failed in that first odyssey, but my journey was just getting started. I suspected it would continue as long as I kept taking steps and trying.

It's a shame that people don't try more often. I can't urge you enough to take that first step and just keep trying. What is the dream you have been thinking of? When will you start taking those initial steps? Are you willing to fail? You will note that all contributors to this book are actually proud of their failures!

The moment my dream of joining U2 evaporated was one of the most heartbreaking of my life. But as you will soon see, I brushed off the dust and kept going. That's tenacity! How cool will *you* be when you take that first step, willing to fail?! Go out there and risk it. Let life punch you in the face. Then tenaciously get up, just like Rocky would. You'll be in great company and one step farther down the path to a much better life!

(My superstar mom and I at Little League, her favorite picture of us. My BRAT! My home on wheels and the greatest little Subaru in history!)

INTERLUDE I

Failing

I just failed! Let's take a moment to celebrate the power in that! I've asked a couple of my guests to share a time when they brutally faceplanted. Not to pick on them, of course, but to highlight the bravery and tenacity they showed in getting back up and moving forward.

Country star Chris Young is a friend of mine who knows something about failing and coming back stronger. He's a determined guy who has run the gauntlet of the Nashville music scene and emerged as a shining example of what unfaltering tenacity can achieve.

CHRIS YOUNG

ON FAILING

No one ever tells you that it's going to be that difficult. When I signed my first record deal with RCA Nashville, I was so excited! It was where Keith Whitley had been signed, and I'm a huge fan. As an artist, I expected hard work, but I had no idea how much work I was walking into. Almost four years into that deal, I had three failed singles. Three times I poured my heart and dreams into a song only to have country fans and radio say, "Meh, no thanks." All this with the whole team at RCA watching. It's not like I wasn't hanging it out there either. I had been in every middle seat on every airline and almost every rental car across most of the USA. I'd been to every radio station that made up the charts at least twice, just to watch each song fail.

I had my fourth radio single out, and I had a feeling it was my last chance. More than three years of giving my all had left me perpetually exhausted, my tank damn near empty. The emotional drain was worse than the physical. It was soul crushing to see my songs—my art—failing out of the charts. When they signed me I was pumped, but three years later all I had done was run into brick walls. I will say this, though: Even when I was dying inside, I kept grinding.

I remember riding in the car with one of my record label's radio regional reps, Josh Easler, and I asked him, "If this song doesn't work, is this the end of my career?" He paused for a moment and said, "Probably." My heart just sank. I lived with that feeling for quite a while. After all I had endured, was this really it? Was my dream over?

Well, guess what? The song we were promoting was "Gettin' You Home"—my first of thirteen number ones so far, and one of the biggest songs I've ever had. Long story short: Never give up on your dreams. In hindsight, I can see that every failure forced me to strive to be better, and, in the end, I *was* better. As it turns out, being an artist with hits isn't easy either. That early struggle was the boot camp I needed to become the artist I am today.

Chris mentioned that "Gettin' You Home" was the first of his thirteen number ones "so far." I smiled when I read "so far," and I smiled even wider when I heard he just had *another* number one song—his fourteenth as of writing this chapter! I love that Chris shines a light on his feelings that failure and struggle were necessary for him to not only get to his dream but to be the man he needs to be to endure the pressures and demands of being a star. Chris opens with the words "No one ever tells you that it's going to be that difficult." It's funny, because here he tells us it *is* that difficult . . . and it's worth it! Chris, thanks for sharing with us, and thanks for being a friend.

(An unreal shot of Chris at a stadium show, the crowd all has their phone lights on, it's stunning. Chris and I backstage somewhere, and Chris dressed up like he's . . . I don't know how to describe it . . . for one thing, he's wearing a fanny pack!)

*All photos and supplemental material can be found on TENACIOUSBOOK.COM

INTERLUDE ONE, CONTINUED

Here's one more story I couldn't resist sharing. It proves that once you've had the tenacity to overcome failure, not even the sky's the limit. Ladies and gentlemen, our next guest is out of this world—and he literally has been.

NASA ASTRONAUT THOMAS MARSHBURN
ON FAILING

In my life there have been so many moments that were particularly hard. Moments where I failed and doubt came pouring in. I'd ask myself, *What am I doing?* Or worse, *Should I just give all this up?* I tend to be introspective; I have these internal conversations and I question myself. That can be great or debilitating, depending on what you do next.

Believe it or not, I started failing math tests when I got into high school. At the time, I wanted to be an artist. I loved to draw and paint. I didn't love math. But then I read an incredible book titled *Thirteen* about the Apollo 13 mission. That changed everything for me. At some point while reading it, I dared to think, *Could I be an astronaut?* Well, I was pretty sure that astronauts didn't fail math tests, so I had to reset my brain—rewire my thinking to train it for those math problems. I had to learn how to learn. So I did.

First, I needed to be extremely honest with myself as to why I wasn't understanding a problem. I'd get mad, frustrated, and even scared. I would think, *I can't do this.* You know what? If I had stayed in that mindset, I could have made that outcome 100 percent true. But what if I didn't? I worked on putting those emotions aside and found that when I did, I could think. Then I'd slowly and coolly break down the problem and reconstruct it. *Why am I missing it? What am I not understanding?* I was working *with* failure instead of letting it beat me down. The key was to turn off my self-doubt. Dwelling on those feelings just keeps you from moving forward. You have to get over your failures. You have to press on. This is so very important.

Putting those emotions aside was hard at first, but it's like a muscle; if you work it, it keeps getting stronger, and I worked it. If you are like I was—and I suspect many of you are—your own doubt might be part of what is holding you back.

Second—and this is just as important—you have to find something you love. I wasn't motivated to overcome my math struggles until I started to dream of space; then I had the motivation. And you know, with that in place, it all felt different. I didn't worry so much about my failures, because the failure was now worth it. I learned to tamp down any anger I might feel toward myself and instead just calmly evaluate where things went wrong. When I did these two things, everything started to click for me. Not just the math, *everything*.

Where did this practice of embracing failure take the kid who was failing math? Two hundred and fifty nautical miles above the earth, hurtling along at a speed of 17,500 miles per hour! That's right, it took me where I had long dreamed of going.

On July 20, 2009, I took my first space walk. My crewmate Dave Wolf and I were getting suited up in the air lock of the shuttle *Endeavor*, which was docked to the space station. Spacewalking is a dangerous business—equivalent to launch and landing as the most dangerous things we do in space. No one has ever been lost on a walk, so you sure don't want to be the first.

It's hard to explain the feelings around your first space walk, but imagine a combination of your excitement as a kid on Christmas morning wrapped around the feeling of walking into the biggest test of your life. You're thrilled but quite daunted.

The moment is so huge, but you lean into your training. You suit up like you've done a hundred times before. You think, *I know this suit. I'm OK.* You gather your tools—*all familiar there too.* You hear the beautiful sounds of the tools floating about, clanking off each other and the walls. But then it's time to let the air out of the air lock. In an instant all the clanking and chiming goes away. The silence is sudden and jarring. *Whoa, who turned off the volume?* With no atmosphere, there isn't anything for the sound to travel across. I wasn't fully ready for that. That's when you know this is *not* a simulation. Tick my nerves up another notch.

As the door opened I saw the remarkable view of the earth below me—the terminator dividing the dark of night from the brilliant new day. It was breathtaking. But in this same moment I sensed the infinite void of space, and I felt very untethered, unsupported. Surprisingly, I felt like I was falling. At first, everything in my body screamed, "*No*, don't go out there!" My training taught me otherwise, but the primitive survival instincts in my brain stem went into overdrive. I was used to zero gravity by this point, but with walls around me, and unlike practicing underwater on earth in the NBL tank, I was floating inside my space suit. Without gravity, there's no pressure on the bottom of your feet or in the seat of your pants. There is no other way to describe it than to say you are falling. You literally are, and it's really frightening on some primal level.

As hard to process as this truly was, I once again leaned into putting emotion aside. My conditioning prevailed, and I was able to move forward. As I exited the craft, there was the whole earth below me, sharper and bigger than any picture could be. It's the most spectacular view you can imagine—easily the most incredible thing I had experienced up to this point in my life.

Remember this: No matter what your dream is, there will be failures. That's guaranteed. You need to accept that up front so that when failure occurs, you'll learn from it and move on. It was that kind of tenacity that carried me from failing math, all the way to my dream 250 nautical miles above the earth.

Wow, as a kid who dreamed of being in space, this one really gets me. I should say I am still a kid who still dreams of space. When Tom describes exiting the station and seeing the Earth below, he is one hundred percent describing a dream of mine. I loved hearing him explain how he felt like he was falling; I have actually experienced zero G training by riding the affectionately dubbed vomit comet, a full size jet that dives straight to earth so its passengers can briefly experience weightlessness. It's wildly disorienting as the ground falls away from your feet. I can't imagine how that sensation might multiply if instead of floating with the plane fuselage a few feet away, the next closest thing was the earth 250 miles below! Thank you, Tom, for sharing this amazing story and reiterating that failure is going to happen; what's important is how you handle it.

So are you getting the message? You cannot be tenacious without failing! Accept it. Heck, embrace it! Try not to fail, but don't let the fear of it paralyze you. Depending on how you handle it, failing will make you stronger, not weaker!

I spent three years as a ski instructor when I was a teen. I would often hear new skiers brag that they hadn't fallen down all day. To me that was an indication that they hadn't tried very hard—that they didn't hang out there enough to risk falling. The ones who pushed their limits fell down but learned more. Ultimately, they would be the better skiers. It's a pretty good metaphor for life. Put me in the group that falls down, please!

(If this isn't an iconic photo, I don't know what is. It's right out of a movie. Thomas in his space suit. A picture of me floating in the vomit comet, weightless as it plummets toward Earth.)

*All photos and supplemental material can be found on **TENACIOUSBOOK.COM**

CHAPTER 6

With or Without U2

> Success is not final; failure is not fatal. It is the courage to continue that counts.
> —Winston S. Churchill

I let myself down . . .

The kid who was mortally afraid of failing had finally tried . . . and failed. Ever since being told I could no longer follow U2, I was sleeping in every day—depressed, disappointed, lamenting the loss. The fire that had burned within me on tour was now an ember at best. I still knew in my heart that I wanted to bring music to people for a living, but I had no idea what to do next. Sometimes when we fail, instead of trying the same thing again, we need to adjust our course, bend our tenacity around the obstacles in our way. I supposed I could still try to sneak into U2 shows, but that would certainly end poorly. My friends on the crew made the management's thoughts clear. No, I would have to find another way. As my best pal and bus driver Mikey says, "There's more than one way around the barn." Mikey usually says this right after missing a turn, but he isn't wrong! Is there something in your life that you have tenaciously been tackling? Are you not getting anywhere? If so, maybe it's time to see if there's another way around the barn? There was for me.

When the phone finally rang, and it was Lawrence, the cinders reignited!

"Yes!" I said—yes to whatever your plan is!

Lawrence laughed. "I told you about touring through Southeast Asia with Stevie Wonder, right?"

"Yes." Lawrence's stories about that tour were amazing.

He continued, "We carried video projectors that were a nightmare to keep running; it's the most complex piece of gear I've ever seen. My thinking is that the kid who spent five weeks living in his car and working for free just might have the grit it takes to master these beasts. What do you think?"

I felt the fear holding me back, but that wasn't who I was going to be anymore. "I'm in," I said. "How do I get started?"

"Great." I could hear the excitement in Lawrence's voice. "They teach a weeklong class on how to run the projectors at the GE submarine plant in Syracuse."

"OK, how do I reach them?" I asked.

Lawrence laughed again. "I guess just call information and ask for the number to the top military clearance GE submarine plant."

It was funny when he said it that way, but I could do that!

Submerging

"Hello, directory assistance, can I help you?"

That's right—back before the Internet, we actually called the operator on a telephone plugged into the wall and asked a human to help us find numbers.

"Yes, could you please connect me to the GE factory in Syracuse, New York."

"Sure thing, hold on . . . Sir, do you know the name of the factory?"

"I don't, no."

"Well, when I look up GE in Syracuse I get dozens of listings."

"Oh, I see. I want the plant where they make the submarine parts. Do any of the names seem like they are related to that?"

"Stand by," she replied. It took a while for her to speak again. Clearly there were a lot of GE numbers in Syracuse. "I'm afraid not, sir."

"OK, thank you for your time."

Back then, directory assistance was a quarter—that was 25 cents down the drain. I thought for a moment and then picked the phone back up.

"Hello, directory assistance, can I help you?"

"Hi, I need the number for GE in Syracuse, New York. I know that there are many listings, but could you give me any of those numbers, please? Perhaps pick one that sounds important?" (The operator laughed.)

"Um. OK. Connecting you now . . ."

Not surprisingly, I did not luck into getting the right number. But the person who answered was able to give me the main administration line. Then, the lady in administration gave me a number for the Military Development office, and the Military Development people gave me the Nuclear Sub buildings' main number, and that guy gave me the number for the projection school. Less than an hour into my quest, I was on the line with GE Talaria Projector Operations! I was going back to school.

I arrived at the hotel the day before school started, dropped my bags in my room, and went down to grab a bite in the lobby restaurant and bar.

As I sat at a table and ordered, I noticed a guy sitting alone at the bar having a beer. I bet he was in the school too. I would have happily joined him, and maybe made an industry connection, but sadly I was still nineteen years old, and too young to sit at the bar. My burger arrived, interrupting my desire in the moment to be older. I have always liked hotel burgers. I still do. They come with chunky fries smothered in salt, the juicy patty is made of actual meat, and heck, I even like the pickle slice they invariably put on the plate.

Food has always been a comfort for me, no doubt to a fault. This meal was both satisfying and delicious. As I took a bite of the juicy burger, I was nervous about what tomorrow would have in store. This marked the first time in my life I would be in class for something I actually needed to know in real life. We are all aware by now of my history of academic failures. I paid the bill and then swung by the bar to chat with the man I spied earlier.

"Hi, any chance you're here for the projector school?" I asked.

"I am," he replied with a grin. "John Fletcher. Can I buy you a beer?"

I didn't want to let on that I was underage, and while I did have a fake ID, getting arrested the day before school seemed unwise. "Hey John, I'm Scott. Rain check on the beer, but I'll see you tomorrow at lobby call."

"Cheers," he replied, tipping his glass.

Early the next morning, about a dozen of us piled into a passenger van that carted us off to the factory. While Lawrence was kidding when he said it was a top-secret nuclear sub plant, it was actually quite secure. They ran background checks and issued badges. It was made clear to us that we were to follow security to the projection area and never venture out from there. The farm boy in me thought this was very cool. We were marched into class and handed two massive three-ring-binder textbooks. *Oh shit*, I thought, staring down at the intimidating binders.

Ever go to the beach as a kid and get distracted while playing in the water, only to look up just as a huge wave was upon you? Well, that was the feeling I had in class. The course, I discovered, assumed a foundation of video knowledge and a base understanding of circuit-level electronics. I had no such knowledge. That information, not unlike a tidal wave, knocked me over, and I was submerged.

I fought to compose myself as my anxiety rose quickly. Just then, John from the bar corrected the teacher on something. *Interesting*, I thought. As class progressed, this happened a few more times. John actually knew more than the instructor. This gave me an idea. I started taking notes detailing everything that I didn't understand.

As we piled back into the van after class, I managed to sit next to John.

"What did you think?" I asked.

"It was more basic than I had hoped," he replied. "I'm not sure I will learn much."

"Yeah, I think you actually taught the teacher a few things today. I have a deal for you: I will buy your dinner and all your drinks this week if you are willing to answer my questions."

"Sure, why not," he grinned. "That'll be fun."

He had no idea what he was getting himself into.

We sat at a table for two, although John wanted to sit at the bar. Embarrassed, I had to tell him that I wasn't old enough to drink, so I wasn't allowed to sit there. After small talk, we ordered dinner, then I pulled out the notebook and started lobbing questions at him. By my third question, he leaned back and asked, "How many questions do you have?"

I sheepishly showed him the pages of notes I'd taken. He rolled his eyes. "Do you know *anything* about this stuff?"

"Sadly, no," I confessed.

He tilted his head. "Why are you here?"

I sighed and started to tell him. If he was expecting a one-sentence answer, he was in for yet another surprise. I gave him a ten-minute summary instead. I touched on all the major points of my story, including dropping out, my fear of failure, Sandy being killed, U2, and living in my car. To his credit, he listened patiently.

"Wow," he said as he took in all this new information. After a pause, he smiled. "We need to get you up to speed, don't we?"

"Yes, please."

John was a great and patient tutor, answering and explaining the finer points of the course for hours each night. I was so grateful, and John seemed to enjoy it too.

On the last day, the instructor handed out the test. Multiple choice! I loved multiple choice. Test makers are inevitably careless about leaving clues in the context.

I labored over my answers and was the last to finish. Imagine my surprise when I landed the second-highest score in the class! John had the highest, of course. He was really proud of me. He should've been—he'd made it happen. As we went to say goodbye that day, he gave me the best news of all.

"Listen, I took the liberty of calling my boss. I told him that there was a kid here who doesn't know his head from his ass. [That would be me!] But I think given a chance, he could learn. I told him about how hard you worked and that you tricked and/or bribed me into being your tutor. I also told him I thought you were worth talking to. It's not rock and roll, but do you want to interview at my company in Washington, DC? We specialize in audio/visual for major events. You wouldn't be on tour, but you would be learning the touring technology."

"Hell, yes!" I nearly shouted. "I would love to!"

Future View

I got back in the BRAT and once again found myself on the road. Not to sneak my way into a U2 show this time but rather to get to a real interview. My Aunt Joan and Uncle Stan lived in DC, and they graciously offered to let me stay at their house along with my cousins

Cindy and Carol Jean. Once again, my trusty Rand McNally *Road Atlas* showed the way. Eight hours later I pulled into their place, just in time for a nice meal.

Sleep did not come easily that night. I was afraid much of the projector knowledge I'd learned at GE had already escaped me. I got up bleary-eyed the next morning and made my way to Future View. I straightened the skinny tie on my "cool" suit. In hindsight, I wasn't much to look at in my ill-fitting attire and with my long hair pulled back in a ponytail.

The owners—two brothers, David and James Hanrahan—interviewed me at length. At the end of the meeting they looked at each other and David said, "Well, we are missing a projectionist. When can you start?"

I am ashamed to admit that I was afraid to say yes. Avoiding their expected answer of "I'll take the job," I instead offered, "I have to move from New York."

They sensed more was going on. I really wish that I was better at covering up my feelings.

"Can I tell you tomorrow?" I asked.

"Could you start a week from now perhaps?" David prodded.

My chest tightened. This was what I wanted, but . . . I smiled tensely. "I'll let you know tomorrow."

Back at Aunt Joan and Uncle Stan's, everyone was full of questions. They were thrilled to hear I had been offered the job and equally confused that I wasn't jumping at the chance. My cousin Cindy started working on me. I was no match for her, and her opening argument proved that.

"Let's go to a bar and talk about this," she offered, smiling. I had a fake ID, but I didn't want to get caught using it and be arrested three states from home.

"I'm only nineteen," I reminded her, surprised that she was already twenty-one.

"When is your birthday?" she asked.

"July 30th." Cindy smiled a now fully mischievous grin. She played her trump card.

"You are old enough to drink in DC. We changed the age to twenty-one, but they put in a grandfather clause, and you and I just made the cut." Cindy picked up the phone.

"What are you doing?" I asked.

"Calling the police," she responded slyly. The information line at the station answered and confirmed that I had indeed made the cutoff.

"Thank you," Cindy replied, her smug smile resembling Angela Lansbury's in the final scene of every *Murder She Wrote* episode, at the very moment when she blows the defense's argument to pieces.

If I move here, I can go to bars legally? I thought. That's huge for a nineteen-year-old who had already been arrested once for underage drinking. (Ask me the story if we ever meet.) I could jump right to adulthood! My mind raced for a brief moment, and when I looked at Cindy, she was still grinning like the Cheshire cat.

I caved. "I'm taking the job. I'm moving to DC!"

The whole family laughed out loud. I had made my decision, not for a reason that I could be proud of, but what the heck, I was committed.

The Toll

So I relocated to DC. The first days at Future View were overwhelming. Since I was the new guy, they put me on every gig no one else wanted to do. That first week I worked ninety-three hours. The next week, the total was ninety-four. That's when the sleep deprivation set in, and it never really left me for a full year.

One night, while driving home from work at three in the morning, I dozed off. I swerved as I caught myself, a bit rattled. A moment later, night turned to day as police lights flooded my rearview. The combination of startling myself and the police stopping me had my heart pounding.

"Step out of the car, please."

The officer was really hard on me. It was apparent he thought I had been drinking. He gave me a few sobriety tests before finally escorting me home, afraid I would fall asleep again.

It also became apparent that taking this job because I could get into bars wasn't very beneficial. I didn't have time for a social life. Living with family was nice though. Aunt Joan would warm up leftovers when I came home late. I am so thankful to Aunt Joan and Uncle Stan for their hospitality. Although both have passed, my gratitude lives on.

As my time at Future View continued, the long hours gave way to shows where I had more and more responsibility. We would get into a shiny white van and drive to the Capitol building, or the Senate or House buildings, or some office nearby, and set up a huge video screen so that the government could watch a presentation related to an upcoming decision. I worked near President Reagan often and got to know his Secret Service people. One of them was a really attractive lady I had a bit of a crush on. I bet that behind that alluring smile she was pretty dangerous. While I never personally met President Reagan, I was a huge fan. He was a tremendous leader and an incredible communicator. Heck, he was the most powerful man in the world. While I have never been tied to a political party, he was my president, and I loved him just as I loved my country. Being in the same room as him was electric.

While all of this sounds exciting, there was an undercurrent. The projectors were so finicky, and I was never fully comfortable running them. The stress started taking a toll on me. Soon there were some outward signs. For example, I found myself getting really angry when I was stuck in the inevitable DC traffic. I would pound my fists on the steering wheel and yell. I started having nightmares about failing to make the projectors work. I was mostly succeeding, but the occasional failure would shatter me. I tried to hide my tears from my coworkers, but, embarrassingly, there were times when I couldn't.

Once, I accidentally erased an incredible speech at a corporate event instead of making a copy. For a full decade, my heart would ache every time I recalled that error. Another time at the Kennedy Center Honors, with President Reagan watching, I hit play on a video and the image that came up on the screen looked terrible. I helplessly watched the distorted video play, before my boss ran up to show me my mistake. After a thirty-second analysis, he'd spotted the problem: A 75-cent resistor had failed. His fix took less than five seconds to implement. He looked at me like I was so stupid, and I absolutely felt as if I was. Honestly, a part of me died inside.

The stress escalated, and soon I was having excruciating headaches. As the pain and fatigue overwhelmed me, I ruminated that this wasn't really my dream. There was no music, no screaming fans. I wanted to give up, but I had made myself a promise to keep trying, so I persevered, even though I was losing more and more of myself inside. There were many times on gigs when I would find a place to hide and just cry. I think it's extra hard working toward a dream when you aren't headed straight for it. Corporate and political events weren't what I felt destined to do. Failing while heading in the wrong direction can make you feel extra hopeless.

The headaches got worse, and I finally found time to see a doctor. He officially diagnosed me with migraines. They had become so bad that I started feeling physically ill, occasionally throwing up. The best way to describe the pain is to draw an analogy to what happens when you sprain a muscle and accidentally move it the wrong way. It's that same stabbing pain, but constant, and relentless, and happening inside your head.

As many other migraine sufferers will tell you, it can make you feel like an artery is about to burst and you're going to drop lifelessly to the floor. At some point, the pain becomes so intense that despite all logic to the contrary, and the fact that you have experienced this before and lived, you convince yourself that this time you'll die.

One of the owners, James Hanrahan, asked me into the office one day to see how I was doing. I admitted that I was struggling and that I was so afraid of letting him and the clients down.

"Want to hear about failing?" he asked. I nodded yes, and James continued.

"I was doing a huge show for the American Advertising Agency in the massive Hyatt Regency ballroom in downtown DC. We shot footage of DC landmarks and edited it into a montage that would play at the opening of the show. I cued it up and paused it. Unbeknownst to me, the tape deck was malfunctioning and started creeping backwards into the raw footage. With full confidence, I spoke into the God mic [a backstage microphone wired into the ballroom sound system]. My voice boomed as if from heaven, filling the massive ballroom. 'Ladies and gentlemen, we are so glad you could join us today. Before we get started, let's enjoy a few scenes from beautiful Washington, DC.' I hit play and instead of breathtaking scenes of the Capitol, the Lincoln Memorial, and the White House, there was just footage of pigeons. I blurted out, 'Where did all of those f-ing pigeons come from?' realizing an instant later that the mic was still open and my profanity could be heard by everyone."

James paused to let his story sink in. "*That's* failing."

He went on, "In the client's eyes, it was a devastating travesty that erased any and all of the goodwill he'd earned by flying hundreds of people in from around the country to be there—a travesty that might get him fired. So, the next time you think you have failed, remember my f-ing pigeons and know that it could always be worse, and that I managed to live through that humiliation and anguish, so it's ultimately survivable."

James was a good leader. I'm not sure how much he helped my stress overall, given how hardwired it was, but to this day I laugh whenever I think about his f-ing pigeons.

Perhaps the stress would be more bearable, I thought, if we could work on some music gigs instead of corporate ones. My tenacity felt as though it had bent to near breaking. I started hanging out with one of our salespeople, Michael. As I recall, Michael used to be Kool & the Gang's monitor engineer, which made him awesome in my eyes. Michael missed music and wanted to get Future View into that area, so we started scheming.

This Bud's for You

Within a few months, Michael had landed us a music tour with the first show in Atlanta. I thought it was called Budfest. I say this, but looking back through the Web I can't find proof of this show's existence that lines up with my timeline, so I must be getting something wrong. Whatever it was called, it was music and I was thrilled! Never mind the fact that I didn't know any of the acts in the show. I could finally escape my skinny tie and hear the roar of the crowd.

Loading our equipment into the stadium gave me fantastic flashbacks to my time with U2. As the massive sound system fired up, I reminisced about riding the golf cart with Bono's cousin AJ. I smiled. This was my dream.

Sadly, our lack of experience doing outdoor shows quickly became evident. We barely got our equipment set up in time. A piece of gear broke, and we didn't have a spare, so I had to cobble a connection together with a short piece of wire and an alligator clip. It didn't want to stay connected, so I spent the entire show nervously hovering over it.

We had older tube cameras, and they did especially poorly in low light, particularly with the dark flesh tones onstage. A couple of fans walked up to me and asked why the images looked so bad. One even told me I should just turn the screens off. I was crushed.

Afterward, Michael tried to focus on the bright side. "Look, we know that we can do better next time." I agreed, and, good news: The next stop on the tour was Washington, DC. The event was at RFK Stadium, right in our backyard. The next day, however, the client called to inform us they had hired a different company for the DC show. We had been fired.

After giving it some thought, I asked the Hanrahans if I could have a long weekend home in New York. What I didn't tell them was that I was about to pull a page from my old playbook. On Friday, I was going to sneak into the DC load in to try and glean what the competition was doing better than us.

I arrived early at the stadium and parked near the backstage entrance. I held a magazine up to the steering wheel, so I looked like I was reading, but instead I was assessing security as stagehands came and went. It didn't seem very tight. I took a deep breath and donned my fake white laminate for the first time since I was following U2. Sneaking in when you are nobody feels really different than sneaking in when you are the guy who got fired from the gig. If caught, I would likely be seen as someone who intended to do harm. I imagined they might arrest me, and, if so, Future View might have to fire me. Was this worth it? I thought about how far from my dreams my life was and how frustrated I had been, then I opened the car door and started walking toward the stadium.

I was a nervous wreck as I passed security, but they didn't stop me! I found a spot out of the way and just observed. In fairly short order, I figured out who was in charge of the video. I walked up to him, smiling, with a plan to play to his ego.

"Hey, this stuff is pretty cool. Mind telling me about what you do?"

He gladly obliged, and I learned that Future View was even more lacking than I'd thought. We had what we needed to do a great job in the ballrooms, but his gear was far superior for outdoor work.

After a while I asked him how one goes about getting a gig like this. He was perhaps a bit too honest. The first thing he said was that the previous company (us) had all the wrong gear and didn't know what they were doing. That hurt, but I couldn't argue. Next, I felt he implied that he'd taken care of the production manager to get the job. Looking for something or someone to blame other than me, I decided that might mean he did something unfair. My look hardened, and my feelings apparently betrayed me.

He questioned, "Who are you, anyway?"

I blurted out angrily, "I'm the previous video company!"

He started yelling at me for being sneaky. Despite having no evidence, I returned fire, angry about how he may have stolen our gig, while somehow forgetting our poor performance as a logical reason for why we'd lost the work. The yelling had gone on for a bit when a third guy showed up.

It was Peter Daniel, whom I was hired to replace when he left Future View to start his own company. The guy I was yelling at had, in turn, hired Peter's company to provide the screens when we got fired. Basically, we lost the gig to a guy I saw as a traitor for leaving Future View!

"Guys, what's going on here?" Peter asked.

I thought for a moment and gave a surprisingly honest answer.

"I think this guy did something I don't like, but you know what? I don't even know. The real reason I'm yelling is that I'm frustrated with my life!"

That answer seemed to surprise everyone, including me. My adversary shook his head and angrily huffed off. (I don't recall who that was, but whoever you are, I'm sorry I was yelling. I was just at my wits' end. In hindsight, our poor performance was reason enough to be fired. I'm sorry I accused you of wrongdoing.)

Peter remained and asked me what was so hard. I explained that I wanted to get Future View into music, but it was a struggle.

Peter wisely replied, "Well, that's great, but do they really want that? And if they did, would they be willing to buy the right gear?"

"Great questions," I said, pondering the answers.

To my surprise, I really enjoyed talking to Peter, and we spent what seemed like a good hour together.

"Peter, it was really nice meeting you, but I am going home to New York for the weekend to lick my wounds. Thanks for taking some time to talk with me, but if I don't go now, I'll get stuck in traffic the whole way up."

"Nice talking to you too," he said, but as I turned to walk away he added, "Scott, I just landed the Rolling Stones tour, and I'd like to talk to you about it."

Holy shit . . .

I stopped walking and turned to face Peter, stunned and speechless. Peter finally broke the silence.

"I know you want to beat the traffic, but if you're interested in the gig, give me your number."

"Um . . . yes, I am interested," I replied flatly. I wasn't playing it cool; I was just too overwhelmed to take it all in. I calmly gave Peter my New York and DC numbers (remember, there were no cell phones back then) and headed for the door.

Steeling Myself

So there I was, sitting in traffic heading north to New York to take a break from my failures at Future View, while also trying to absorb the bombshell Peter had dropped on me . . . kicking myself for how lame my reaction was. Traffic on the East Coast is hit or miss, and I missed. With no traffic, the trip would be six hours, but this time it was over nine. I had plenty of time to consider the possibility that Peter presented as well as to regret not being prepared for the conversation. I ran the scene over and over in my head.

When he offered me a chance at my dream gig, I was all but despondent. What the hell was the matter with me? Would Peter even feel like he should call me? I will say that sitting in New Jersey traffic is a perfect backdrop for such dark thoughts.

I finally pulled up to my dad's house in rural upstate New York. Stepping into the cool night air felt amazing. Off in the distance I could hear the creek gurgling despite the best efforts of a million crickets all vying for attention. It was too dark to see the water, but as I turned my head to listen to the babbling brook, lightning bugs danced before my eyes, flashing their own message. I stretched and took in the sensations, drinking in the feelings this mountain home stirred.

The crickets, lightning bugs, and I all had something in common. We were calling out, hoping for a response. I had been sending up SOS signals to the universe, and it seemed it had finally responded with Peter's stunning statement: "I just got the Rolling Stones tour, and I'd really like to talk to you about it." That was just what I needed to hear, but I had been too weary to properly reply. I was near my breaking point, and I just wanted to go home. My roots had called me, and here I was.

I turned my eyes to the stars. The whole Milky Way opened up before me. I smiled. There above me was my first love, space. As a child I so longed to travel there. I studied astronomy and was heartbroken when I learned that my asthma would keep me from becoming an astronaut. I still loved looking skyward, even though I had traded my astral ambitions for a different kind of star. It felt great to be home, and I already felt better.

I entered my old room at my dad's—the room I had covered with space posters as a child. The room I'd filled with model rockets and dreams. The place felt huge back then, but now I was struck by how small it really was. In the old familiar kitchen, I poured a glass of cold milk and cracked open the seal on a box of local Freihofer's Chocolate Chip Cookies. There is nothing like a bite of the soft, chewy cookies you grew up with after some time away. I took a minute to savor it melting in my mouth. The answering machine light was on, yet I didn't let myself get excited about it. I had left Peter in show mode. There was no way he would have called already. I pressed the button and reached for another cookie.

The answering machine kicked into gear and a digital voice said, "You have one new message." The tape rewound. Then, with a loud click, it popped into play mode.

"Scott, this is Peter Daniel with Performance. After talking with my business partners, we want to interview you right away. Any chance you can interview tomorrow? I know it's Saturday, so I get it if you can't."

With the cookie still hanging out of my mouth and my eyes pried wide open, I grabbed my bag and snuck back past my sleeping father's room. I spent one last moment being serenaded by the crickets, taking in as much of "home" as I could, and then I got back into my car. I was going to drive all night to make it to that interview.

I pulled over twice on the way for a nap. I had taken the cookies with me, and, of course, my blood sugar crashed sometime after eating the last one. I arrived back at my aunt and uncle's house shortly after dawn. I set the alarm for 10 a.m. and fell into bed. I woke up, wiped the sleep from my eyes, and called Peter. He wanted to meet at their office. I hurriedly cleaned up and made the forty-five-minute drive to Performance, drinking three Mountain Dews on the way. Besides exhaustion, I felt real guilt, as if I was cheating on Future View. My lack of satisfaction there was not their fault; they had been so good to me.

A smiling Peter greeted me and informed me that his partner Lee Griffin couldn't make it but that his other partner, Greg Gurner, would join us. Greg was intense right out of the gate with a serious handshake. He locked eyes with me. "So you think you have what it takes to tour with the Stones," Greg asked, holding my hand hostage for an awkwardly long time. He successfully established dominance and, in my tired state, threw me a bit off. This interview, I gleaned, was not going to be a cakewalk.

Whereas the interview with the founders of Future View over a year ago was all about character, Peter led right away with a discussion of technical skills. Besides being president of the company, he was also their sharpest technician. He really knew his stuff and asked all of the right questions. I answered honestly, even admitting shortcomings.

They wanted to know my motivation, so I gladly shared my story. As I was talking, Peter surprisingly filled in some blanks for me. I told him that my friend Lawrence had learned about the projectors on tour with Stevie Wonder in Southeast Asia while helping their projectionist. As soon as I spoke those words, Peter laughed and exclaimed, "That was me!" He was clearly pleased.

"If that's true, then I have been following you around," I replied. "Future View hired me to fill the void you left."

They both laughed at this, and then Peter narrowed his gaze. "Well, maybe you should keep following me."

A couple of hours into the interview, the Mountain Dew was wearing off. I was losing steam, and I desperately needed to use the restroom for a second time. I once again asked to be excused.

"Again?" asked Greg, ever happy to poke me for chinks in my armor.

"Yeah, sorry, I had several Mountain Dews on the drive."

Peter reacted, "Oh God, that's right, you went to New York. You must have driven all night to get here."

"Yes, but I was happy to." For the first time, Greg looked impressed.

When I returned, I felt a shift in the conversation. Perhaps they just felt sorry for me after realizing my exhaustion, or perhaps they were impressed. Either way, they both took the intensity down a notch, and in my state, I was grateful.

After three hours of questions, there was a long pause. Peter and Greg looked at each other and nodded. Peter turned to me, smiled, and asked, "Scott, would you like to go on the Rolling Stones *Steel Wheels* tour?"

This time I did not hesitate. "Yes, I would!"

Rear View

When I awoke Monday morning, my mind was swirling. I had just accepted my dream job, but I was conflicted about leaving Future View. Touring the world with music was my dream, but how could I abandon the people who had taught me so much? And worse, how could I go to work for their competitors?

I arrived at Future View and asked for an audience with the Hanrahans. I found myself shaking as I sat down to talk with them. With a quivering voice, I told them what had transpired. I stressed how much I appreciated all they had done for me and told them the thought of leaving felt awful. But I also expressed my frustration with our lack of ability to do music-based shows.

I was torturing myself over the decision to leave, and they were just listening attentively. They weren't acting angry at all, which made me want to be loyal to them even more. Finally, my guilt overwhelmed me. In an unexpected burst, I told them if they could show me a path where Future View would start doing music, I would stay. I was relieved and crushed by what had just come out of my mouth. Trading my dreams for loyalty yet again.

The Hanrahans paused for a long time. Then James sighed and said, "You should take the gig." He frowned and continued, "If we keep you here we will get one, maybe two years out of you before you realize that we aren't ever going to do what you dream of doing. You will grow to resent us."

He pause before adding, "It's your dream, and it's an amazing opportunity. We just ask one thing as you go."

I nodded, ready to accept his terms whatever they might be.

"Please speak kindly of us as you move forward."

That is a wish I have happily honored.

Rolling

Bus driver Mikey was right: There is more than one way around the barn. My tenacity had bent and headed off on a tangent, and though I was frustrated by the detour, I dug in and worked hard, using the experience I gained to become better qualified to fulfill my dream.

In fact, this tangent created my chance meeting with Peter. Never underestimate the value of being in the right place at the right time! Again I ask, are you also hitting the same failure button on repeat? If so, might there be another path? Tenacity is stubborn, and it gets back up when it falls down. It is also smart enough to know there is always another way forward. Be tenacious, be brave, be stubborn! But be smart and patient enough to favor a detour over a blocked road.

Someone who knows exactly what I am talking about is my life-long friend, Kate Snow. We've been hanging out ever since we met at a Huey Lewis concert, before either of us knew what we wanted to do with our lives. Nowadays you all know Kate as a television journalist for NBC News, where she is an anchor for NBC *News Daily*. She is also a senior national correspondent and contributes to various NBC platforms, including *Today* and NBC *Nightly News*. If anyone can tell us about finding another way around the barn, it's her.

Thanks for your willingness to share with us, Kate.

KATE SNOW
ON BEING TENACIOUS

Scott is actually the guy who knows all about barns! How many times so far has he mentioned growing up on a farm?! All teasing aside, Scott and I go back—way back—to high school in upstate New York. I grew up in a slightly bigger small town than his, with an apple orchard out behind my house. Back when I met Scott at age sixteen, I had no earthly idea what I wanted to do with my life. And if you had told me then that I'd become a network news anchor living just outside "the City" (that's what Upstaters call New York City), I would've said you were crazy.

I didn't get to where I am by chance or by accident. I got here through really hard work, some talent, and a whole lot of tenacity. And not just regular tenacity, but the kind of flexible tenacity that has to bend and curve and take a detour every once in a while. Let me tell you a few stories.

Let's start with videotapes. Anybody remember what a tape is? But first, some background. Around the time Scott was touring with U2, I had seen a flier in my college dorm advertising an organizing meeting for an off-campus radio station. I convinced my friend Monica to walk there with me because I thought it would be *so* cool to be a radio DJ and play music. But when I raised my hand, someone said, "No, we don't need any more DJs. What we really need are news people."

Hmm. News? I had never taken a journalism class or even written for my school paper. But sure, why not? So I signed up to cover city council meetings, car crashes, and other hyperlocal news. Turns out I was pretty good at it. I developed the basic skills of a reporter, and by my senior year of college I was the news anchor during the "morning drive" hours. I tried to get a job in news radio before graduation but ended up collecting rejection letter after rejection letter and literally hanging them on the walls of my shared apartment. Why? Because if we had five rejection letters we could go to The Palms and they'd give us a free pitcher of Schaefer. With no job offers (and lots of pitchers), it was an obvious decision to go on to grad school.

Once I finished school, I did finally land a job. It was an entry-level position as a behind-the-scenes producer at CNN in Atlanta. My role was to book guests. I would find a guest, interview them by phone, then write up a bunch of suggested questions and hand them to an anchor. Then the anchor would read my words! An amazing job for a twenty-three-year-old, for sure. But it wasn't what I actually wanted to do. I wanted to do what I had done on radio. I wanted to connect with the audience. I wanted to be the person in front of the camera. I wanted to report.

Here's where the first big lesson in being tenacious showed up in my life. The year was 1995. And back then, to get any job as a TV reporter, I knew I would need to make a tape (you know, like a VHS tape) and send it in an envelope through the actual mail to a small local station. Now, I had never been on TV at this point. Radio, yes. TV, no. But because I worked at CNN headquarters, I had a lot of twentysomething friends in low-level jobs who could help me. After my day ended as a booker, I begged those friends to teach me how to edit tape at night. (This was back before cell phones and editing your video to post on TikTok even existed.) I begged another friend who was already a local reporter in Atlanta to take me along with her on weekends as she covered actual news, such as murders and robberies. I shadowed her and learned how to craft an on-camera "standup" (the part where you earnestly look into the camera and describe things, often while walking). I taught myself how to craft a script for a story. And within a few months, I had enough edited stories, which had never actually aired anywhere, to show a news director what I might be able to do for their station if they took a chance on me. Did I mention I had no actual experience as a TV reporter?

I remember going to the library and taking out the *Broadcasting and Cable Yearbook*—this thick directory that contained the name, call letters, and address for every local station in the country. I targeted places where I thought I could stand to live. Some were in upstate New York near my parents. Some were near Atlanta (and my boyfriend). Others were in places that just sounded like cool places I could call home for a while. I loved the Southwest and West, so I sent tapes to stations out there too.

I am not lying when I tell you that I sent out about one hundred VHS tapes. *One hundred!*

And then I waited . . . and waited. I remember interviewing at a station in Fort Myers, Florida, with a gruff news director who very quickly pronounced, "You'll never make it as a reporter." I wish to hell I remembered who that guy was. I'd love to call him.

In the end, do you want to guess how many job offers I got?

Three. That's right. Ninety-seven rejections and three offers. One was in Helena, Montana, where they offered to pay me less than my little brother was making as a pizza delivery guy. One was in Columbus, Georgia, where a military base dominates local coverage. I almost went there just because it was a close drive from Atlanta where the boyfriend was. But I ended up choosing KOAT in Albuquerque, New Mexico. Only I wasn't based in Albuquerque. I would be the "bureau" in the small city of Carlsbad in southeastern New Mexico. I was a one-man band, meaning I carried all of the gear necessary to get me on TV. (And in the '90s that gear was *heavy!*) I would find stories to cover, drive a powder-blue K-car to the scene, shoot the video, do the interviews, and then return to a closet (literally) in a local cable office to edit my story.

Taking that job was, in hindsight, one of the best decisions I ever made. It was grueling and lonely and exhausting. And it taught me skills that I use to this day.

I moved all over New Mexico, to Roswell where the aliens landed, and then eventually to the mother ship in Albuquerque. I met my now-husband Chris there, and we moved back to Atlanta so I could take an entry-level correspondent job at CNN, the network where I had once booked guests. (Always, always keep in touch with people from past employment!)

I pushed and pushed to move up to Washington, DC. That happened in 2000. We had our first child in 2002, and when I was on maternity leave my contract was coming up. I carried a breast pump in a shoulder bag and interviewed at every major network in New York. ABC News hired me to cover the White House for *Good Morning America*.

Now here's a story I don't often tell.

I'll never forget my very first live shot as a White House correspondent. I was standing on the West Lawn in August of 2003 when I heard a voice in my earpiece. "Look at her. She's so pasty and white," the voice said. "She looks terrible." It was the unmistakable baritone of the anchorman. "Can't someone go up and pinch her cheeks? Get a little color in there," I heard him say. No, really . . . he said that.

I instantly felt my cheeks start to redden from the sheer embarrassment and shame. Mission accomplished; I was no longer pale. But I felt like a failure on my very first night, before the broadcast had even begun.

"I can hear you," I said out loud to the camera.

"I know, Kate," he answered. "I know you can."

Another time, when most of the ABC News on-air staff was in the newsroom practicing for election night coverage, that same anchor singled me out in front of everyone in the room and said, "Your legs look better in pants than in skirts." And another time he criticized me for wearing a red jacket. A fellow female correspondent gave me a quick, compassionate look that telegraphed, "I'm with you." Years later, when I covered the Me Too movement every day for months . . . I thought back on all of this and winced.

Those comments were misogynistic, to be sure. But they didn't stop me. In fact, they probably made me work even harder.

The following year, I started hearing rumors that ABC might be starting a brand-new weekend version of *Good Morning America*. This was my chance! It was the opening I'd been waiting for. I called the head of on-air talent and told her I really wanted to be considered for the position of anchor. I'd be willing to move to New York.

"We'll keep you in mind," she said.

Fast-forward a couple of months, and I hear that they've hired a male anchor for this new GMA Weekend show and are searching for a female co-host. Again, I raised my hand. "We'll keep you in mind."

It was springtime, and Chris and I planned a trip to Oregon to visit my sister and her family. We were in a car with our young kids strapped into car seats, driving from Portland out to the beautiful Oregon coast, on a winding highway with towering pine trees shading the road. All of a sudden my phone rang. It was the head of on-air talent.

"Kate, I just want to let you know that we're moving forward with our search for a co-anchor of *GMA Weekend*. This is really just a courtesy call to inform you that we'll be doing some screen tests tomorrow in New York. I know I'm catching you on vacation and there's no need for you to change your plans for this.

Besides, we think you're more of a 'Washington reporter,' not an anchor," she said.

I paused.

"But . . . my vacation is over, actually," I began. (Um, it wasn't). "If I could get to New York by morning would you let me do a screen test?"

"Well, I guess so."

"Great! I'll be there."

I hung up and looked at my sister. "I need to cut this trip short and take a red-eye back to New York tonight. I have to book a flight!"

Chris agreed that he could stay with our son while I flew all night to arrive in New York City by 7 a.m. I will never forget what I did next. The suitcase I had with me was packed with vacation clothes—shorts, T-shirts, bathing suit. So I took a cab straight from LaGuardia Airport to Saks Fifth Avenue and bought an entire outfit—from shoes to a pants suit (early 2000s!), a shirt, and a handbag. I showed up to the screen test on zero sleep but somehow I aced it. The only part I remember was having to ad-lib about Avril Lavigne.

They ran focus groups for what seemed like an eternity, showing my screen test to real-life viewers to get their reactions. I was just about to give up hope when I got the call.

"You got the job. You're moving to New York."

For pretty much my entire career to that point, I had relied on hard work and tenacity—never giving up and pushing myself to the limit. It got me my first job after all those rejected tapes. It got me to the White House. The goal-setting helped me ignore that sexist anchorman. And it landed me my dream job.

A quick summary of some highlights at ABC: I covered Hillary Clinton's 2008 campaign, anchored live in Africa trailing animals on the Great Migration, pulled g's with the Thunderbirds, partied with Richard Branson, interviewed Bono . . .

But five years into that amazing job, I ran into a wall. *Hard.*

It was the summer of 2009, and Diane Sawyer was leaving the weekday *Good Morning America* program to become the anchor of *ABC World News Tonight*. ABC was looking for a new weekday anchor team, and I desperately wanted to be a part of it! I told anyone who would listen that I wanted to be on the new team. I had barely taken one day off a week, toiling away on weekends, missing my kids (Oh yeah: I had *two* now!), and working crazy hours. I wanted that Monday-through-Friday gig. And to be honest, I thought it was mine. One of the bookers even told me she was already planning guest interviews for me to do when I moved to Monday through Friday.

So imagine my heartbreak when the president of ABC News came to my office and sat down.

"Kate, I'm sorry but we're going in a different direction."

I fell apart. I started sobbing—like, snot-dripping-from-my-nose sobbing. I felt like everything I had done for all those years had counted for nothing. I was being passed over. I wasn't good enough. (Damn, the TV business is a subjective and judgmental environment, and that self-talk was mean.) I felt humiliated because I was crying in front of the big boss.

What am I supposed to do now? I thought.

I guess . . . find another way around the barn.

ABC didn't want me to leave. In fact, they came to me with a really nice offer to do the same weekend job I'd been doing. I said no. Rightly or wrongly, I felt like I would be trapped on weekends and couldn't see a path out. It felt like it was a dead end.

So I had my agent call NBC. After a series of meetings, they made it clear they would hire me away from ABC. But there was

> a catch: I would not come into NBC as an anchor. I would be a correspondent for *Dateline*. Professionally, this was basically a lateral move. Some of my mentors urged me not to do it. "Don't switch networks unless you're getting the brass ring," one famous TV anchor said to me at the time.
>
> I didn't listen to them. I listened to myself. In my heart, I felt like starting fresh at a new network would be a clean slate. I knew that a detour was better than sitting at a roadblock.
>
> It's been fifteen years now that I've been at NBC News. I've held many different roles here. It has been an amazing journey—better than I ever could've imagined. I have reported from the biggest history-making moments. I've contributed to *Dateline*, another primetime, long-form show; *Nightly News*; *Today*; and our streaming platform NBC News Now. For eight and a half years I anchored the Sunday edition of *Nightly News*. And now I anchor *NBC News Daily*.
>
> But I'm most proud of the reporting and investigations I do that shine a light on issues that never get enough attention. I gravitate toward difficult subjects like sexual assault, mental health treatment, substance use, threats to children, and inequities in our systems. To balance that out, I also tell "good news" stories and sit down with people at the top of their game for a series called *The Drink with Kate Snow*.
>
> I'm honestly not sure I ever would have done all of this work if I had not made that "lateral" move to NBC. And right now—as I type this—I am once again an anchor of a network (and streaming) broadcast. Only I don't work weekends anymore.

I love Kate's story! It's inspiring on so many levels. Tenacity, as she has lived it, is driving the bus and never taking your hands off the wheel.

When Kate hit a traffic jam somewhere on the way to her dreams, she opted to take a daring off-ramp to a whole new network—against the advice of her peers. Kate steered away from her dream for a stretch, to find a less obstructed route. As you just read, this bold gamble paid off and she found her way after all! That's flexible tenacity! I have mad respect for her journey and appreciate her sharing it with us.

Thank you, Kate! I am honored to consider you a lifelong friend.

Remember: Banging your head against the wall repeatedly isn't tenacity; it's stubbornness! Be like Kate and don't be afraid to bend your tenacity. Look where it got her! And me? My detour intersected with the biggest tour in rock and roll history!

(Kate anchoring at NBC. Kate, a few friends, and I in a pile in someone's dorm room in 1987!)

*All photos and supplemental material can be found on TENACIOUSBOOK.COM

CHAPTER 7

Rolling with the Stones

Failure is success in progress.

—Albert Einstein

The lights dropped and the crowd went insane; I mean it was *nuts*. Fifty-five thousand fans erupted into a frenzy. The Stones were back. There it was again: the roar of the crowd, the sound of pure joy that forever changed me at that first U2 show. I turned my head away so Pete wouldn't see the tears in my eyes.

A jungle rhythm emanated from the massive speakers as the juggernaut that was the *Steel Wheels* tour came to life. Hundreds of lights blinked on, their beams slicing through the air as smoke billowed out of the beast. Now near deafening, the rhythm reached a crescendo, then abruptly fell silent. An instant later, it punched back up for one last round punctuated by an incredible explosion. Dozens of pyro concussions ignited, producing a shockwave that pounded the air out of your chest!

Simultaneously, a wall of flames one hundred feet wide and over thirty feet high threatened to sear your retinas! Even from my position eighty feet away, the heat seemed to burn my face. I knew what was coming and I was still overwhelmed. Stunned, the once roaring crowd hung in the aftershock for the briefest moment, then a breath later the epic guitar intro to "Start Me Up" ripped out of the PA as Keith Richards strolled onstage with his trademark swagger. The crowd erupted! Mick then bounded out with the energy of a teenager as Charlie hammered away on his kit. Ronnie and Bill sidled out to join them, and it was game on. Fifty-five thousand people simultaneously losing their minds. *Holy shit!* Is this how I am going to spend the next thirteen months of my life?!

Flying High

I think airports are great. I have always loved them. As a kid, we packed up sandwiches and drove to the nearest one to watch the planes take off. We wondered where they were going, and I often imagined I was on board. Now, a dozen years later, I stood in Albany International Airport, and it was my time to fly. I was soon soaring above the clouds at a speed my little Subaru could only have dreamt about. Before I knew it, New York City sprawled out below my window. What a sight.

I grabbed a cab to the Stones rehearsal at Nassau Coliseum, a wonderful coincidence. You may remember this was the first stop on my U2 "worst plan ever" odyssey. When last there, I snuck in, scared to death I would be arrested. Not this day. I walked straight into the arena bowl.

I had pondered how the team would fit a stadium show inside this smaller venue, but I was not prepared for the spectacle that awaited me. The monster that was the *Steel Wheels* stage filled my entire view. It took a minute to catch my breath. The set stretched the entire length of the arena floor the long way, then climbed up into the seats. It had impressive width, but the height was remarkable. The stage was over one hundred feet tall—almost as lofty as the arena itself! It looked like a towering industrial building still under construction, or maybe a scene of postapocalyptic destruction. There were two gargantuan, smoking steel pipes jutting from its facade, huge ramps, and runways connecting different levels that were divided by massive, oversized girders. It even had a working elevator to take Mick to the top! I stood there in total awe while it hissed and belched smoke and fire as if it were alive!

Suddenly, moving lights ignited, cutting through the atmosphere like a hundred lightsabers engaged in a chaotic duel. And then the sound . . . subwoofer tests rumbled and growled, making the entire place shake. It was a monster, and we were going to spring it from its cage and ride it across the globe!

I allowed myself to take in the moment. It seemed a lifetime ago that I had experienced that paradigm shift at the U2 show. All of the struggle, heartbreak, and tears I endured along the way—and better yet, all of the small victories, friends made, and lessons learned—landed me here again.

I had indeed arrived, though one challenge persisted. Despite all that had transpired since then, I still had serious doubts. I didn't feel ready. I questioned if I even deserved to be there. It's one thing to take those crucial first steps toward your dream when you have nothing to lose, and quite another thing when you feel you have *everything* to lose. Once again, I was nursing fears.

I gazed at the remarkable scene around me for a long while and then set out to find the production office. The lovely production assistant handed me an itinerary book and a radio. She smiled and said, "One last thing," then handed me my laminate. A Rolling Stones backstage pass! Two and a half years after waiting on U2's techs at the Howard Johnson's, I was officially on tour. And a massive tour at that!

I walked into the belly of the arena and found Peter. Over the next couple of hours he explained our responsibilities. It was our job to set up and align the three massive video screens. One of them was 120 feet in the air! It was a good thing I'm not afraid of heights. Each of the screens had four of GE's state-of-the-art projectors. That's well over a million dollars of technology per screen (adjusted for inflation). The two stage screens had thirty-five-foot-long fabric "tunnels" flown behind them to block out any ambient light from washing out the screen. Imagine a funnel-shaped sock stretching thirty-five feet back, completely enclosing the light path from the projectors to the screen. This massive fabric tunnel was ratcheted into place with tension so it looked solid when it was properly deployed. I was concerned that these huge structures were frighteningly susceptible to wind.

When I was working with Future View, it was enough of a challenge to point one single projector at the screen. But now, for the huge screens to be bright enough, we had to overlap four projectors. That meant more than four times the work and four times the chance of failure. All this had to be done working one hundred feet in the air, at times in torrential rain and high winds. Lawrence wasn't kidding—I think this is the worst job on the tour.

We flew the video screens into place before calling it a day. I walked across the lot to the very same Marriott Hotel from that first U2 show. I stood in the same parking spot under the same tree that my BRAT had nestled under. I felt myself getting emotional thinking back to that first night crammed into the back of my Subaru. Wow, I had come a long way.

The Machine

The orchestrated effort to move the massive stage around the planet was incredible.

The *Steel Wheels* tour was actually a well-coordinated dance involving seven independent traveling systems, each with their own tour itinerary. The production was so big and took so long to build and move that it required redundancy. There were four full sets of the massive steel structures designated A, B, C, and D. Each one took a week to move, so they would leapfrog around the country. If the Stones were playing on the "A" stage in one city, the "B" structure was already built and almost set for a show in the next city; the "C" structure was being built in the city after that; and the "D" structure, which had just completed a show in the previous city, was being torn down. Four sets of the massive stage and four sets of steel crews were always employed in four different cities at once to keep this show running.

Then there were the lights, sound, and massive decorative pieces and elevators—two fully redundant sets of all of that as well. They were designated as the Red and Blue systems, and that gear and those people also leapfrogged, doing every other show. Think about it: At any given moment the 450 crew members were dispersed in teams throughout four different cities.

Finally, there was a seventh team dubbed the "universal team." They consisted of three tractor trailers filled with equipment and thirty-eight people deemed essential enough to be at every show. Somehow, even though I was the new kid, I was on the universal team. Although I was the youngest of the 450-member crew, I was one of the few needed in every city, often flying cross-country to hop from stage to stage for the shows.

At the head of this circus was an incredible man named Michael Ahearn. Michael, who looked a lot like a cross between Jerry Garcia and Santa Claus, was the overarching production coordinator. Beneath him, there was universal production manager Jerry Gilleland and Red and Blue team production managers Paul Chavarria and David Stallbaumer, respectively. Last but definitely not least, there was the legendary British stage manager, Roy Lamb. Let's start with Roy, because Roy sure started with me.

We had loaded the Red system out of the arena in Nassau at a leisurely pace, focusing on our process rather than stressing speed. The next stop was Philadelphia, where, uniquely, two stadiums were located right next to each other. The Red system was built in one, the Blue in the other. There we practiced a load-out to see how fast we could strike the universal system and get it to the other stadium. Stage manager Roy had decided that our projectors would load quickly on the first truck.

An announcement came over the radio that the clock had started; it was time to tear down and load out. The projectors needed to be rigged to a chain motor that would lower them into a case waiting below. Unfortunately, the projectors were positioned so high that the trip down and up with the motor took a lot of time. The motors, which were designed to carry a huge load, traveled at a mere sixteen feet per minute. I soon realized that we were going to be late. Before I knew it my radio crackled to life and Roy Lamb's voice barked out, "Where are my f-ing projectors!"

"It's going to be a bit," I sheepishly replied.

"No, it f-ing isn't," Roy barked back. "I need those f-ing projectors, and I need them now!"

I didn't know what to say. I had my finger on the motor control button, and the projector was making its way down at a snail's pace. It was seventy feet to the deck below—six trips up and down, and another six trips on the other side. It would take almost an hour just for this one task! Roy wanted our gear ready in forty-five minutes. We were over thirty minutes late, and Roy's nerve-shattering scream came in hot. Pete knew what we needed: smaller and faster motors. We could get some, but it wouldn't be for a couple of cities. I had started off on the wrong foot with Roy. That wasn't good.

It was a mad rush to load into the stadium across the street. I found myself working all night to get the twelve projectors aligned. I finally headed back toward the hotel at 9 a.m., completely exhausted. I slept during the day, heading back to the gig at 5 p.m. for dinner and the show.

At 9 p.m. I stood in the middle of an ocean of people, all excited to see the Rolling Stones' first show in over a decade. I climbed to my perch on the third floor of the tower in the middle of the stadium and sat at the controls as the radio squawked, "Go for house lights." The sound and stage presence of this iconic band was something to behold. As described in the opening of this chapter, the jungle rhythm, the wall of flames, the pyrotechnics . . . the Rolling Stones did not disappoint, and after all I had endured to get here, I was moved to tears.

Drowning

We had two incredible shows in Philly before striking for the next city.

Not having the new faster motors yet, things did *not* go well. Peter apparently knew better than to answer Roy when he started barking for us on the radio. I keyed my mic and once again said that it would be a while, as our motors could go only so fast. Roy was having none of it and resumed screaming at me every few minutes. I was failing him. He didn't want to hear about the slow motors. My worst fear was coming true. I was keenly aware that there were more than a hundred radios out there. They were all hearing my name as Roy demanded, "Where is Scott f-ing Scovill, and my f-ing video projectors!"

I knew that as the youngest person on the tour, I was already under scrutiny. Roy was letting the whole tour know that I was royally messing up.

With my nerves shattered, I walked away from the semitruck door as it closed, our gear finally loaded. I did have an exciting moment coming, so I tried to shake off the funk. I was about to take my very first tour-bus ride. This bus didn't have a space shuttle image painted on it, but it was still amazing. I climbed aboard and cracked open a beer in the front lounge (think rolling living room). Pete, a few other bus mates, and notably Jerry Gilleland, the universal production manager, were already unwinding. The conversation was great, and thankfully there was no mention of Roy's yelling at me. Jerry, in particular, asked me a lot of questions. I got the sense that he was going to look after me a bit.

Our driver, Charlie, fired the big engine up, and the bus started rolling. Nobody paid much attention to it. I suppose to them, this was old hat. To me, it was amazing. The kid who had driven his tiny Subaru BRAT down seemingly endless highways night after lonely night was now sitting up front, drinking free beer, and rolling toward another country on the biggest tour ever!

Charlie hollered back, "Don't forget to bring your passport to me since we have a border crossing tonight." I handed Charlie mine and sat alongside him in the captain's chair. It was exhilarating sitting high over the road and watching the world roll by. As we passed cars, we could see people looking at our big, shiny bus and probably wondering who was inside. *Me . . . I am*, I thought, busting with pride.

Oh, and great news: The faster motors arrived in Toronto! But sadly, my hopes that we could finally make our stage manager happy were almost immediately dashed. To fit more than sixty thousand people in the stadium, we would have to position the projectors stage left inside the Jumbotron (the venue's huge built-in video scoreboard). This delicate operation was doable but, of course, it would take time. The load-out took too long. It was even worse than before! I finally turned my radio down. I worked for a while in silence, but the next thing I knew, Roy had climbed up into the Jumbotron and was standing over me yelling, "I need those f-ing projectors . . . yesterday!"

"Yes, sir," was my simple response.

"I mean it," he grumbled. "You and me are going to keep having f-ing problems, aren't we?"

"I hope not, sir. Today is different with the scoreboard in the way."

"Well, it feels like the same f-ing movie to me! I need those f-ing projectors! Now turn your f-ing radio back on!"

"Yes, sir."

I was shaking even after Roy left. After all of the struggle and sacrifice to get to here, I was failing big-time. My dream was fast becoming a nightmare.

Is there anything worse than the feeling that you are flunking at the very thing that is so important to you? I think not. While touring with the Stones, I was exactly where I wanted to be. That gave the test of each moment gravity. Success felt like magic, but the weight of failure felt catastrophic. My fear of this ending in a fiasco never left me. It darkened even the brightest moments.

Motoring

I finally got the projectors out of the scoreboard and retreated to the bus for a beer. Exhausted, I climbed into my bunk a bit early. I had been really nervous that I would get carsick (bus sick?) once we got moving. Nope. Gratefully, I slept like a baby. By the way, a crew bus has a lounge both in the front and in the back. The middle is where the bunks are located. Typically, there are two rows of three high bunks per side—twelve total. Bunks are like little coffins. The sounds from the motor, highway, and ventilation system combine to make great white noise so you aren't distracted by the conversations or music in the lounges. The noise and the vibration from the road put me right out. I drifted off with a quick thought: *Pittsburgh will be better.*

Unfortunately, Pittsburgh did *not* start off better . . . the weather was terrible. As soon as the show started, it began pouring. Remember those thirty-five-foot-long tunnels made of tautly fastened fabric? Well, as it turns out, this fabric stretches when it gets wet. At first I could just ratchet it tighter to compensate, but eventually pockets of water started to form. I watched in horror as the weight of the puddles pulled the fabric down, inviting more water to gather. Soon, huge, heavy, rain-filled pockets were hanging down, blocking the top of the image. This not only distracted the audience, it was dangerous—the weight threatened to tear the stage down.

The solution was a bit crazy. I strapped together two long wooden poles with a razor knife taped to the end of them. Then I climbed the wet, eighty-foot steel posts in the midst of the storm, clipped my climbing harness on and hung upside down in the tunnel, hoping to reach the water pockets. Even with the length of two wooden poles, I wasn't certain I could reach the hanging puddle, which was looking more like a lake by then. I extended my body as far as I could and stabbed at it. Damn, I was just a hair too far away. Finally, soaking wet, I leveraged my legs against the slippery steel and leaned out even farther, lashing until my spear hit the mark and a deluge of water poured from the massive, ruptured bulge. As it drained, the pocket shrunk and disappeared out of the picture. Success! I rappelled down, ran to the other side of the stage, climbed up the wet steel again with my spear, and repeated the process. I shudder to think what might have happened if the weight of that water had caused a collapse.

There was some good news: Having the new, fast motors at our disposal meant a decent chance for a quick load-out. At the last downbeat, we sprang into action, and forty-five minutes later all of the projectors were down. With my gear staged by the trucks, I spotted Roy. In a bold move I grabbed my radio and keyed the mic.

"Where the eff is Roy f-ing Lamb! Scott f-ing Scovill has his projectors ready to load. Where the eff is Roy f-ing Lamb!" Roy scrambled to grab his radio, but just as he went to key the mic he got suspicious. He slowly turned and scanned the horizon until his eyes landed on my grinning face, about fifteen feet away.

Roy nodded and keyed his mic. "Am I to gather that Scott f-ing Scovill has his projectors ready?"

"Yes, sir," was my proud reply.

Roy put down the radio and walked toward me, smiling. "Faster motors?" he asked.

"No, sir. I just finally started listening," was my sarcastic reply.

He laughed knowingly, then gave me a wink and said, "You just might work out." I nodded. "Now get them on the f-ing truck," he commanded, eyebrows raised.

"Yes, sir," was my happy reply.

That night having beers on the bus with the guys was really gratifying. Jerry asked if I had sorted myself out a bit with Roy. Clearly he heard me fake yell at him on the radio. I proudly recalled the interaction. Perhaps the best part of the evening was Peter describing the scene as the water was collecting dangerously in the tunnels.

"I was watching from the tower out front, and these huge shadows were drooping into the image on each screen, like huge boobs. I'm watching them get bigger, thinking, *Oh, this isn't good. That's a ton of weight.* Then there is a quick shadow . . . it strikes a few times, then finally hits its mark. All of a sudden this massive boob shadow is draining a huge stream of water. You could see it superimposed over the image of the band. And I'm like, *OK, the screen just needed to take a leak, I get it.*" Everyone laughed. "When ya gotta go, ya gotta go," Peter continued to more laughter. "A few minutes later, I watched the same movie play out on the other side. The other screen took a leak, too, and I think we all felt . . . relieved."

It was hilarious . . . now that it hadn't torn the stage down! I recounted my perspective of hanging upside down eighty feet high in the deluge with a duct-taped spear in my hand, trying to bust a boob. This garnered more laughter. I felt for the moment like I truly belonged. It was a moment of victory I desperately needed.

The next city was East Troy, Wisconsin, the only amphitheater on the schedule and thus a unique setup. There were no tunnels. Instead, we hung front projection screens on both sides of the stage.

Without the tunnels, I had to wait for dusk to align the projectors as the crowd walked in. After alignment, I left the projectors in a test pattern. They just happened to have the company name, Performance AV, on them. I then went to catering to grab something to eat. The crowd had already seen the pattern, so why not leave the logo up? It looked cool. Boy, was that a rookie mistake! I was called on the radio by the man himself, the boss of all the bosses, Michael Ahearn.

"Mr. Scovill, how much is your company paying to sponsor the Stones this evening?"

I was confused, but even without the details I could tell I'd screwed up. I didn't have to think long. "You want me to remove the test pattern?" I asked.

"No, I simply want to know how much you will be paying for your ongoing sponsorship. Thousands have already seen it. What is that worth?"

"I'm on my way to remove it," I replied hurriedly.

"Perhaps if you have a moment you could grace me with your presence . . . right after removing the logo."

"Yes, sir." *Shit*, I was getting called to the principal's office.

I shut off the pattern and ran to Mr. Ahearn's office as fast as I could. I stood outside for a moment to collect my breath. There he sat. As you may recall, I described him as a cross between Jerry Garcia and Santa Claus. This description was still spot on, even when he was angry. He gestured for me to sit and lowered his reading glasses, looking over them at me disapprovingly. He finally spoke after what seemed like an eternity.

"Young Mr. Scovill . . . just how young are you? Remind me."

"Twenty-one, sir."

"Twenty-one. I assume that at this spry young age this is your first tour?"

"Yes, sir."

"Do you think that maybe the biggest tour in history is an interesting place to find someone with your *sparse* résumé? I'm wondering if you shouldn't have more *experience*."

My heart sank. I didn't know what to say. He just gazed at me, then finally continued. "It is my understanding that some people are starting to get attached to you. Not me, but some people. I guess that for now, you will have to gain that experience here. *For now.* Did we gain any experience today, young Mr. Scovill?"

"Yes, sir. We learned that our logo does not belong on the screens."

Mr. Ahearn's face brightened, suddenly glowing like Saint Nick's. "Excellent! Well now, that's progress," he said sarcastically, before pausing again. Then, furrowing his brow, he graded my reaction and said, "You may go, Mr. Scovill."

"Yes, sir." As I stood to walk out, I felt sick. Michael had emphasized that I was on the tour "for now." Was I in jeopardy of being fired?

"Mr. Scovill," he called out. I stopped and turned around. "I think I might be starting to like you too."

Perhaps he saw how impacted I was and felt sorry for me. I could feel half the weight lift off of my shoulders. "I hope so, sir."

I called Peter on the radio. No doubt he'd heard Michael summon me. I went to where he was and filled in the gaps he had missed. He was not happy. I had embarrassed us and shown my lack of experience. The half of the weight I felt relieved of just minutes ago landed right back on my shoulders. Dammit. I was so afraid I would fail technically that I was now failing in *every* way.

The next five cities—Cincinnati, Raleigh, St. Louis, Louisville, and Syracuse—started me down a dangerous path. Peter needed to tend to the business of running the company. No easy task while you are on tour. As such, he increasingly left me alone to implement the projectors, and I was struggling. Twelve of these beastly machines spread out around the stadium was a lot of responsibility. Several times I had a part of a projector stop working, dimming the image that was already difficult to see in all the light. We had several shows where I did my best, but I was confident it wasn't good enough. My fear of failing started winning. Every night I looked at the screens at showtime and felt inadequate. I was convinced my work was less than the crowd deserved. My dream job had turned into a nightmare.

Gathering Moss

In Syracuse, I finally broke. I was one hundred feet in the air working on the stage-right tunnel, grappling with the tension on the fabric and falling behind schedule. My body was exhausted from the odd hours, and my muscles ached from fighting with this huge, heavy beast. I took a moment to rest, and a thought hit me.

I was just three hours from home . . .

I longed to go home and hug my mom. I had had enough. I was floundering and I knew it. I started crying, a little at first, but soon that gave way to full-on sobbing. I was suspended by my harness, and the sobs sent my body bouncing up and down. Horrified that the crew would see this weakness, I tried to calm down. Sometime later I managed to stop the tears, and I made a decision. The next city was DC, where Performance was based. We had a day off without a show. I would call a meeting and tell my bosses—Pete, Lee, and Greg—that I quit. That they had the wrong man. That I wasn't good enough.

Stumbling

My intention when I set out to write this book was to help you by sharing my story for better or worse, as you can learn from both. This was definitely a "for worse" moment. I no longer believed in myself. Instead of letting my tenacity drive me through the challenges, I told myself that I was in over my head. Instead of embracing the struggle, I convinced myself that I didn't belong there.

In any great endeavor, you must believe in yourself. You also must have faith in the workings of tenacity. You need to remember that failing is a part of that process but that you cannot suffer ultimate failure unless you stop trying. Be strong enough to fail, learn, make little adjustments, and try again. Since the *Joshua Tree* spark, I had been a champion of this process. Now, suddenly I was slipping. I think I know why. It was the gravity of the Rolling Stones.

What does that mean? Despite progress in overcoming my fears over the past year, when I found myself operating at the highest level I felt the pressure increase exponentially. For the first time, I was responsible for something that mattered to me. It all felt so heavy that I forgot what had gotten me there. I stopped believing in myself. And I forgot believing in tenacity. If only I'd had the sense to just keep doing what had gotten me there, I would have succeeded. Instead, I folded.

Have you ever failed because you didn't give yourself enough credit? Have you ever done everything right to get somewhere you wanted to be, then screwed it up because you got too nervous?

Are you being tenacious now? Or, by some chance, are you quitting? Are you telling yourself that you can't? Or that you shouldn't? Or that you are in over your head? And if you are thinking those things, are they true?

Stop that. Tenacity doesn't quit.

Believe in yourself. Believe in being tenacious.

Quitting

A few days later in DC, I stood in the company office with Pete, Lee, and Greg. They had assembled at my request, seemingly having no idea what I wanted to talk about until I blurted it out.

"You need to replace me." I paused, fighting back tears. "This is the most important thing I have ever done, and I am screwing it up every night."

Greg and Lee seemed shocked. They looked to Peter to see if what I was saying was right. Was I screwing it up? Peter looked at me incredulously. "Scott, you aren't screwing it up."

I could hear so many things in his voice. Frustration. Disbelief too. But also caring.

He said it again softer. "You aren't screwing it up. You have done great through a lot of challenging situations. The reality is that the gig is brutal. There will be times when things aren't perfect. That's why we have multiple projectors on each screen. You have been handling it fine."

I was reluctant to accept any of this, but what he said next is something I will never forget.

"There is more to the job than making the projectors work. Everyone knows that you are young, that it's your first tour, and that you have a really tough gig. But you have made people like you, so they are rooting for you. That's half the battle. If something is less than perfect, they can still tell you are doing your best. Scott, people like you. That people like you is at least half the gig. In that half, you are doing extremely well."

I distinctly remember thinking, *People like me? So what! I'm talking about failing and Pete is talking about my popularity. I'm failing!*

At the time, I thought Pete's words were nuts, even though they resonate incredibly with me now. As an inexperienced, scared twenty-one-year-old, I didn't really accept them. Letting my fear win in that moment meant it would be a long climb back up the cliff I had jumped off. I finally spoke, trying to bring the conversation back to sanity.

"But the projectors . . ."

Peter interrupted, frustrated again. "The projectors are doing fine. You are getting by. And you are getting better every day."

The third owner, Lee, chimed in. At this point I hardly knew him. "The people part can be the most important thing. I totally agree with Pete. If they like you, that's really important." Greg nodded. Their answers were unexpected. I relented, agreeing to stay on the tour.

Luckily, my bosses did not accept my resignation. I offer this example to show you that I let negative thoughts and fears undermine me. I forgot to live with tenacity. I failed . . . but with a little nudging, support, and guidance, I agreed to keep going. By the way, it's OK to get help along the way.

With our slow load-outs, I had failed to make Roy happy. Then I'd failed to show good judgment in putting our logo on screen. I also failed at being the best projectionist I could be on too many nights. In hindsight, though, I can see that failing is a major component of tenacity. Eventually I made Roy happy. His lesson that nothing less than great will do was not lost on me. Thank you, Roy. Michael Ahern calling me out about the logo on the screens taught me to be more mindful of the big picture. Thank you, Michael. Though I didn't always make the projectors perfect, little by little I was learning and making fewer mistakes. Still, I couldn't seem to overcome my fear of failure, my demons. But with a little love and encouragement from my bosses, I agreed to keep trying. The day I tried to quit, I gleaned a lot about the importance of being likable. There is gold in failure. It's a great way to learn.

Ed Sheeran, the brilliant singer and songwriter, gave this moving testament to tenacity:

> You learn nothing from success. Nothing. You learn everything from the failures. And this is the thing that annoys me about the state the world is in at the moment. No one talks about failure anymore. It's like shame. Like failure is shame. "Oh, let's bury that and not talk about that." No one goes, "Oh, what did we learn from that?" Whereas with success, everyone shouts about it. But there's nothing in success. Success happens from failing hundreds of times. It doesn't just happen overnight. You have to be rubbish.

And you have to have people laugh at you. And you have to have people go, "Oh, go on, get a real job, this isn't really going to work." And you have to believe that eventually it is going to get better.*

In fact, Ed famously shares a YouTube video of him singing "Addicted," a song he wrote and performed at age fourteen. (As of the writing of this chapter, the video is still there!)† To say it's definitely not his best work is an understatement; it's pretty awful! But five years later, at age nineteen, after countless failures and the lessons they taught him, he released "The A Team," a smash hit that was nominated for a Grammy and "Best British Single" at the Brit Awards.

That he boldly shares singing awfully at fourteen and speaks out on the subject of failure says so much to me about his character. Ed appreciates failing because he sees the value in it, and he doesn't mind using his own failure to inspire others to accept theirs and to move past it toward success.

My friend Cameron Herold has strong feelings about failing as well. You may not know his name, but trust me, he is a rock star in the business world. Listen to this: His entrepreneurial journey began at a young age, and by thirty-five, he had helped build his first two $100 million companies. But his greatest achievement came as chief operating officer (COO) of 1-800-GOT-JUNK?, where he engineered the company's spectacular growth from $2 million to $106 million in revenue and from 14 to 3,100 employees—all in just six years!

With those incredible successes, Cameron realized that the experience he had amassed was something he wanted to share with

---

* Ed Sheeran, "Ed Sheeran on the Power of Failure," *The Howard Stern Show*, YouTube, June 2, 2023, 1:47–2:41, https://www.youtube.com/watch?v=SwegMPrTHBc&t=30s.

† Ed Sheeran, "Addicted," from *The Orange Room* EP, YouTube, December 25, 2016, https://www.youtube.com/watch?v=6YS03WG2t1Q.

others so they could achieve their dreams too. He founded both the COO Alliance and the Invest in Your Leaders training organizations. Through those ventures, Cameron has coached some of the biggest names in business. Known as the "CEO Whisperer," he has a reputation for guiding his clients to double their profits and revenue in just three years or less!

Cam also shares his wealth of knowledge from the stage. He is a top-rated international speaker and has been paid to speak in twenty-nine countries and on all seven continents (yes, including Antarctica). *Forbes* magazine publisher Rich Karlgaard stated, "Cameron Herold is the best speaker I've ever heard . . . He hits grand slams."[*] Wow! Cam's reputation as a speaker is actually how we came to meet. I asked a mutual friend to introduce us in the hope that Cameron would mentor me a bit on public speaking. He agreed, and that meeting culminated with him insisting that I write a book—and now I have!

Cam, tell us about being tenacious, and better yet, tell us about failing!

CAMERON HEROLD
ON BEING TENACIOUS

First off, let me say that I fully believe being tenacious is the mechanism behind my success. It is a defining characteristic for me, and one that I value above virtually all else. As such, I loved the idea Scott had for this book, and I am so happy to throw in my two cents.

My dad was an entrepreneur. My grandparents were both entrepreneurs, and they gave us these lessons as young kids. I remember my dad telling me something when I was quite young.

---

[*] Rich Karlgaard, *Forbes*

He said, "If it's worth having, it's worth asking for. If it's worth having, it's worth pushing for." That landed, so for me, I'm like a dog with a bone. If I've got a vision about something, I just don't give up. Like, I have to go after it. In every single business I build, there's someone saying no—the banks are saying no, your competitors are saying no, your suppliers are saying no. This is where the test is, the tough times. But you can't give up. You just gotta figure that shit out.

Being raised to be an entrepreneur by an entrepreneur, I probably had fifteen different little hustles by the time I was nineteen. Then, at twenty, I started with a group called College Pro Painters, which went on to become the largest residential house painting company on the planet. At College Pro, being tenacious was one of the three traits we looked for when hiring eight hundred franchisees every year. And what we wanted in these franchisees was this:

> The dog-like work ethic to get over, under,
> and around any obstacle put in one's path.

That's what we'd look for in the interview process. In other words, we wanted tenacity. I have a favorite story from my time there, or should I say, the end of my time there.

I had ranked very high in tenacity on our tests. I'd been one of the top franchisees. I was the strongest general manager, but I had a single bad year. It was 1993; the markets crashed, the economy crashed, and I had a brutal year—just awful.

Then, in '94, I went out and opened the West Coast of the US, and I crushed it. I'd hired Kimball Musk to work for me (Elon's younger brother). I also hired his cousin, Peter Reeve, who built Solar City. I absolutely had the best year ever. I applied for a vice president role, and the president of the company said no because of the bad year I'd had before.

I'm like, "That's bullshit. You knew that everybody had struggled that year. You can't pin that year on me when I followed it up with the incredible year I just had." I was angry, but I collected myself. I thought for a second and told him, "I want to read you a quote by Theodore Roosevelt." It was this:

> It is not the critic who counts; not the man who points out how the strong man stumbles, or where the doer of deeds could have done them better. The credit belongs to the man who is actually in the arena, whose face is marred by dust and sweat and blood; who strives valiantly; who errs, who comes short again and again, because there is no effort without error and shortcoming; but who does actually strive to do the deeds; who knows great enthusiasms, the great devotions; who spends himself in a worthy cause; who at the best knows in the end the triumph of high achievement, and who at the worst, if he fails, at least fails while daring greatly, so that his place shall never be with those cold and timid souls who neither know victory nor defeat.*

I read him that quote and continued. "Don't you dare criticize my last year and say that's not why you're giving me the VP job. I know you're giving it to the founder's younger brother. So eff you. I resign." And I resigned.

---

* Theodore Roosevelt, "The Man in the Arena," Theodore Roosevelt Digital Library (Dickinson State University), https://www.theodorerooseveltcenter.org/Research/Digital-Library/Record?libID=o307754.

About two months later, I joined Brian Scudamore at 1-800-GOT-JUNK? and built one of the most successful businesses in the last couple of decades. I had the tenacity to overcome what had happened, and I knew how to do it. I just had to dig deep and prove it. So I dug out of a rough thing, moved to the West Coast of the United States from Toronto, and f-ing *slayed* it. When life knocks you down, you get back up and find a way.

My dad told me when I was quite young that I'll never be the smartest person—the one to figure it all out—but my R and D could stand for Rip off and Duplicate. So, my tenacity isn't like, How do I figure it out? I look to who's figured it out already and decide how I can do what they're doing. Can I just take the ideas that other people are doing and do them well?

As such, I definitely carried the tenacious guideline over to 1-800-GOT-JUNK?. As COO, I put tenacity down as one of the three traits that we looked for in every franchisee. But we did it a little differently there. We would interview and then rate candidates on a bell curve of one through five, 10 percent could get a five out of five, 20 percent could get a four, 40 percent could get a three, and so on. You had to be in the top 10 percent to get a five out of five.

One of our VPs was interviewing a candidate, and he said the guy was a five out of five on tenacity, and I had given him a one. So clearly, we saw something different. I'm like, "How did you rate this guy as a five out of five? He's like a bricklayer."

The VP defended him. "He's a hard worker."

I'm like, "No, he's a bricklayer. He has a hard job. He quit in school. He never followed his teacher's instructions. He never got a coach. He didn't try after hours. He's quit every sport he's ever been in. He's not tenacious. He ended up in a shitty blue-collar job and has to work hard."

The VP says, "Holy shit. He's not a five; he's a one."

The lesson is, don't mistake working hard for being tenacious. You need to work smart, right? You need to take the path of least resistance instead of just going in with blind determination. Blind determination is not smart; you're just like the fly that keeps smashing into the glass trying to get out. You're going to end up dead on the windowsill.

Speaking of smart, do you know that I carry my university transcript on my cell phone to show people I wasn't that smart? Brains are not why I've succeeded. I've succeeded because of the dog-like work ethic to get over, under, around any obstacle. I've succeeded not because I was brilliant but because I was smart enough to be tenacious.

I think about when I was just starting in business during my first stint at College Pro Painters. At twenty-one years old, I had twelve full-time employees. My friends had time during the day to go and play, and time after hours to play. I had to grind it out, do my accounting and estimates, figure out marketing, worry about payroll, get up early in the morning to fax the order to the paint store, then get to the paint store and drop off the supplies so that all six of my job sites had the materials they needed before the crew even got there. That wasn't necessarily fun, but I knew that the rewards would come.

Here's another example of the grind. Spoiler alert: This is where the failure comes in. Back in 1999 and early 2000, I was building an Internet company while I was living in Seattle. My wife was in Vancouver, Canada. I was driving from Vancouver to Seattle on Monday morning, staying in my condo until Friday night, then driving home to Vancouver. I did that crazy commute as the company exploded. We were hiring hundreds of people. It was nuts, but we could see what an incredible opportunity we had. All that sacrifice seemed to pay off, as we sold the company in January 2000 for $64 million. It was an all-stock deal that wasn't going to close until June.

Then, in March of 2000, Steve Ballmer proclaimed there was an Internet bubble, and the stock market started to crash. By the time we got out, our $64 million valuation was worth $3 million. We basically lost everything. I was sitting with the CEO, Steve White, on the fourth floor of our office in Seattle. And Steve, funny guy, looked out the window, and he says, "Kind of sucks. We're only on the fourth floor."

I'm like, "What are you talking about?"

He goes, "We'll only break our legs if we jump."

It was brutal. We ground ourselves to a pulp, sacrificed everything, and for what? I resigned and was leaving to go back up to Canada. As I stepped into the elevator, one of the employees tapped me on the shoulder and asked, "Are you OK?"

As I turned around to answer him, I collapsed on the elevator floor and started shaking and crying. I was on the verge of a clinical nervous breakdown from stress and not taking care of myself.

I went to a doctor the following week just to get a routine physical, because my wife and I were buying a home in Canada, and I needed a checkup to get insurance.

The doctor said, "What's going on?"

I'm like, "Everything's pretty good. I do have this weird metallic taste in the back of my throat."

He said, "Well, what do you mean?"

I said, "I don't know. My neck and shoulders are always tight. It feels like I'm chewing on aluminum or tin foil. I have this weird chemical taste in the back of my throat. That's the best way I can describe it."

He asked again about what was happening in my life. I said, "Not much. The stock market crashed. We lost the company. My wife's pregnant. Just quit my job. She's quitting her job. My mom's got cancer. I'm moving from the US back to Canada."

The doctor was like, "Wait, wait, pause, pause." He did this test: If you get 150 points, you have a 50 percent chance of a heart attack, and if you get 250 points, you have a 90 percent chance of a heart attack. I had *435* points. I was melting down and the stress was causing that weird chemical secretion. I didn't notice it, because I was full throttle. And then I'd drink at night, and I wasn't getting exercise. I had no time for that.

Why am I sharing this example? I was falling apart and this company was a failure. True, but I learned from it! I brushed off the dirt and kept going. These failures all taught me something, and as I have tenaciously moved forward, my experience has culminated in the success of 1-800-GOT-JUNK?, and COO Alliance, and Invest in Your Leaders training. The struggles have made me the speaker I am today, and they are the reason to read my books. So you can learn from my failures, just as you are learning from Scott's.

It took a while, but I've learned to take care of myself as well. I'm healthy; I've lost forty-two pounds. I quit drinking. I go to the gym; I work out with a trainer. If I showed you photos of what I looked like back then, it's crazy. But that was an extreme situation. My grandpa always said, "Keep your nose to the grindstone, then come up for air." I usually live by this sage advice, but in this case I took the risk and paid the toll. No regrets, but I do recognize that I am lucky I survived, and I am glad that I have learned to take better care of myself.

So, all that to say this: Being an entrepreneur is hard. Being tenacious is really the only way through, and because so many

> people don't have it in them, that leaves the spoils to those who won't give up. You can get there if you employ tenacity like I did, like Scott has. Read on!

Fantastic, Cam! The vulnerability you showed sharing your defeats as much as your victories is what makes you such an inspiring leader, communicator, and author. Thank you!

I strongly recommend that you entrepreneurial readers check out Cam's books, and if you ever get a chance to hear him speak you will be fired up!

As for me, back on the Stones tour, I had given up, which is the worst kind of failing. But thanks to that pep talk from people who had my interests at heart, I got back to work. It took me a little time to process what my bosses had said, and eventually I realized they were right. Just like in Cameron's story above, I had learned a lot of invaluable lessons. Being likable mattered way more than I had realized. Trying hard and caring was noticed. And so long as you showed improvement and didn't make the same mistakes twice, little hiccups along the way were forgiven. I stayed the course and learned those damn projectors. But more than that, I had learned to be tenacious.

As the tour rolled into the next year, my confidence built and my nightmare receded. I was finally living my dream of touring the world with music. This drove home the greatest lesson of all: Tenacity works!

I spent an incredible month in Tokyo with the Stones. We toured all over Europe. It was wild. Then Europe again, this time with David Bowie. My career was off to an amazing start. I so wish there was room in the book to share those adventures. Maybe someday they will appear in a book of their own.

In the meantime, please remember *not* to let the pain of your mistakes erode your tenacity. Learn from them. Grab the gold and move on. This story, and indeed life, has taught me to embrace Ed Sheeran's words. You learn nothing from success. You learn everything from failure. Sure, try to be successful. Try not to fail. But don't fear failure. Fear can freeze you in your tracks. You need to keep moving, keep trying. When you fumble, learn and move on tenaciously, recognizing that failure is an essential ingredient of success.

<blockquote>
I refuse to let my fear hold me
down just like a prisoner,
I'd rather make mistakes than just stand still
—lyrics from the song "Try,"
written by Scott Scovill, Victoria Shaw, and Madeline Stone
</blockquote>

(Cameron, Scott with long hair! The infamous video tunnel, and my Rolling Stones backstage pass.)

*All photos and supplemental material can be found on TENACIOUSBOOK.COM

INTERLUDE II
Arriving

In the last chapter, tenacity finally paid off and I arrived at my dream. I will never forget the incredible kickoff to that first Stones show. Just as the flames and explosions ignited, baked tears of joy ran down my smiling face because I knew I had arrived. Let's take a second to remind ourselves why we are tenacious by checking in with two of my friends who've also had incredible moments of arrival.

First up is my pal Terry Crisp, AKA Crispy. Terry played hockey in the NHL before they all wore helmets. (I tease him that this explains a lot about him.) His path is remarkable, and he absolutely should write a book. Sadly, I doubt he will; like all Canadian hockey players, he is so humble. As he shared the story below, I kept having to pull him back from talking about how great everyone else was. I'd say, "Hey pal, that's wonderful, but I want to hear about you too." Even with that nudging his message is riddled with gratitude, and grateful is what I am to know him and his amazing wife, Sheila. They are amazing people with *huge* hearts. They light up the room wherever they go.

May I present one of the greatest gentlemen I will ever know, Terry Crisp.

TERRY CRISP'S ARRIVAL

I always wanted to be a high school teacher. That was my goal in life. Back then, every Canadian boy dreamed of winning the Stanley Cup. But that's just a dream. I was going to be a teacher. But I started playing and just kept going. Why not? I was having fun.

Well, the next thing you know, the Boston Bruins signed me to a contract. There were only six teams in the league way back then [in 1965]. If you didn't belong to the good old boys' club, you didn't get a shot. So every year, I went to training camp, made the team, got a place to live, and played maybe one game before being shipped to the minors in Oklahoma. That felt miserable because I didn't think I should have been sent down.

They did the same thing for the next two years, and I was ready to quit hockey. But I got married to Sheila, the love of my life. Sheila said, "Like hell you are. You love the game. You're not going to go through life saying, 'Well, I could have been a hockey player, but I got married and had kids instead.'" She said, "That ain't gonna happen."

Next year, the NHL suddenly went from six to twelve teams. I got my chance in St. Louis, which was by far a real break for me. I was playing under Scotty Bowman, the best coach in the world, in my estimation—and many, many others agree. In St. Louis, we went to the Stanley Cup Finals for three years in a row. What an experience that was. Suddenly, you dare to imagine you could win the Cup. I don't care who it is—what team it is—as they move through the playoffs, they put 1,000 percent into it and are all banged up. They'll have hidden injuries; I sure had mine. Hell, we wouldn't tell the coach or the trainer because we wanted to play.

So, we went to war three years in a row with the Blues, and our record was 0-12. We never won a single playoff game in three years—none of them. With each loss, you would just feel sick; your heart would just go *boom* and hit the floor. I am proud to say we gave them a run. We gave them all they could handle, but that final buzzer would sound and your heart would drop.

If you know hockey, you know tradition dictates that the teams line up and shake hands. There's one team going down the line feeling grateful, victorious. We were the other team, going through with our guts just knotted because it was gone—you might never get the chance again.

Three years, 0-12, and that's when I got traded from St. Louis to the Islanders, and then on to Philly, playing for the second-best coach ever in my opinion, Fred Shero. I got to play under and learn from Scotty Bowman and Fred Shero. And if that's not a good grounding, then I don't know what the hell is. So here I was now in Philly, the would-be school teacher, just playing the sport he loves, until one Sunday afternoon we're playing the Boston Bruins. If we win this game, we've won the Stanley Cup. The Bruins had a wonderful team. There was Bobby Orr, Phil Esposito, Gerry Cheevers—you could go on down the line. It was a great team. But we had a great team too. Well, we found ourselves at the end of the second period winning, 1-0.

I'll never forget waiting for coach Shero during that second-period break. Now, Freddie was not much for words, but he always had something to say. We're all waiting, and he didn't come . . . didn't come. We're getting anxious. We're looking at the clock. Ten minutes to go . . . eight minutes to go . . . no Freddy. Five minutes, no Freddy. Shit, we need to get out there and warm up, get the skates going. At about four minutes before we've gotta hit the ice, Freddie comes in. He walked in the room, walked up to the blackboard, and just stared at it. Finally, he slowly turned and looked at every player in the room, right in the eye—*right in the eye*—without saying a word. He turned around again, put the chalk down on the blackboard, and walked out.

What just happened? What just happened?

This man just told us all what we needed to know: *I've taken you as far as I can take you. It's your game, boys.*

Twenty minutes later, and holy cow, we won! We were hoisting Lord Stanley. It was crazy. The fans came down on the ice—the whole hoopla was down there. I broke through that mosh and went where my mom and dad and wife and kids were sitting, just to wave to them and blow kisses to them. Winning the cup was my Mount Everest. That was my moment. It comes, and now you're thinking you should be out there celebrating. You should be going crazy. But no, the first thing that popped into my mind was my mom and dad and my wife and kids. I went and found them first, then I joined the celebration.

You know, there's a hockey team out west—a junior team. They're called the Princeton Posse, and their motto is "You are who you travel with." I'd love to put that on a T-shirt with a big biker motorcycle on the back. Because when you think about it, the people you pick to be your friends, that's most times who you are.

Thanks to some amazing teammates and coaches, it all worked out. But most importantly, after many years, I'm sitting here in Nashville, Tennessee, with my wife, Sheila. And we have three wonderful children up in Calgary, Alberta: Tony, Jeff, and Caley; and ten grandchildren. All through that sport called hockey. You are who you travel with.

Crispy, thank you for sharing that amazing moment of arrival as you finally won the Stanley Cup! You *are* who you travel with, and I feel so lucky to have you and Sheila as friends. You both have this wonderful positive energy around you. People love spending time with you, and so do I. Needless to say, it takes a mountain of tenacity to win the cup. Terry teased some of it, but since I had asked him to focus on his moment of arrival, he did just that. He really should write a book so we can hear it all.

Terry, by the way, went on to win the Cup again the next year. When he retired as a player, he went into coaching and won the Cup with Calgary as their head coach. Later, he moved into broadcasting and was the Nashville Predators color commentator, where over the decades, millions enjoyed the game through his unique perspective.

Thank you again, pal. You are the best!

(Crispy sporting three Stanley Cups, Crispy with Dierks and me after an Iceholes game.)

*All photos and supplemental material can be found on TENACIOUSBOOK.COM

Interlude II Arriving, continued

As I've mentioned before, when I was a little kid my bedroom was all about space—posters, toy astronauts, model rockets—and all of this even before *Star Wars* came out. My uncle Bob and Aunt Ginny gave me amazing books on astronomy, and my mom bought me a telescope. I was going to be an astronaut! Then, sadly, I discovered I had asthma, and my dreams of NASA slipped away. Nonetheless, I loved everything about space. I still do. Space nut that I am, I couldn't resist inviting another astronaut into these pages to inspire us.

Ladies and gentlemen, NASA Astronaut Cady Coleman has graciously agreed to share some of the early challenges she faced in her pursuit of space travel. And, best of all, she also recounts her moment of arrival—the stellar payoff for all her tenacity. Take it away, Cady.

NASA ASTRONAUT CADY COLEMAN'S ARRIVAL

When I first dreamed of becoming an astronaut in 1982, there had been just over sixty people who had been in space, and of those, only two were women! That's out of 4.6 billion people on the planet. It's easy to think nobody like me gets that job. I mean, what are the odds, right? More than one in a billion if you do the math! But – you just can't think that way. If you push aside that doubt, amazing things can happen. That's why I like to be public about my journey, especially because it wasn't always a straight path. No, it's been full of detours and obstacles, and I want people to realize that the path to a dream is rarely straight or easy for anyone.

Even after I was selected as a NASA astronaut (!!!) in 1992, there were significant challenges. One was the extravehicular

(EVA) space suit for spacewalking, which had been designed years ago to fit men. At 5'4", even the small suit was too big for me.

To practice spacewalking, we trained underwater at the Neutral Buoyancy Laboratory (NBL) where an enormous swimming pool holds mockups of the space shuttle and station. After donning our three hundred pound suits, a crane lowered us into the pool. Once submerged, weights were added to our suits to make us neutrally buoyant, allowing us to float without rising or sinking. For spacewalking, it's as close as we can get to simulating zero gravity on Earth.

Spacewalk training is physically grueling for anyone, but as a smaller person, operating in the suit was particularly tough because even the smallest suit was just so much bigger than me. But I did well despite that. I qualified in that too-large suit with above average grades, and I was ecstatic and proud to be selected as a spacewalker for my first two missions on the space shuttle. While no spacewalks turned out to be needed on those missions, it was important to be ready to go outside to address any emergency.

But then after my second mission, with Space Station construction underway, NASA made a decision with critical implications: They would eliminate the small space suits for Space Station missions (which would soon become the only missions, with the end of the Shuttle program). At that time, every astronaut who flew on the space station had to be a qualified spacewalker.

During the announcement, they said something that I still remember: "But don't worry, we've looked ahead at the manifest, and we have all of the space walkers that we need." In my mind, I responded with, *So if we can't qualify in the medium suit, a third of the women astronauts will be grounded—possibly for the rest of our careers. And it sounds like you won't even miss us!*

The decision had been made, and there was no debate. I will say this: I loved my time at NASA, and I loved the amazing people that I worked with there. But these moments, as painful as they are, are worth discussing so we can learn from them. I wish we lived in a world where everyone realized that the best person for the job might not be someone like themselves. It's a learning process to realize that people who are different from us—in the way they look, think, see things—are some of the most valuable people on a team because they complement our own strengths. Sadly that's not our reality yet. But little by little, people are speaking up and helping the world to change.

By this time, my dream of being an astronaut had evolved into a determination to fly on a long-duration mission on the International Space Station. The elimination of the small suit was like hitting a brick wall. But while I was frustrated and angry, somehow I was undaunted. I would climb that wall.

Proving to myself and others that I was capable of performing in that medium suit was daunting, exhausting, and often painful. Even when a suit fits, you have limited mobility and reach. And while it may look soft—like a giant marshmallow suit – it is actually inflated to a pressure of 4 PSI. Every single hand squeeze or limb flex is met with significant resistance. Most importantly, in a suit that is much too large, none of your joints are in the same place as those same joints on the suit. So, for one example, to use my left arm to manipulate a tool, I have to slide over within the suit to get my elbow in position to bend my arm. In the process, my right elbow is now totally out of position. So forget about using both arms at once!

> In addition to determination, I had a strategy. To maximize my ability to work in the suit, I made sure I was impeccably prepared for every other aspect of the spacewalk—every detail of the plan, and how the tools and the equipment worked. Importantly, I stayed cheerful and enthusiastic, at least outwardly. It made it easier for people to work with me and helped me keep my perspective.
>
> In the end, I qualified for spacewalking and I spent 159 days on the space station. I didn't know it at the time, but if I hadn't found ways to qualify in the medium suit, I would have waited to fly in space again for at least *eleven* years.

That's awesome, Cady. Your response to the challenges you faced is inspiring. Instead of using them as an excuse to strive for less, you leaned in extra hard and overcame those obstacles.

The physical struggle of the oversized suit and the challenge of excelling as a female in an environment customized for men were no match for your determination and tenacity. You went on to have other missions on the shuttle, and of course, you achieved your ultimate dream of living on the International Space Station.

If you have not yet read Cady's wonderful book *Sharing Space*, you must! Her story is fantastic, enlightening and inspiring. I wish I had room to share more of it here.

We are so grateful to you, Cady, for sharing space with us. Somewhere within me there is still a little boy who dreams of the stars; thank you for being a hero to him and to so many other dreamers.

Incredible stories like Terry's and Cady's are why we endure the hardship, rejection, and pain of failure. This is why we gladly spend our most precious commodity—time on this earth—exerting efforts toward a hope, a vision of what we might be. This is why we dream.

Because dreams can come true.

Now, back to the book in progress. We have just learned to be tenacious. What ever shall we do with this new power? Put it on the shelf and admire it like an award? Or take it for a spin?!

(Cady on the ISS; look at that hair! Cady in her massive suit at the Neutral Buoyancy Laboratory (NBL))

*All photos and supplemental material can be found on TENACIOUSBOOK.COM

CHAPTER 8

Building to a Crescendo

If your dreams don't scare you
You have the wrong dream.

—Richard Branson

My boss Lee timidly handed me a sheet of paper—an itinerary full of fairs and festivals. I read the heading: *Alan Jackson*. I looked up at my boss, Lee. "Any relation to Michael Jackson?"

Lee laughed out loud. "No! Alan Jackson is a country singer."

My eyes rolled. I shook my head in disbelief. "Does he wear a cowboy hat?"

"Yes, a big white one, like a good guy!"

By now, you know how my tenacity was sparked, how the flames were fanned to fruition, and how I endured occasional failure again. You also know about several of the amazing payoff moments. But the story has even more twists and turns than that.

After the Stones, I kept rolling. David Bowie, Whitney Houston, Paula Abdul, Ozzy. I was indeed living my dream. I became a master of my craft. I was seeing the world. I was helping to bring music to screaming fans. This was the life!

What do you do when being tenacious makes your dream come true? Keep dreaming—and *keep doing*. Take all that you have learned and deploy it again. There is no limit to where it can take you! As I just hinted, my life was about to take a sharp left turn. My rock and roll fantasy was about to be traded in for a pair of cowboy boots. What might the now confident, tenacious Scott Scovill find starting over in country music? Read on!

Neon Rainbow

In 1992, Alan Jackson's manager, Barry Coburn, had hired set designer Ian Knight of Led Zeppelin fame to design Alan's upcoming show. He had seen and decided the technology on Paula Abdul's tour was exactly what Alan needed. In contrast to Garth Brooks, who was swinging from the ceiling like a wild man, Alan Jackson refused to move from the mic stand. So we were hired to, as Barry told me, "Move the world behind Alan."

My parents had several country eight-track tapes that I was exposed to as a young man, but I hadn't listened since. In anticipation of being Alan Jackson's video director, I studied the music. I must admit I struggled at first. The structure and even some of the instruments were strange to me. What the hell was that sound? (It was a steel guitar.) Still, I studied hard until I felt fairly prepared.

On day one of the tour, I was standing side stage with the band, waiting for the show to start. Alan's then-twenty-year-old *violin* player, Mark McClurg, poked his bow at my notes accusingly. I looked down at where he was pointing. In bold letters, I had written "Violin." I turned and looked at Mark.

"Wrong," Mark said, with a crooked, tobacco-stuffed snarl.

I quickly reviewed the song in my head. I was sure there was a violin solo there. "Do you not perform the album version of the song?" I asked.

Mark was dumbfounded by my question. He shook his head in disbelief and snapped, "This ain't no violin; this is a *fiddle*," Mark continued, now thumping me in the chest with his bow. "We can't figure out why yer here . . . Alan says yer a Yankee who don't know nuthin' 'bout country music. Look at you—a New Yorker with long hair! Ridiculous."

Just then the house lights went to black. Mark turned and strolled onstage to the roar of the crowd. Time to do my first show; thanks for the pep talk, fiddler.

I struggled with the music's flow throughout the show. An exhausting hour and a half later, the house lights finally came up, ending my frustration. My then-video-directing mentor, Bob, offered only one bit of feedback. He looked at me, shook his head, and said, "Well, you failed me." Then he turned and walked away, heading to the airport and out of my life for a few years. You know how I feel about failing, so you can only imagine how that landed on me.

The old me would have crawled under a rock after a comment like that, but not the tenacious me. I studied show tapes obsessively, favoring that over sleep. Slowly, the music started making sense. By week two, there were reviews that noted how strong the video work was. Still, one opinion was glaringly absent: Alan's.

By the third week of silence, I convinced myself that Alan and I did not belong together. I decided to be proactive and asked the road manager, Tony Stevens, if I could meet with Alan.

"Sure, just go on the bus and say hi," was Tony's offhanded response.

"So could you arrange that?" I asked.

Tony stopped what he was doing, made eye contact with me, and smiled. Then he repeated, "Just go say hi."

I was confused. No one would ever just drop in on any of the stars I had worked with before. If you walked onto a rock star's bus unannounced, you would be fired immediately.

Tony, seeing my confusion, reiterated, "Don't knock. Just walk in so he doesn't have to get up."

I walked out to Alan's bus thinking this must be a setup. I knocked twice and then walked right in, cringing at what felt like a huge invasion of privacy.

There was Alan Jackson, an imposing figure at six feet five. I braced myself for the challenging conversation ahead. Alan raised his eyebrows. He was clearly surprised to see me, but he smiled. I was new to the Southern lifestyle, but I had already learned that most people (other than ~~violin~~ fiddle players) would be polite whether they liked you or not.

Alan spoke first. "Hey video man," he said, seemingly happy to see me.

"Hey singer," was my reply. I wasn't trying to be sarcastic; it just came out as a logical response. Alan didn't seem to mind.

"What can I do for you?" he asked.

"Well, I'd like to be honest, if I may."

"Sure," he nodded.

"I have been here for over two weeks, and you haven't said a word to me. If we aren't communicating, I don't see how I have any chance of making you happy. It was made clear to me from the start that you didn't want me here. I'm thinking we should part ways and find you someone who knows country music. I will continue to do my best until we find someone you would feel more comfortable with. Frankly, I don't really want to be here either."

Alan frowned, sizing me up, then sighed. "You sing?" he asked.

I was confused by his question. "No" seemed the obvious answer.

"Good. I don't direct video." He paused, collecting his thoughts. "I wouldn't know what to say about video. I'll admit that when I saw you I thought my manager was crazy. There you were, a Yankee from New York with hair down to your ass. They told me you were fresh off the Ozzy Osbourne tour. I heard you didn't know anything about country music. My fiddle player told me that you had written *violin* in your notes instead of *fiddle*."

I nodded in agreement. Alan paused, seemingly weighing his next words.

"Well, three weeks later, and I never want to do a show without you."

What?

"Did you just say you never want to do a show without me?"

Alan nodded. "Man, all I hear about is how cool all of the things you are doing on screen are. It seems like every time I turn around there is something new. What you do helps make the show exciting and lets me just sing."

This was not what I expected at all. I was ready for a big, spoiled star to tell me to take a flying leap because he didn't think I was country enough. Instead, Alan was genuine, thoughtful, complimentary, and appreciative.

I struggled to respond. "I guess that I could stick around for a while," I offered.

Alan nodded, not really happy with my answer. "How about for the rest of the year, and we talk about it again in January?" he asked.

It was August. That was a long time to hang here, but Alan had surprised me, and Lee wanted me here. "Sure, I guess I can do that."

Before I go on, I'd like to say that this was the start of an incredible relationship between Alan and me, and between his people and Moo TV. We spent over two decades together; in show business, that is an eternity! He was becoming the legend that he is today, and I am so fiercely proud to have played my role and to have called him a friend. Thank you, Alan, for everything.

Heel, Toe, Do-si-do

A rock tour hits the road and packs in five shows a week for months before taking an extended break. In country music they mostly tour on weekends. I looked at the schedule and realized I was going to have at least a few days off every week in Nashville. What the heck was I going to do? I hadn't had any free time for years.

Now, many of you reading this have likely been to Nashville. It's a huge party with never-ending waves of tourists sloshing in and out from all over the world. It's fun! But that was *not* the Nashville I moved to in 1992. Downtown Nashville was dangerous. The bars had metal detectors. Fighting and muggings were commonplace. I was strongly advised to never go downtown, and I never did. No, the Nashville I landed in was different.

In fact, it had just entered its line-dancing phase. The first weekend I was there I discovered a huge dance hall called Rodeo's in a strip mall. The scene inside was so bizarre my crew and I felt like we had fallen into the cantina from *Star Wars*. There we were, huddled together: Jerry from San Jose, who was half Asian, half Irish; Schmaba (pronounced Shmah-bah), who was 100 percent American Indian and hailed from Oklahoma; Robbie, a Puerto Rican from the Bronx; and me, a six-two rocker from upstate New York with hair down to my ass. We were quite a sight. We stood, dressed in all black and sneakers, surrounded by guys wearing cowboy boots and starched, vibrantly colored Garth Brooks rodeo-style shirts and girls in Southern skirts or tight-fitting Wranglers.

As the music played, they all swirled around, two-stepping in couples. When the next song started, they would cheer and fall into line. Every single person knew every single step of the line dance. If you have never seen a line dance in action, it's impressive. The whole dance floor instantly organizes in rows and does each step of a complex dance in unison. This was mind-blowing to my crew and me. By this time I had been to twenty-five countries around the world and had hardly seen anything as strange as Nashville in 1992.

Just a few days into my Music City adventure, my crew and I once again found ourselves at Rodeo's. Out on the dance floor, a girl caught my eye, and I was mesmerized. She wore tight jeans and a puffy, starched blouse. More notably, she had a huge smile and a thick mane of curly black hair. She was beautiful, and boy, could she move, dancing with a precision that blew me away. At a shade over five feet tall, her dance partners would just whip her around. At full arm extension, they would yank her back and she'd collide with them at impressive speed, only to bounce off spinning in some other direction a moment later. They would swing her between their legs and flip her up over their heads. It was amazing.

After I'd watched her for a good ten minutes, she took a break, and I just had to introduce myself. She eyed me up and down, deciding if she wanted to talk to me.

"It's my birthday," she told me in her heavy Mississippi accent. "You should buy me a drink."

We downed a shooter, and before I knew it I found myself slow dancing with her out on the floor. I wasn't much of a dancer, but I could slow dance. A song later, the pace picked up, and after a minute or so of my desperately trying to two-step, we laughingly agreed that it could wait for another time when the floor was less crowded. We talked for a good hour, but then they gave last call. I didn't want it to end.

Outside, I found myself climbing up into her jacked-up jeep. She had offered to drive me home. She paused as she went to turn the key, having second thoughts.

"What's my name?" she asked with a challenging tone.

Shit! She had told me, but I was terrible at names. I froze. She took her hand off the keys and repeated the question, this time with a wry smile. "What's my name?"

I did my best. I remembered it wasn't a common name. "It starts with an S," I stated matter-of-factly, and I could see that I was correct.

"And?" she asked hopefully.

After a long pause I knew I needed to at least take a stab at it. "Shea?"

She leaned over to my side of the jeep, opened the glove box, grabbed a piece of paper, scratched something on it, and handed it to me with a grin.

"One letter gets you my number," she laughed out loud, completely pleased with herself. "Now get out of my jeep."

I looked down at the paper. "Shayla! Dammit, that's right."

"Too late," she said, still grinning. "Call me."

I climbed down out of the jeep. "I will."

"You better." Shayla smiled as I closed the door and watched her drive away.

Remember that part where I was going to leave Nashville in January? Spoiler alert, Shayla and I dated for many years. If you want to escape planet Nashville, don't fall in love with the adorable redneck girl.

By the way, mentor Bob and I patched things up eventually—I am grateful for the time he invested in me—and fiddle player Mark McClurg and I have been good friends for years. Despite our interesting start, I soon found him to be a great guy. What's up, Hog!

Zoo TV

Shayla made my free time in Nashville interesting. But days off on the road were tedious. Unlike the Stones or Bowie, Alan didn't have deep pockets yet. Days off during the Stones tour were spent at five-star hotels in the downtown areas of exciting cities. On Alan Jackson's tour we were generally at a Holiday Inn off a highway exit. If we were lucky, there would be an Applebee's within walking distance.

I was at just such a hotel about two months in when a strange phone number set off my SkyPager. For those of you too young to know what a pager is, before cell phones we had small electronic boxes clipped to our belts that could display one line of text. People would call your pager and enter their callback number to let you know that they wanted you to call them. Mine worked worldwide, this was cutting edge, and I felt very cool when it beeped. Anyway, mine beeped. I called the number, and the person on the other end of the phone explained that U2 was going on tour again and that they were taking the cutting-edge video screen technology that I had helped pioneer on the Paula Abdul tour. They heard that I was the only guy who could get it right, and they wanted to hire me. My heart jumped . . . and then sank.

"Who is doing your video?" I asked.

"Nocturne," they replied. Nocturne, while a good company, was a competitor of Performance. This was my dream, but if I said yes I would break Lee's heart, disappoint Alan, and abandon my crew. I knew that my answer would have to be no.

"I'm afraid that I can't," I said, my words a self-inflicted gut punch.

"I don't think you understand," he countered. "This is going to be a groundbreaking tour. There is so much state-of-the-art video that they put TV in the name. They are calling it the *Zoo TV* tour. It will be great for your career."

"I can't," I repeated. "I'm already on a tour, and I am very loyal to my boss."

"What tour?" he asked.

"Alan Jackson," I replied.

"Who?"

It was exactly the reaction I had expected. He had never heard of Alan.

The person from U2's tour continued to argue, but I held firm. I explained my respect and friendship for Lee and why it just wouldn't be ethical for me to go to work for a competitor. Also, it wouldn't be right to leave Alan. I thanked him for calling and hung up.

The next day I was awoken by the beep of my SkyPager. It was the gentleman from U2's *Zoo TV* tour again. He expressed that they really needed me and asked how much I was currently making.

"It's not about money," I replied.

"It could be about money, but it's also about doing something groundbreaking—the *Zoo TV* tour."

"For me, it's about loyalty and ethics," I countered. "I can't say yes no matter how attractive the offer."

He continued to press me, saying how amazing the band was, how the tour was going to so many exotic places, how it would be first-rate hotels and recognition. He was certain they would offer me a lot more money than "what was the name of that tour you're on again?"

I have to be honest, sitting there in the crappy Holiday Inn I felt myself weakening. I fought the temptation the best way I could think of: I switched from defense to offense. My tone became harsh.

"You know, I keep explaining to you that I can't do this for ethical reasons. That my boss has earned my loyalty. None of that seems to register for you. I could never work with someone who doesn't understand loyalty or ethics. As such, I could never work with you. Never call me again." I hung up the phone, a bit shocked at myself.

I bounced off of the walls in my room for a bit as the reality that I had just told my dream job to get lost settled in. In an attempt to get out of my thoughts, I went to the hotel bar. This was not just a Holiday Inn; it was a Holidome. Billed as mini-vacation getaways, Holidomes had a bar by their indoor pool. I plopped down and ordered a beer, the smell of the freshly chlorinated pool all but overwhelming me. I quickly downed my first and ordered a second, then a third.

Alan Jackson's lighting director, Jimbo, walked by and then backed up, looking at me puzzled. "You OK?" he asked.

"Yup," I answered dryly.

He tilted his head. "OK, I've just never seen you drink in the middle of the day."

"Well, it's been a weird day."

"How come?" he asked.

"It doesn't matter," I replied despondently.

"It might help to talk about it."

I didn't think I wanted to, but words started pouring out, probably fueled by the alcohol. I told Jimbo everything that had happened, briefed him on my history with U2, and wrapped it up with this: "I just told my dream job to get lost."

Jimbo looked confused. "I don't understand. Why would you want to be on the *Zoo TV* tour? It may be cutting edge, the biggest video tour in rock, but you are directing a cutting-edge tour, the biggest *country* video tour ever—you have Moo TV."

It was a play on words for Jimbo. The country equivalent of Zoo TV would apparently be Moo TV—the sound a cow makes. In that moment I failed to see the real sense in what he said, and in the mood I was in I'm afraid I was harsh with my reply. "Moo TV? That's the dumbest thing I have ever heard . . ." But then it occurred to me to ask, "Can I keep it?"

Jimbo shrugged. "Sure." Then, having enough of my negativity, he shuffled off.

Regretting how grumpy I had been with Jimbo, I ordered another beer and brought it to my room, sparing any future passerby from my wrath. I plopped down on my bed with a sigh. Lying next to me was a new set of director-chair seat covers I had just purchased. I'd ripped the seat out of the one I had during the last show. They were out of black at the store, so I was forced to get white. I was frustrated by this, as I knew they would get dirty fast, but today, in this state, the clean white canvas sparked an idea.

I pulled out a black magic marker and carefully traced out block letters.

MOO TV

Satisfied with the label, I then drew cow spots on the rest of the cover. Perhaps it was just the four beers and the pungent fumes from the magic marker, but I was quite pleased with my handiwork. There! Now I was officially on the self-declared *Moo TV* tour with that artist good ol' what's his name. Who needs *Zoo TV* with U2? We are *Moo TV*!

Moo TV

The name was catchy. Within days of placing the new cover on my chair everyone was calling our tour the *Moo TV* tour, and my personal nickname became "Moo." Soon there were industry articles about it. Later that year, my employer, Performance A/V, won the prestigious Pollstar Award for "Video Company of the Year." Our work on the *Moo TV* tour was cited as being a notable part of Performance's success. Moo TV was contagious.

I continued to work hard on Alan's show. While the rest of the crew finished their duties and had free time in the afternoon, I would tenaciously spend hours making the screens look perfect. On days off, without compensation, I worked on creative ideas for the screens. For example, when Alan sang the song "Working Class Hero," I visually placed him in the inner workings of a machine with huge gears. And during the song "Tropical Depression," waves washed around the band's feet on the screens. These kinds of visuals are commonplace today, but back then, they were unlike anything the audience had ever seen, and the reviews evidenced that. Our show was described as groundbreaking, cutting edge. This was exactly what Alan wanted to hear while trying to keep up with Garth. We were moving the world behind Alan in exciting ways.

Perhaps my favorite description came more than a decade later. I was appearing at a conference, speaking just before Brad Paisley, who was the keynote. As always, Brad delivered a heartfelt and compelling talk. He is such a good and genuine guy. After his talk, Brad did a Q&A. A lady stood up and asked, "Visuals are always such a strong part of your live show. Where did your love of video come from?"

Brad smiled. "I hesitate to tell this story," he said before pausing. "Is Scott still here?"

Surprised, I waved from the crowd. Brad gestured toward me, shaking his head before continuing, his tone at first apologetic.

"I probably should have told him this story already. Growing up in West Virginia I was a huge Alan Jackson fan; I still am. I saved up some money and went to one of his shows. I was fascinated by everything, eager to learn from a master. Looking at the stage before the show I was disappointed that it didn't look like much. I was hoping it would be a big, cool set. I saw nothing, just a bunch of gray walls. The house lights dropped, the crowd went wild, and as the band kicked in, every one of those gray walls came to life. They were video screens! The first song was 'Chattahoochee,' and the image of Alan waterskiing the Chattahoochee River filled every screen larger than life. Alan stood still at the mic, but behind him 'Waterskiing Alan' was doing flips on the screen. It was incredible.

"Song after song Alan held court for the arena, simply standing at the mic. He sounded amazing, but it was visually exciting because of the screens that surrounded him. I decided right then that if I ever got to have a show like Alan's, I was going to lean into the power of video. I guess it's no wonder that years later Scott and I ended up working together."

I loved hearing Brad give Alan and me credit for sparking his interest in video. It's always wonderful to hear that your work is appreciated. Building on my tenacity had made me a great director and show visual designer. (I was awarded Visual Designer of the Year one year.) And, as you just learned, this landed me a great client in Brad. Better yet, he is a great friend, and my life is so much richer because of that friendship. These are the spoils of tenacity. The more you deploy it and the more you build on it, the more you receive.

What can you tenaciously build toward in your life?

Speaking of the spoils of being tenacious, it is remarkable to me that I also get to work with one of my heroes, Peter Frampton. As a child, my music-loving Aunt Barbara gifted me a vinyl copy of *Frampton Comes Alive*. This was the first-ever music that was mine! Owning that legendary album was a key step toward the love of music that has shaped my entire life. (Thank you, Aunt Barb!)

Magically, Peter has let our teams at Moo Creative and Moo TV help craft his show visuals for the past fifteen years, one of the great honors of my career. Peter is just an incredible human who has traversed a remarkable path and done incredible things. His *Frampton Comes Alive* album has sold more than seventeen million copies. It was the number one album in 1976 and became one of the best-selling live albums of all time.[*]

Did being tenacious have anything to do with his success? Let's ask Peter himself. Ladies and gentlemen, it is my honor to introduce one of the nicest humans ever, the legendary Peter Frampton!

---

[*] "Peter Frampton Album Sales," BestSellingAlbums.org, accessed December 5, 2025, https://bestsellingalbums.org/artist/10318.

PETER FRAMPTON
ON BEING TENACIOUS

It's been quite a ride—being number one in the world, the biggest ever, all those superlatives that one gets. I went through and hit all those points. It's fantastic at the time, but it's like, OK, now, how do you top that? You know, yours is the biggest album in the world for two years. And it was a very heady experience being there and being in this kind of protected bubble, surrounded by who I thought, at the time, were the best people to advise me.

Well, perhaps not; they advised me in all the wrong ways. Mistakes were made. Big mistakes. Foremost, I was pushed into doing another record virtually within a year of releasing *Frampton Comes Alive*, which was ridiculous, because you're only as good as your last record. Why not let that one sit? That's a good one to be as good as. If you just wait a little bit longer, you can keep that album and yourself on top. Well, in the rush, with my life as crazy as it had become, the next album, shall we say, failed to meet expectations.

I had, over the years, through my work with Humble Pie and other acts, built a following. Suddenly, with this wild new success, I was something of a sex symbol. The girls were screaming at me, so the guys didn't like me anymore. My core fan base largely died off in those two crazy years. Then the follow-up album came out, and the new fans just moved on. It all went south so very quickly. I remember being in a situation with a celebrity—I won't say who—and a photographer wanted to take a picture of us. This celebrity literally couldn't get out of the frame quick enough, because they didn't even want to have their picture taken with me. That was memorable. People were telling me, "Oh, your career is over." Then I was dropped by my label, A&M. That was so hard for me. Yup, mistakes were made, but hey, don't get me wrong: I did some very bad things too.

Many years later, I still couldn't get anything to click. It was suggested that I should form a band again, so I tried that with Steve Marriott, the lead singer from my old band Humble Pie. Hey, it had worked once, right? Well, it wasn't really working, and then we tragically lost Steve at only forty-four years old.

I'm a very positive person. My cup is always half full. For me, when you get knocked down, you get back up. You brush yourself off, and you get back on the horse, the bike, the elephant—whatever you were riding. You get back up and you do it again. But this was harder to come back from. People had a negative opinion of me. I had to dig up through the dirt before even getting to the bottom rung of the ladder again, you know? It was awful. I'm not trying to say, "Oh poor me; woe is me." I'm just saying it's a fact, you know, that that's the way it was. From 1978 to 1992!

Well, you need a little tenacity to get through all that. Good news, though: There's nothing a Frampton likes more than a challenge. So a bit after we lost Steve Marriott in '92, I got the old band together, and we went back on the road. We were going to do six weeks of clubs to dip our toe in the water. Let's not beat around the bush here; we didn't know if anyone was going to come to the shows. Well, anyway, it was phenomenal. I mean, you couldn't jam any more people in there. The people, it seemed, were giving me a second chance. And so that six weeks turned into six or seven months, and by the end we were playing to over ten thousand people in huge amphitheaters!

Then, all of a sudden, I get a call from my dear friend David Bowie. We went to school together; he is another lifelong friend.

He asked, "Will you play guitar on my next record?" I said, "Let me think about that. Yes!" I said, "This is great."

So I got to play on the *Never Let Me Down* record. And while I was in Switzerland doing the album, David said, "Would you come on the road and be one of my guitar players?" I said, "Oh my God, yeah." I had no idea what that would do for my career, but what it did was reestablish me as the guitar player David knew I was. My image had become more teeny-bopper, and David recognized this for the problem that it was.

He said, "Peter the guitar player is forgotten."

When that tour was announced, my world changed again. We are out there doing shows, and you know, Prince is in the audience. Mick Jagger's in the audience. People like that—it was pretty heady stuff. But it was the best gift—career gift—anybody had ever given me. David was saying to the world, *I sanction him the guitar player. Peter is a guitar player.*

And so, as it happened, my label came back. I had a deal again! Bowie had said to me, "You need to play more guitar," so when the label asked me, "What's going to be your first record back with us?" I said, "An instrumental record."

At first, there was dead silence, crickets. But then one of them said, "Oh, I get it. I get it." OK. That album, *Fingerprints*, was a labor of love. I went all around the world with the Shadows, the Stones, all my influences, all my friends, and Bowie was advising me on players and the like. Well, I poured my all into it, and in the end I was quite pleased.

Lo and behold, I go to the mailbox one day, and I get out two envelopes, both from the Grammys. And I think, *Wow, they're giving me a couple of seats.* So, I opened the first envelope, and it was a Grammy nomination for the single "Black Hole Sun" from *Fingerprints*. And I went, *Oh my God.* And then I opened up the

> other one, and it was a nomination for the whole *Fingerprints* album. Guess what? I won the Grammy for the whole album!
>
> Remember, you can always start again. There's a couple of songs about that on the new record that we're in the middle of making. You can always start again, even in the middle of the day. You can take a break and start again. Take a nap, get up, have a cup of coffee or tea or whatever you drink, and start again. Do it tenaciously. Just always remain a very positive person, that no matter what is going on you always do your best at everything you can and never give up.

Thank you, Peter! You are just the best!

Peter's journey was like a roller coaster ride. One minute, you're climbing on board and shooting straight to the top. The next thing you know, you're plummeting, and all the twisting and turning kicks in. After coming back down to earth, Peter applied tenacity, and what did that get him? A return to sellout crowds, and even a Grammy. What a life!

To experience Peter's whole journey, grab a copy of his book *Do You Feel like I Do: A Memoir*. It's such a cool book. I was floored reading about Peter and David Bowie jamming with guitars in the school stairwells. Having worked with them both, I know they truly are two of the most incredible people I've had the good fortune of knowing, of course as artists, but even more so as human beings. Someday ask me about how Bowie singled me out as the youngest kid on the tour and would ask my advice on his yet-to-be-released music. Talk about mind-blowing.

Long story short, get Peter's book—better yet, get it on Audible and hear Peter tell his story. That's what I did, and I loved it!

Speaking of listening, I still love listening to *Frampton Comes Alive*, *Fingerprints*, and all of Peter's music, and I've heard a sneak peek of his latest album (2026, yet to be titled), and it sounds amazing.

Now, where was I? Oh yes, I had gone country.

Gone Country

Things were going really well in Nashville, and my boss Lee could not have been happier. When he came to town for a visit, we went out for a wonderful steak dinner at Morton's. He was effusive about the job I was doing and excited that there was such a buzz around Alan's tour.

"I knew this would be good," he declared, raising his glass of wine.

Lee and I enjoyed some great meals together. He had a taste for the finer things and loved sharing them with me. What I said next made him even happier.

"Lee, I think we should open a Nashville office."

His eyes lit up. "What happened to 'I want to get out of country music?'" He was grinning now.

"Well, no one is good at what we do here. I feel like with some effort we could own this town. Besides, I really like working with Alan." (And I was in love with Shayla.)

With enthusiastic support from Lee, I started working toward opening our Nashville office. I labored tirelessly and, you guessed it, tenaciously. Lee, who had already taught me so much, tripled down on investing in me. He had a great mind for business, and I tried to take in all that he was sharing. Expanding our stake in Nashville was exciting!

I was simultaneously growing creatively too. I wanted to buy bigger and better tools to help me make even more novel content for shows. The gear I needed was expensive. It would cost about $50,000.

The best financial way to make a purchase that large was to start a new company to get the tax benefits. With that plan in mind, it was time to ask Lee.

I began, "I think there is something special in what we are doing for Alan. Other tours are hiring their music video directors to make content—or sometimes their brother-in-law who went to film school. But none of those people get it. They are all conditioned to tell a story inside a rectangle (the TV). What they forget is that the onstage screens are just a part of the show—the footage shouldn't always tell the story. Sometimes it should just be scenery, or colors, or words. Sometimes the screens should be off, allowing the audience to redirect their attention. Nobody is thinking that way. If I had better tools, I could improve Alan's show even more."

Lee nodded, so I continued.

"The gear I want is going to be $50,000 though. For tax reasons, it makes sense for me to start a new company and buy the gear that way. Can I have your permission to moonlight?"

Lee was surprisingly serious. He confused me with his answer. "I don't think so." He paused, then added, "That doesn't make sense to me. I don't want you to do that."

Off-balance from that unexpected reply and Lee's serious tone, I relented. "OK," I said. I waited for him to perhaps explain a little more, but he didn't.

For the next few weeks it felt a shade awkward. Lee and I didn't talk as much as we usually did. We eventually met for dinner, and Lee quickly brought up the elephant in the room. "Have you thought any more about starting a company?"

"Honestly, yes. I think it's a good idea, but I do respect your decision."

He nodded. "I told you no because I was afraid to lose you. I feel like what you are describing is necessary. You would be pioneering a whole new industry. I think if you start this it will grow, and that makes me nervous that I'll lose you." He sighed. "I would like for you to do this, but I want to be your partner in it—fifty-fifty. And I will pay for half of the gear. I will help you get clients."

I shook my head no. "I'm not sure I like that. If I take half of your money and the company fails . . . I would rather not have that pressure."

"Well, I think it's a good idea, and I want us to do it together. Besides, did you say it was $50,000 worth of gear? Half of that isn't much money to me overall."

It was clear that he genuinely wanted us to do this. Since he was also my boss, I was already accountable to him. Besides, we knew that we worked great together. What the heck. We shook hands, and just like that Lee, my boss and mentor, was now also my partner.

"What should we call it?" Lee asked.

"We already have a name, Moo TV."

He shook his head no. "That's silly."

"Yup, it is silly, and for some reason no one ever forgets the name."

Moo TV it was, and we soon found that Lee was right. We became popular and began to grow. It was a great pairing; we provided the technology and the creative in one stop. The artists loved it.

Baby Steps

Lee also grew to love the name Moo TV. Even more, he loved watching my country transition. I remember he came out to visit while the tour was in Montana. Lee looked at me funny upon seeing me walk up.

"Why are you walking like that?"

"I pulled my groin last night in Cheyenne riding the mechanical bull," was my matter-of-fact answer.

Lee about fell over. "No!" he said incredulously.

"Yup," I rode it about twenty times. Mean son of a gun."

It was true. I had spent a day off in Cheyenne in a country bar. The locals were thinking about starting some trouble with me, long hair and all. But my awful attempts at the bull had them cracking up. It was a great day, but twenty short-lived rides later I could barely walk.

Lee absolutely did his part to anchor us in Nashville. He was a natural salesman but would never be described as one. He loved what he did, and he loved talking about it. As such, people wanted to work with him. I hope I am the same. If so, I learned from a master. One of our greatest sales moments came within our first year in Nashville, 1993. Lee heard about something called Fan Fair (now CMA fest). It's a four-day event in June that literally every single country artist attends. Lee arranged a meeting with then-CMA head Ed Benson, and we insisted that we provide our services for free for the first year. Boom! It was a huge hit, and that started a seventeen-year run where I was the video director for Fan Fair / CMA Fest. It was a wonderful place for me to not only meet new acts but also hone my skills as a director.

Our video production area was that little trailer backstage that Storme described in the foreword. What Storme forgot was that we put huge black cow spots on the white trailer and posted our trademark logo on a big board to the side of the door. Thanks to that and the catchy name, Moo TV was known by everyone in country music within that first year. I have such great memories of directing legends like Willie, Waylon, Dolly, and Johnny. I also directed the newer powerhouses of the day, Billy Ray Cyrus, Randy Travis, Garth, Reba, Brooks & Dunn, and of course, Alan Jackson. I am very proud of my time directing there.

Fifty-fifty partnerships can be tough, as the two partners need to agree or no decision can be made. I remember early on Lee and I having a rare disagreement where both of us were sure we were right. Tension was starting to build. This was uncomfortable and unwelcome.

"Fine," I said. "We will do it your way, but the next time we are in deadlock we will do it my way."

"OK," Lee replied.

"So you understand that the next time we disagree, you will have to do it my way?"

"Well, I don't know about that," Lee replied. I could see he was imagining that might be tough.

"Perfect, since you worry that you might be more upset about the next time, we will do it your way the next time." Lee's expression told me he knew there was a catch. "Thus, we will do it my way this time," I added, grinning. It seemed fair to me.

Lee nodded, almost starting to acquiesce. Then he caught himself. "I want this time," he said, eyes narrowing.

"Then we do it my way next time," I replied.

"OK," Lee smiled.

The great thing was that it would be a long time before we disagreed again. We really saw eye to eye most of the time. That day eventually came, nearly a year later. I proudly stood up and declared, "I invoke my right to win this argument. It's my turn."

Lee scrunched up his nose, nodded, and begrudgingly agreed that we could move forward the way I wanted, even though he thought it was a mistake. "I guess that's the deal I made," he conceded with a half smile.

"Yup, but good news: The next one is yours!" Lee was now fully smiling.

It was a wonderful partnership.

Over the next several years some amazing acts joined our roster, including Tim McGraw, Martina McBride, Vince Gill, Amy Grant, The Judds, Faith Hill, Wynonna, Shania, and, as you know, Brad Paisley. They all wanted Moo TV!

Being tenacious had built me a great life. I found real balance, something that was sorely lacking during the previous decade. I had great friends. I had purchased a beautiful home where I threw a huge monthly pool party. I had money in the bank. Work was great, and Lee and I were closer than ever. These were golden years, the spoils of my tenacity.

A Box of Rain

I received a phone call one day from a friend and coworker Barry Otto. I was in Florida on Alan's tour.

"Hey Scott, I have something to tell you, but I need you to sit down."

His voice was shaking. I was standing in a parking lot; the pavement was radiating heat like a skillet in the Florida sun. It was definitely not conducive to sitting. I fibbed a little, anxious to hear the news. "OK, I'm sitting."

Barry struggled to speak again. "Earlier today there was a carjacking. Lee was shot in the head and then run over. Lee is gone."

Lee is gone.

It hit me as if I had been shot too. It was too much to process. My vision blurred as the tears started to pour. I couldn't speak, I couldn't think.

Lee is gone? It couldn't be.

A week later I found myself in Annapolis, Maryland, carrying the casket of my friend, my business partner, my mentor. It was surprisingly heavy. It banged against my thigh as I shuffled through the wet grass. I was cautious to not fall and drop my friend. *I've got you, Lee.* Would this be the last thing I could do for him? We had been looking after each other for so many years. For the rest of the afternoon, I did my very best to help his fiancée, Ginny, through the day, holding her arm, having a tissue when needed. There were times when the tears streamed down my face, but even as they flowed I tried to share my strength so she might feel safe. It was horrific for me; it was devastating for her. Ginny had lost her great love. They had known each other since college.

We put Lee to rest and headed to a celebration of life some loved ones had organized at a waterside restaurant Lee had frequented. One of Lee's friends had piloted Lee's sailboat, *The Box of Rain*, down to the dock. That boat meant the world to him. As we all headed in that direction to throw rose petals in the water alongside the boat, it was pouring. There it was; Lee's prize possession. I thought back to Lee teaching me how to sail it in the massive Annapolis Bay, sharing the water with dauntingly huge sea vessels. I'd steer as Lee, always the one with a taste for the finer things, would go below to prepare some wine and cheese. As I threw my rose petals alongside it's hull, the Grateful Dead song Lee had named the boat after echoed in my head.

🎼 A box of rain will ease the pain, And love will see you through.*

My business manager, Alice (AKA Momma Moo), made the trip up. She really is like a mother to me, and I am so grateful. Surprisingly, Shayla insisted on coming up as well. Even though we had broken up some time ago, she'd insisted on being there. I still loved her. I don't know how anyone stops loving anyone.

My mind drifted back to the last conversation Lee and I had. He was always so efficient on the phone. When he heard what he needed to hear, he would just hang up, no goodbye. It wasn't harsh, just one of his quirks—a cheerful tone and then . . . click.

During our last phone call, he asked if I could do something he thought was a good idea. I responded that I had already done it the

---

* Lyrics from "Box of Rain," by Phillip Lesh and Robert Christine Hunter day before. Lee replied gratefully, making me feel proud. I waited for the click. After a moment I asked, "Anything else?"

"Yeah," he said, with genuine appreciation. "Thank you."

"You are very welcome," I replied. A moment later I heard the click.

Smiling, I'd placed my phone back in my pocket. I loved making Lee proud. Who would I make proud now that he was gone? The last of my tears fell as exhaustion finally took me.

In Memoriam

Three months passed, and I was still lost. My compass was gone, my friend and mentor had left, my training was incomplete. I was overwhelmed with emotion and drowning in responsibility. My employees at Moo TV and Lee's employees at Performance in Nashville were all looking to me for guidance. I just put my head in the sand. I had spent ten years in Nashville, building a company, a life. Without Lee it all felt wrong, ruined. I wanted to run away.

Despite the scolding I had given the guy from U2 on the phone a decade ago, others had reached out inquiring as to my interest in a position on every U2 tour since. I had, of course, always declined, favoring what Lee and I were building. Maybe I would just go on the road with Bono and the boys. Moo TV was too much for me without Lee.

The phone rang and it was Bailey Pryor, an incredible friend and longtime Performance employee.

"How are you?" he asked. I had grown to loathe this question. Of late, it was just an invitation to lie. I was, of course, doing terrible.

"I'm OK, pal, how are you?"

"Doing OK, all things considered. Look, I've been thinking . . . wondering what you were going to do. To be honest, I was afraid that one day I would just hear that you had run off on the U2 tour."

Bailey knew me better than I realized.

"Anyway, I was thinking that maybe you could just start an equipment and video company like Lee's. I've taken the liberty of asking the employees, and they all say that if you did they would come work for you. Then I asked the clients, and they all said they would, too, and they asked how they could help. I have no idea what you would do about equipment, but I just thought that this would be a way you could keep a part of Lee alive."

Those last words hung in the air. *Keep some part of Lee alive?* Hearing this, I simply had to try.

> You might be scared as hell,
> But the only ones who really fail
> Are the ones who never try
> —lyrics from the song "Try," written by
> Scott Scovill, Victoria Shaw, and Madeline Stone

The Gauntlet

I had enjoyed running the Nashville office of Performance for Lee, but the thought of actually building a beast like that from scratch was terrifying. I had none of the expensive equipment I needed, no money to buy it, and no clue about what it took to build a big, capital-intensive business. The creative company, Moo TV, was started with $50,000. That was a drop in the bucket compared to the costs of buying the massive screens and cameras this new company would need. But I had to try.

We'd keep the name. Everyone loved Moo TV. But this version would have to start small—just the Alan Jackson tour at first. All the other business would have to go to our competitors, and that hurt, even if we could get them back some day. I needed well over a million dollars' worth of gear—again, money I didn't have, so I got creative. I applied for credit with Sony to buy cameras;

they approved me for about $70,000, which would get me two, but I needed three. I also applied for credit with the projector manufacturer; they approved me for the three video projectors, about $120,000 with accessories as I recall. I then got a $50,000 line of credit on my house. Finally, I applied for a small business loan, and I believe that added around $75,000.

Mind you, I was approved for each of these as if they were the only loan I was taking on. If any of them found out about the others, they would likely rescind their offer. Thus, I let them all sit on hold, approved but not active. Then I got really crazy. I had seven credit cards, all recently brought to a zero balance. I had a history of running up credit card debt in the past, but I always paid at least the minimum amount due on time. Thus, to the credit card companies, I was a great customer. I called them one at a time and told them if they would max my limit I would cut up all of the other cards. I got them each to give me limits of over $30,000—*seven* of them. I also had about $25,000 left in the bank after buying Lee's half of Moo TV from his estate for $35,000. Beautifully, upon word that I was starting a company, Lee's mom had his brother Neal deliver Lee's $35,000 back to me, along with an incredible note saying how proud Lee was and how he was looking down on me. Yeah, that made me cry.

This all worked out to being just under $600,000 in credit. Alan Jackson and our corporate client, Gail & Rice, gave us deposits for future work on good faith. That was another $100,000. Wonderful... but still well shy of the million needed.

If the credit card debt was crazy, the next idea was equally nuts. Everyone was discovering that old equipment could turn into cash on eBay at about the same time. Unlike today, back then it was not unusual to find secondhand equipment at a quarter of the price of a comparable modern unit. This cheaper used gear is how I would make the almost $700,000 I had collected into a million-dollar-plus tour.

I set up a massive, automated search for every item I needed—literally fifty searches, each laying out the parameters for used equipment I had to have. When completed, I could click one button to conduct one mega search. Back then, the Internet was painfully slow, so you could hit the button and make dinner while the fifty pages loaded. I was executing this mega search every night, placing all the things we needed in my overflowing eBay cart: big items over $10,000 and smaller items I might need one hundred of—everything a video company needed to launch a huge tour. At the end of a week, I started buying items but not paying for them yet (back then, eBay allowed a week to pay, as I recall)—hundreds of items costing hundreds of thousands of dollars. My business manager, Alice (Momma Moo), thought I was nuts, and she was right.

I woke up early one morning in late December of 2002 and jumped off the financial cliff. I had orchestrated the mayhem to hit on the same day. Back then, banks didn't communicate in real time. No one would know what I had done until it was too late. I called Sony and executed the camera loan. I did the same with the projector loan, and then the small business loan. Then I started paying for everything on eBay—*everything*. By the end of the day, I had spent it all—the loans, the equity in my house, the lines of credit on my cards. I was over half a million dollars in debt, with literally a tractor trailer of questionable used gear heading my way.

Several of my lenders panicked. The phone calls started coming in with questions like, "Do you even realize how much debt you have taken on?" and perhaps even better, "Do you plan on leaving the country?" They shut my credit cards down for future purchasing, and since no money was coming in yet, I got behind. This triggered huge hikes in my credit card interest rates. It got scary!

For the record, I do *not* recommend this as a way to finance a business. It was a Hail Mary from a desperate guy who couldn't think of anything else. It could have easily cost me everything I had, including my beautiful home.

On the Road Again

Thanks to the herculean effort of our crew, Barry Otto and Andre Nolan in particular, we somehow pieced together a full touring system. A university cut us a deal on the third camera for the first shows in exchange for giving their students opportunities to learn, something that we gladly did for years.

The design called for three ten-by-fourteen-foot screens stacked on top of each other, thirty feet high, displaying three different images. Without permission, I decided to blend those three images into one thirty-foot-tall seamless screen. It would be harder to do but would be unlike anything anyone had ever seen. We loaded in rehearsals and Alan's production manager, Craig Stahl, was beside himself seeing the unapproved design change. He was a great friend who worried that I wouldn't be able to get the tour working. Now I was telling him I had made it even harder and deviated from the agreed-on plan.

"God, Scott. What if management would rather have the three screens?"

"This can still do that. Three single images will be easy to project on the screen."

"OK, and it can be one image too? How does that look?"

"Well, we haven't been able to make it work . . . yet." I thought poor Craig was going to have a heart attack.

"Alan will be here tomorrow. This needs to work now!"

"It will," I assured him. I knew the plan was good; it was just complicated.

Despite my promise, we went through rehearsals in Nashville without it properly functioning. We loaded into Peoria, Illinois, the day before the first show. We were late, staying well after every other crew member left. But the amazing Andre Nolan (crew member and video engineer) executed the blend cue and it finally worked. We did it!

As the lights dropped and Alan Jackson walked onstage, we faded up the screen and there he stood. His imposing, six-five stature was now an unreal thirty-feet-tall image on the screen behind him. It looked incredible! Alan and his management were thrilled, Craig Stahl was equal parts impressed and relieved, and the reviews were stellar. We had done it.

For $700,000 we had pieced together a show that looked like millions! Somehow this crew pulled other people's broken and discarded equipment together to make an incredible machine. We were the Millennium Falcon of the video business—a piece of junk held together by gaffer tape and dreams. But when the lights dropped, we delivered! My gosh, Lee would be so proud.

Heck, I'm proud of what we achieved—*fiercely proud*. But it would not have been possible without the trust of my next guest. In the more than three decades I have had the honor of knowing him, he has been relentlessly creating and defending classic country music. This tenacity has landed him as a multiyear Entertainer of the Year and even earned him a spot in the Country Music Hall of Fame. I am so honored this icon wanted to say a few words about tenacity, and I am humbled that he chose to speak more about me than his own legendary accomplishments.

Ladies and gentlemen, Alan Jackson!

ALAN JACKSON

Scott Scovill, well, I've known you since you were just a wild young man on the road with a good-lookin' woman on each arm every day. You've come a long ways—*we've* come a long

> ways together. You're a real pioneer in live video, especially country music. You've really helped bring all of my music to life on the road for years. All of that propped up my show out there, and that means a lot to me. My fans have enjoyed those videos for years and all of the magic that you brought to the stage with it.
>
> You've really built great companies and helped country music a lot. I just appreciate all of your dedication to my career and life on the road and all of the hard work and friendship over the years.
>
> Congratulations on all your accomplishments. You deserve it, and I'm happy for you, man. I'm glad to have been a part of all of that, and I think it's great that you are sharing your experience in this book. I was a witness to all of your tenacity, and I'm grateful to have been a benefactor of it. Thank you.

No, thank *you* Alan, for everything. I cherish the time we had together. When we met, you had three songs that had made the charts. As of today, that number is sixty-six, with thirty-five going to number one. You have sold over seventy-five million records and have two Grammys and shelves full of major awards. Your journey has been beyond incredible—all the while relentlessly resisting the pressure to conform to "modern" country music and carrying the torch for the classic country music you and your legions of fans love. I have incredible respect for you, pal.

Oh, and it's your fault that I moved to Nashville! And I love it.

As the new company grew, the challenges kept coming, but each time we rose to the occasion. Moo TV grew to be the market leader that it is today. Industry magazine *Pollstar* awarded us Best Video/Visual Company an unbelievable ten years in a row.

Funny story: We were nominated seven years straight before we won. It was nerve-racking to sit there and stress over the possibility of winning, only to end up disappointed. That said, by year seven losing had become old hat. I would patiently wait for the announcement and politely smile and applaud for our competitor. On the seventh year the announcement was made, and I did my part, smiling and clapping.

Just then my buddy Rob hit me. "Holy shit! You won! Get up there!"

I was stunned but I sprinted to the stage to receive our award. Standing in the spotlight, in front of over a thousand peers, and in the camera's eye, I am told that I gave a brief but moving speech. I say I am told this because I don't remember.

Furthermore, as I walked backstage with our award I suddenly found myself dizzy, slumped against a wall and sliding down it dramatically. Oh God, was I having a heart attack? A stroke?! My breathing was shallow, I was sweating, and my vision had blurred. All this, but my chest didn't hurt. After about twenty seconds I started to feel better. OK, it's not a heart attack. I don't think it's a stroke either. So what the hell? I looked around and no one was near me. Nobody had noticed. I pulled myself together and continued walking back to where the press were taking pictures and conducting post-award interviews. After completing that, I returned to my seat for the rest of the show feeling fine. What the devil had happened to me? Piecing it together, I came to this hypothesis that I was afraid of public speaking, and I'd actually had an anxiety attack.

Well, as you know, I don't like being afraid of things anymore, so I tackled that possibility head-on. I called a respected friend at Belmont University, Jeff Cornwall. Jeff's fancy title was the Jack C. Massey Chair and Director of the Entrepreneur center. I told him what had happened, and asked if I could speak to a class at his school.

He happily arranged this, so a few weeks later I was wandering the halls in search of my classroom. I was a bit lost and on the edge of being late when I came across a crowd in the hallway. I asked one of the students where the room I was looking for was. "Here," he said, "but you won't be able to get in; it's full."

I was confused. "So wait, why are all these people in the hallway?"

Suddenly realizing who I was, he replied, "Oh, to see you."

There were so many people there my heart sank. I would not be speaking to a class of thirty or so students as I had expected. No, I would be speaking to *three hundred*! Well, if there was any doubt that I had a fear of public speaking (called glossophobia, by the way), my doubts were quickly confirmed. Once onstage, I started sweating, then my hearing began to fade, and my vision went blurry again. I clenched every muscle, fighting to stay conscious. Somehow I did that, and unbelievably I was able to speak. It was *not* inspiring.

With my glossophobia confirmed, I did what the tenacious do. I brushed off the dirt and called another nearby university. I asked if I could speak for a small class of less than thirty-five. I did this, managing to stave off the fear. I repeated speaking to smaller classes and eventually got pretty good at it. With fear now a memory, I loved sharing my story and my life experiences, and I am proud to say that the CMA put me on a small speaking tour of colleges around the US. Helping those kids was an incredible reward for facing that fear, but it gets even better.

Sometime later, I had the honor of directing a multinight shoot for Garth Brooks in Las Vegas. The first night's crowd had seemed a tad reserved for a Garth show (granted, it was a Thursday), so with no warning just before the Friday show was to begin, Garth asked me to "fix the crowd."

"What?" I replied as he was walking away.

He stopped and turned. "Do your thing, fix the crowd," he stated dryly and turned again.

"Wait!" I yelled. "I don't have a thing with the crowd—you do."

Garth stopped again, slowly turned, and with a wry smile said, "Yes, you do," making one final turn, he walked away. I stood there next to Brian, the production manager, completely stunned. "Do you know what he means, Brian?"

Brian laughed. "Not really, but in fifteen minutes I'm going to give you a mic so you can fix the crowd." Then he walked away, grinning.

As I stepped onstage I knew there was a real possibility that I would pass out. There were 18,500 people out there. Taking in the 360-degree view, I could see that the new arena was sold out. I walked onstage, heart pounding through my chest. The spotlight hit me and I caught a glimpse of my head on the sixty-feet-wide screens. And you know what? To my surprise, I loved it! I spent the next five minutes riling up the crowd, and it was intoxicating. I sprang offstage on cloud nine, sprinting to the TV truck to direct the show. Ducking through the curtain to backstage, I came face-to-face with Garth. He grabbed me.

"You killed that, big guy!"

I grinned and replied proudly, "I did my part, are you ready?!" Then I turned to the band, "What about you guys?" (as if it was my job to fire them up too). They graciously played along and we all stood there hollering in the hall. What an amazing thing to be a part of. I could not love Garth more—he is the best.

Thank you, Garth, for trusting me to "do my thing," whatever the hell that is. I am so very grateful that I tackled my fear (tenaciously!) instead of accepting that public speaking wasn't for me.

When I sent Garth this story asking his permission to recount it in the book, I also asked if he wanted to throw in his two cents on tenacity. I received this back from him a few days later:

> **GARTH BROOKS**
>
> It's not enough to be tenacious alone . . . you have to surround yourself with people who are hungry to better themselves as well. That's why I have partnered with people like Scott . . . he dreams on a higher level . . . he performs on one too.

I sit here hesitant to type. It feels self-serving to include such a compliment in my book. Apparently, since you just read it, I must be too proud to not include it. I do love the message that tenacity loves a good team effort, and I can attest that Garth has an amazing team around him. He is an incredible leader. I also wanted to point out that he signs his name without capitals. That is a great glimpse into the man he is. He is the second-highest selling artist of all time behind the Beatles but still remains remarkably grounded. I am so grateful for the time I have spent working with him.

Thank you, Garth.

Meanwhile, Moo TV was growing. Moreover, I grew as an entrepreneur, learning the value of systems and delegation. Catching the entrepreneurial bug, I started new ventures. Among them were The Steel Mill (a large rehearsal facility) and Moo Creative (the reimagined creative branch of Moo TV). Along with a few partners, we bought CenterStaging out of bankruptcy (a huge music compound in LA). I found that once I had tenaciously fought my way through to Moo TV's success, repeating it and building further successes was ten times easier.

Remember, if you develop your tenacity with your eye on a goal, you can keep going past that dream and use what you have learned on many other ventures. Take that tenacity and build on it!

(A recent pic of Peter Frampton grinning at a show, an epic pic of him playing a stadium in the 70s, and a pic of us backstage somewhere. Alan's 30' screen during a show, Alan and I on the set of the "Country Boy" music video. My mentor Lee Griffin and I, and a pic of me and Garth.)

*All photos and supplemental material can be found on TENACIOUSBOOK.COM

CHAPTER 9

Heartbreak and Silver Linings

Going through things you never thought you'd go through will only take you places you never thought you'd get to.

—Morgan Harper Nichols

October is one of my favorite months. My linebacker build finds great relief when the sweltering Tennessee summer finally wanes. The humidity lifts, and temperatures drop into the high 60s. Never afraid to don a wild outfit, I enjoy Halloween, but easily my favorite reason to dress up in October is Oktoberfest. I make an annual pilgrimage to Munich, and I arrive in style. That's right, I wear full-on lederhosen—you know, the leather shorts with the suspenders—and even the goofy socks and traditional shoes. Some say they look ridiculous, but I choose to think I look amazing! As this chapter starts, I am neck-deep in Oktoberfest 2017, and I am joined by my dear friend

Dr. David Haase. David is wonderfully outgoing and is as funny as he is fearless.

Oktoberfest is a party like no other. Hundreds of thousands of fun seekers from around the globe pack into massive tents to celebrate life. Powered by pure German beer, their appetite for that golden beverage and the shenanigans it fuels is ravenous. To quench this thirst, angelic beer maids decked out in their traditional German dresses carry as many as a dozen massive beer mugs through the mosh of humanity with the grace of ballerinas. The rhythmic heartbeat of this dance emanates from the oompah bands at center stage. They alternate between classic German songs and masterful remakes of pop and rock tunes. Ever heard a tuba join in on Journey's "Don't Stop Believin'?" I have, and it's worth a flight to Germany—or at least it seems worth it after beer number eight! Despite the copious amounts of alcohol consumed by all, this is a harmonious and joyous place, and for me, it's heaven. If I seem to wax poetic on the subject, or if it sounds a bit over the top, please forgive me. You see, I am in love with Oktoberfest.

David and I had been swimming in this ocean of joy for three days. The stroke was simple: We sat at a table with a dozen or so complete strangers and shared a drink and a laugh. Next, we repeated the drink and the laugh until these strangers became our new and dearest friends. This generally took all of five minutes. Finally, we spent the next three hours having the time of our lives getting to better know our new best friends.

When the tents cleared out for reseating (as they did every four hours), David and I went to get a bite to eat—some delicious German sausage, or better yet, some schnitzel—and then we headed back to a different table in a different tent and repeated the process . . . all day long. It may sound crazy, but I promise, it is magical.

Forgive me, but this chapter skips the part where I detail the tenacity it takes to drink twelve of those huge liter mugs in a day. Though I will happily give lessons if you meet me in Munich next fall.

Instead, the chapter takes on a slightly different format. The subject matter is quite heavy, and, as such, I have decided to point out the tenacity at its core once the story's silver lining has been revealed. But first . . .

Shocked

I woke up on what was our last day at Oktoberfest to a text from an employee who is very dear to me. It was short and bewildering.

It simply read, "Active shooter."

My confusion was brief. More texts started coming in, and a few phone calls later, a picture of utter horror had taken shape. The Route 91 Harvest music festival on the Las Vegas Strip had been in full swing with a capacity crowd. Three of our acts were there. Jake Owen had just finished his performance, Chris Young was in his bus backstage, and Jason Aldean was mid-song before a throng of thrilled fans. Seven of our staff members were also there diligently running cameras and doing everything it takes for Jason to be seen on the big screens.

Unbeknownst to all, a man had just smashed holes in two windows of his thirty-second-floor rooms at the Mandalay Bay hotel overlooking the concert. His two adjoining rooms were stocked with five suitcases of guns and ammo. At 10:05 p.m., he opened fire on the unsuspecting crowd. For ten minutes straight, magazine after magazine—one thousand rounds averaging over a bullet a second—rained down on the concertgoers. The helpless crowd had no idea where the gunfire was coming from or where to run. It was a massacre.

I know this phrase is thrown around a lot, but upon hearing this I was quite literally in shock. I had no idea what to do, but I was trying to hold myself together.

After an hour or so of desperate phone calls, I was able to confirm that all seven of our employees, our artists, and their teams had made it out alive. But what was next? They were already saying as many as fifty were dead, a number that would climb over the next few days and eventually land at fifty-eight. Nearly one thousand people were injured; 413 had gunshot wounds. I was shattered. We would later learn that the shooter, a sixty-four-year-old man from Mesquite, Nevada, named Stephen Paddock, was found dead in his room, an apparent suicide. No motive has ever officially been determined.*

The violence and senselessness was just too much to comprehend. I sent David a text to please come to my room. When he walked in, I didn't know what to say.

He looked at me with concern. "Oh, no. What happened?"

I exploded into tears and couldn't speak. David crossed the room and hugged me as I fell apart. I struggled to regain some composure and was finally able to tell him what I knew. He listened, simply saying, "I am so sorry." David, as luck would have it, was exactly the friend I needed in this devastating moment.

He and I spent the next couple of hours working out how we could help the survivors. As he offered some sage advice, one moment in particular stood out. David looked at me, nodded, and said, "PTSD. They are all going to have PTSD." I didn't think I knew much about PTSD, so I asked him to explain. As it turns out, unknowingly, I was an expert on the subject. After David described the symptoms to me, I relayed to him some of my experiences after my business partner and friend, Lee Griffin, was killed sixteen years earlier.

I should mention that David is a doctor, and while not a psychiatrist, his opinion is backed by education, experience, and brilliance. He raised his eyebrows and nodded again. "Scott, you had PTSD." Hearing this from my trusted friend should have been impactful, but

---

* "Five Years After Las Vegas Shooting, Survivors Find Healing in Community," PBS News, October 1, 2022, https://www.pbs.org/newshour/nation/five-years-after-las-vegas-shooting-survivors-find-healing-in-community.

honestly, on top of all the day's events, it was just one more thing I couldn't process at the time.

"OK," I replied. "But what do we do about *their* PTSD?"

David and I split up so he could research counselors. A while later, he came back to me with the name Ginger Poag. Ginger had worked a mass shooting in Arizona, but she now lived in Nashville. I swiftly called her. After she shared her experience with the Arizona shooting, I felt she was the right person to help guide our people through this difficult time. As much of an impression as her qualifications made on me, the fact that she was so clearly moved after hearing about the shooting made a stronger impression. We needed her big brain, but I suspected our people were going to need her big heart even more. I asked her if Moo TV could contract her to take care of our people.

"Absolutely" was her reply.

She asked for how long. "Forever" was my gut reaction. We should pay for their counseling for as long as they need it. She noted that it may take a while for some. I understood. These kids had been through hell, and we were going to stand by them. The next step she recommended was to gently herd them toward her.

Meanwhile, my team in Nashville hired a counselor to advise our primary staff on how to care for our victims when they returned to the office. It was recommended, for example, that we not speak to the survivors about the shooting unless they brought it up first. And if they did bring it up, we were told we should let them lead. We shouldn't ask questions, because in doing so we might inadvertently take them to a memory they aren't ready to face. Furthermore, we should let them know that we care about them and are there to listen.

The counselor also advised that one of the best things we could do is talk about a time before the shooting. Why? Human beings need to breathe about every ten seconds; we need to eat when we are hungry; and we need to feel safe. The last of these foundational needs isn't easily met for PTSD victims. They don't feel safe, and that fear can manifest in surprising ways. We were advised to share memories that specifically took them back to a time when they felt safe. Both counselors were clear about one thing: This was going to be a long road, but with love and support, hopefully they would all be OK.

I headed back home still feeling helpless. It occurred to me that maybe there was something else I could do that might help. David had dropped what should have been a bombshell on me when he said that I had PTSD after Lee's death. I was already so devastated, having just heard about the concert shooting, that I couldn't wrap my mind around that right then. But on the long flight back from Europe, it started to sink in. You see, with the revelation that I had PTSD, so many things started to make sense. I think the only way to explain this is to revisit the darkest time in my life.

Why do that? Why dive back into the darkness I had somehow gotten past? Why dredge up all that hurt and pain? Well, for two reasons:

One, for you, the reader. I think there is real value in sharing our hurt with each other. These vulnerable moments can be great teachers. Sharing may perhaps help you better understand yourself or someone in your life.

And two, as a way to better understand myself. There was some trauma in my childhood that warranted me engaging in a fair amount of self-analysis. In some ways, I am wired to look inward. It started at a young age when I was trying to figure out why my dad was yelling at me. I was desperate to understand. What had I done to make him angry? As an adult, I realized that he was yelling for reasons that had nothing to do with me, but his actions in those formative years conditioned me to look within for an explanation. This origin story is sad, but I am grateful for the gift of introspection. I love looking at and understanding myself better. This introspection has helped me see that my dad was yelling because of what I believe was an undiagnosed personality disorder and that it wasn't my fault. And now, later, in life,

I use that introspection to work at being the best version of me I can be—something I'm really proud of.

So, for those two reasons, let's march on into the darkness and see if we can find that beautiful silver lining.

Lee Griffin

The year was 2002 and we were twelve months removed from the 9/11 terrorist attacks. Life was more or less back to normal. I was touring with Alan Jackson as his video director. As you know from the prior chapter, my phone rang on an otherwise bright afternoon in Florida. It was my coworker Barry calling. He was clearly shaken up. His voice was trembling. He finally mustered the strength to tell me that my business partner, best friend, mentor, and father figure, Lee, had been shot and killed in a carjacking.

In that moment, my world came crashing down. I loved the guy. What followed was a long and deep depression. The important details I chose not to share until this chapter include some of my symptoms of PTSD. It seems fitting that I withheld this information until now, as back then, I didn't know what I was dealing with. Its effects were so crazy that I tried to dismiss them. I think it is most appropriate to share my PTSD experiences here, in the chapter covering the time that I finally began to grasp what had happened to me.

With the death of a loved one, there is mourning, sadness, depression, a malaise. These symptoms are not unlike PTSD. As such, it would be hard to say whether those feelings so prevalent in me were caused by anything other than grief. But in my case, there was more. Little by little, my condition took a scary turn. I started having strange and frightening thoughts. I think they are best described through an example.

One evening, a few weeks after Lee's death, I was sitting alone in my home in the Nashville suburbs. The TV was on. I wasn't big on

TV prior to Lee's death, but it had become an escape for me. The sun was out, but the warm light and the long shadows indicated it would soon set. As I watched, I suddenly got a distinct feeling that my life was in danger. It was a jarring thought, but without basis, I pushed it to the back of my mind. I wrote it off as just a crazy trick of the brain.

A few minutes later, it came back, but this time I envisioned someone outside of my home, in the woods, with a rifle. I could see myself through the scope, drifting in and out of the crosshairs. I could tell right where he was!

Wait, I told myself. *This is nuts. There is no man outside wanting to kill you.* I knew it was crazy, but despite my best attempts at logic, my thoughts drifted between assessing my mental status and being pulled irresistibly back into the feeling that someone was there to kill me.

This battle between fear and reality continued as the sun set. I realized as it darkened outside that it would be easier for the gunman to see in the window, so as a defense, I stood up to draw the blinds. "You are really losing it kid," I said out loud as I started to pull them closed. Just then, a shot of fear went through me like a bolt of lightning. I realized this was the moment the mystery gunman would likely pull the trigger, before the blinds could fully hide me. My fight-or-flight reaction kicked in so hard that I nearly passed out. I jumped back from the window and hugged the wall. My knees buckled beneath me as my heart pounded through my chest. Anyone who has ever had a close call or been in a car crash knows that awful feeling when the adrenaline surge leaves your chest thumping and your mind racing. It feels like a heart attack.

I was grateful that the "would-be shooter" didn't kill me. I also simultaneously knew that he wasn't really there. Logic and these manifestations of fear were at odds. *Was I going crazy?*

With the blinds closed and feeling very disoriented, I sat back down on the couch. I turned off the TV and the lights so "he" couldn't see me. Sitting there in the dark, I struggled to get a grip.

I understood without a doubt that there was no gunman, but I also started spinning a story that Lee had been killed for a reason and that, as his business partner, I was next. My logical brain knew what to think, but my feelings betrayed logic for a fear so vivid that I could see myself through the assailant's scope. I thought I was going mad, and with everyone looking to me to hold Moo TV together, I hid this and other events from even my closest friends and family.

Now, over a decade later, David was telling me that I had PTSD, that I wasn't "crazy," and that these sorts of manifestations are common after trauma. How much of a relief would it have been back then to know that I wasn't going insane? Thankfully, the visions subsided within a few weeks, but for a time, on top of the devastation of losing Lee, I thought I had lost my mind.

It struck me on that flight from Germany that this was where my silver lining opportunity lay. I resolved to share what I had learned with our people. They might never have a PTSD episode, but if they did, I could at least assure them that they weren't going crazy.

Silver Linings

Back in Nashville, we had gently nudged all of our crew from the shooting into seeing Ginger or the Vanderbilt therapist provided by the tour—or both. I was touching base with them when I could, trying to casually check in. When the moment would present itself, I would share my PTSD story. Sparing the scarier details, I would stress that as low as I sank after Lee's death, I had made my way back up and stayed on top of the world for years. If they had some PTSD symptoms, they could take solace in knowing not only that they weren't crazy but that the symptoms would pass.

Jason Aldean had decided to go forward with his tour after taking only one week off. He expressed that if he didn't do this right away he might never be able to. He needed to hop back on the horse and tackle the fears and even the guilt he felt, but he told his crew that if anyone didn't feel up to joining him, that would be OK. I expressed to Aldean's team that if anyone wanted to talk, I had some PTSD experience, and it might be beneficial for them to hear about it. We let it be known that I would roll my tour bus to the first show and that if any of the staff felt uncomfortable or that the show was too much, they could leave the tour and ride home with me.

Out on the road the tension was high, but Aldean's team was stellar. Production manager Drew Brown and tour manager Jake LaGrone were superstars of compassion and thoughtfulness. I was impressed by Jason as well. He and I talked about the tragedy briefly that weekend. He carried himself with strength and focus—just what his team needed. As a young artist, he was living his dream daily, relatively carefree. When tragedy was thrust on him, he manned up and rose to the challenge. He was a leader, and they needed that.

While out there, some of Jason's crew did ask me about my PTSD. I was careful to share what I hoped was just enough to help. Several felt compelled to share their experience during the shooting. Listening to these perspectives was devastating. Their words took me there to that horrific scene.

As the lights went out for that first show, I wondered how many of the road crew and band were fighting flashbacks or simply frightened. Was anyone manifesting a gunman like I had all those years ago? As I stood watching from the side of the stage, I was surprised as Miranda Lambert walked up and gave me a hug. It struck me how touching it was that she had flown out to support Jason.

I think very highly of Miranda. I've had the honor of working with her a few times over the years, and she wears her big heart on her sleeve. She might hug you, or she might yell at you first and then hug you. She lets her thoughts be known, but she is full of caring. I appreciated that about her. I decided to express my gratitude by saying, "Hey, it's so great that you are here for him."

"I am here for all of you," she quickly blurted out, but then her shoulders slumped a little bit. "But I'm really here for myself. I had to see that this could be done safely."

I nodded understandingly. The poor thing was living with the fear that her next show might be the next shooting. It hadn't hit me how far-reaching the fear was. Hats off to all of the performers on the day they first returned to the stage after the shooting. Jason was doing just that, and he was also assuring that well over ten thousand people would be screaming with joy, not terror. The first show went well, and to the crew's credit, they all stayed for three scheduled shows. Touring crews are a resilient bunch.

I started periodically checking in with the guys, remembering that talking about old memories was a good thing to help them regain a sense of safety. I wrote notes to remind myself what might be good topics for each one. I looked down at my notes as I went to call Jeff Horr, an awesome guy. Jeff is the screen tech, the man in charge of making the massive screens work on Aldean's show. The note was one word: *Andre.* I smiled as I picked up the phone. Jeff answered, and we spoke for almost an hour about fun old times with his lovable brother-in-law, Andre. I really enjoyed the talk. The next day, Jeff called me.

"What's up buddy," I asked.

"Well, boss, I have to admit that when I saw you on caller ID yesterday, I didn't want to answer. I didn't want to talk about anything related to Vegas. I did not expect to spend the next hour cracking up with you over old times. After I hung up from that call, I thought, *Man, that was not what I expected, but it was great.* As I thought more about it, it occurred to me that you probably had that conversation planned. I wanted to call you and say how much I appreciate all that you've done for us. Heck, you even have me seeing a therapist! If you had told me a year ago that I would be seeing a shrink, I would have told you that *you* were crazy. But I have to tell you, I don't think I could do this without her. Thank you."

Jeff's gratitude meant the world to me. It was such a relief to hear that I was indeed doing some good.

Jeff continued, "I know that you told me that you never knew you had PTSD and that you never saw anyone about it, so I was thinking maybe I could help you the way you helped us. Can I recommend that you go see Ginger about your PTSD?"

I hesitated, not expecting this. "Jeff, that was fifteen years ago."

"I know," he replied, "and you still get torn up when you talk about it. I feel like all of this is really affecting you. She's doing a world of good for me, so will you please consider taking some of your own medicine?"

My eyes welled with tears. What could I say? "OK," I replied, choking back sobs.

At this moment, I feel compelled to say something directly to you, the reader. This chapter has been emotionally difficult to write. I have been dreading it. Despite those fears, the words have flowed easily up until now. But I have been sitting here at this paragraph break for a while, hesitant to move forward because beyond here there is a lot of pain. I don't like going back. Addressing our pain, our darkest moments, requires tremendous fortitude and tenacity.

On a happier note, reliving Jeff's caring really touched me. Why is it that we can go through hell and not break, but then when faced with kindness we fall apart?

Thank you, Jeff. I love you, pal.

Gingerly

Ginger has a huge smile. She exudes warmth and caring. As I sat down with her, I felt ready to share, learn, and hopefully grow. I took a deep breath and told her what the past few weeks had been like. I told her how I relived my trauma after Lee's death many times by sharing my story. I let her know that through others' stories, I experienced the Vegas shooting from a dozen different angles. I know I wasn't there, but I felt the horror, and it was weighing on me. My heart broke for those who experienced it far more vividly than I had.

We talked about how I was feeling, how it was hard to breathe, and how my eyes watered easily. I express that I had been doing my best but that I still felt helpless. The tears flowed as I admitted the sense of responsibility I carried for all of my crew guys being there that day. Ginger nodded and made me feel like what I was relaying was normal. Then she asked me to tell her about what happened to Lee. I took another deep breath and collected myself.

As you know from earlier chapters, Lee Griffin was a great man. He truly cared about people, and it showed. Lee was beloved by his friends, his clients, and his employees. He had real empathy and knew what people needed. Lee saw something in me and nurtured it, giving me countless opportunities to grow and the guidance necessary to succeed. He was a mentor, but he was also a great hang, full of fun stories we would share over a steak with a glass of fine wine. He was a father figure to me, and a wonderful one at that.

When Lee was killed in that carjacking, it broke my foundation. I told Ginger about the details of his death and the awful realization at his murder trial that he had lived briefly and horribly after the head wound. I told Ginger about carrying his body to its final resting place. I told her about my PTSD and how I thought I was going crazy because I was haunted by visions of a gunman pursuing me. I explained that I thought I could somehow keep some part of Lee alive by continuing his work at Moo TV. I shared that I had fallen apart years later when I realized that no matter how hard I worked, it wasn't going to bring him back. I laid it all out for Ginger. Eyes full of tears, I finally looked at her and waited.

"You did have PTSD," she affirmed, "and it seems likely that it is indeed back on some level."

I sighed. This was the answer I expected. "What now?" I asked.

Ginger was warm and reassuring. She expressed that I would be a good candidate for something called EMDR (Eye Movement Desensitization and Reprocessing) therapy, explaining that it could almost reprogram my brain. Through this process, we would locate misplaced feelings and put them where they belonged.

"Is this anything like hypnosis?" I asked skeptically.

"Not at all," she replied. "It works in different ways. You are consciously working on reprocessing memories.

"It sounds . . . spooky," I replied uncomfortably.

Ginger laughed. "It kind of is. When I was in school, I took a course on EMDR with the sole intent of writing a paper to debunk it. I thought it sounded ridiculous. A few days into the course it was my turn to try it, and it blew me away. It really works."

She showed me the LED light fixture that makes your eyes chase back and forth and also showed me optional paddles that you can hold as they alternately vibrate. She said both worked the same way on the brain and that the patient could choose which one they wanted to try.

I shook my head, smiling. "Spooky" was still my one-word reply. Again, she laughed.

I had already grown to trust Ginger. I took a deep breath and told her I would try EMDR. Pleased, she said we would start in the next session. Ginger then took a minute to tell me how special all of my guys were and that while I may feel helpless, the therapy I had enabled would be important for them, just as it would be for me. I left feeling nervous about EMDR but hopeful.

A few days later, I walked back up the stairs to Ginger's office, as ready as anyone can be to crack their brain open, so to speak. Again, I was greeted by that huge smile as she asked me how I felt.

"Hopeful," I replied. "It's a funny thing to be told you are still broken over something that you thought you had gotten over more than a decade ago."

Ginger nodded. "I think it's important that we explore this," she said.

She set out the light bar, but I felt like I would rather have the paddles, so she handed those to me. She explained that the paddles would start vibrating and keep doing so for a bit. She also said that this back-and-forth vibration in my hands would alternately activate the two hemispheres of my brain, helping stir up the memories. All I needed to do was hang on and let my thoughts drift back to Lee's death.

"Still spooky," I reiterated.

Ginger smiled and nodded. The paddles started to shake. I felt silly. The alternating vibration was strong. It all seemed ridiculous. These paddles were going to help fix me? I tried to relax. My thoughts went back to the moment I heard that Lee had died. I was recalling how crushed I was. I then recounted telling one of our camera operators that Lee had died. God, he cried so hard. *We* cried so hard. Then the vibration stopped.

Ginger asked about my memories, and I repeated them to her.

"Good," she said, offering a little guidance to nudge me on down the path. I closed my eyes and the paddles started again. I drifted back and thought of the funeral. Lee's friends had asked me to help carry the casket. I was worried that someone else should carry him, but his friends insisted. There is something really powerful about actually carrying a friend to the grave. I thought about his girlfriend, Ginny. They were going to be married. I thought about how I tried to be so strong for her that day.

The paddles stopped. I took a moment to analyze the process. My brain had seemed cloudy when it started, confused by the vibrations. When thoughts did eventually come, they were fairly vivid.

They flowed easily. Still, as much as I wanted this to work, I didn't understand how it would. Ginger, however, said I was doing well. "Keep going," she encouraged me.

I closed my eyes a third time, and the jarring paddles started their strange dance. I drifted back to the worst memory this time: I was there at the carjacking as it had been described at Lee's murder trial. The details revealed by the testimony had painted an all-too-vivid picture. Lee was outside of his beautiful historic home in Annapolis, Maryland, loading his car for a weekend at the beach with Ginny.

As it had played out in my head a thousand times, the two young men, cranked up on the drug PCP, walked up to him brandishing a pistol. Startled, Lee turned, thrusting the ironed shirts that he had in his hands toward the young man with the gun. The gun went off, and the bullet struck Lee in the head. He fell to the ground. The two carjackers got in his Jeep, turned, and ran Lee over as they tore down the street. The lady who lived next door heard the shot and ran outside to find Lee. He struggled to hang on to life, but the wounds were overwhelming. After a few minutes Lee let out a final forlorn sigh, releasing what would be his final breath. His neighbor tried to administer CPR, but his wounds were so severe, they didn't allow for that. Lee died. *Lee died.*

And the next thought that popped into my head locked me up. Ginger saw it on my face and stopped the paddles. I opened my eyes, tears streaming down my face. I couldn't speak.

"Take your time," Ginger said, seeming to understand. That final thought just kept repeating itself in my head, but I couldn't bring myself to say it. A minute later and I was still unable to speak.

"Take your time," Ginger repeated patiently. "It's OK."

I took a breath and finally got out two words: "I lived." And then I exploded into tears, completely hysterical.

Minutes later I was still struggling to breathe. *I lived?* Why were these words, this feeling so overwhelming? Confused by my reaction, I looked to Ginger for understanding.

"You have survivor's guilt," she said. "It's common, and these are feelings that don't belong to you. We are going to put those feelings where they belong."

I didn't know what to think. Why did I feel guilty for surviving? Why were these feelings so powerful? How could I have gone all these years without knowing that I carried this weight?

EMDR is indeed spooky . . . in a most impactful way.

What the hell had been happening in my brain? I felt gutted, but I resolved to keep on working toward the truth. Ginger said these feelings don't belong to me. Good—I didn't want them. Ginger explained that if desired, she could likely get me to where I felt relatively no pain over the memory. Giving this some thought, I respectfully declined. I told her that I feel I need my pain, that my pain is what enables my empathy. I explained that I have always felt the mind is a comparative instrument. How can we truly know or appreciate joy if we don't truly know pain? My pain is very much a part of who I am. Ginger smiled and agreed to honor my wish. We decided that we would get rid of the misplaced guilt but leave the pain intact. This memory should hurt.

Over the next year and more, Ginger and I would tenaciously work on just that. I can say with confidence that we put my survivor's guilt to rest. When I recall these memories nowadays, my heart still aches for Lee. It aches over the injustice of it all and over the loss. These memories hurt me to tears, as they should. What I don't feel is guilt or fear. The day finally came when Ginger told me I didn't need to come in anymore. I smiled broadly.

"Did I graduate?" I joked.

She beamed back at me and said, "Yes, you graduated." I gave her a huge hug.

You, dear reader, may be asking, "Hey Scott, we see the tenacity, but what's the point in sharing all this darkness? Where's the silver lining?"

Good question! So much of being tenacious comes down to facing your struggles, fears, and pain. Most times the challenge exists in the outside world, but this time it was within me. I had to tenaciously go after the bad wiring in my head—those misplaced feelings. It was a painful, arduous journey. The silver lining in this gray cloud, for me, has been using my experience to help others.

The message is simple: When you encounter life's toughest challenges, actively mine for *your* silver linings and then share the wealth. Invest it in others, and it will come back to you many times over. Read on to see what happened when I invested my silver lining.

PTSD and Me

I love being there for others. I had hoped sharing my PTSD story with the victims of the shooting in Las Vegas might do some good. It just felt like the right thing to do. And I believe it really helped some of them. As such, I was compelled to say yes when the entrepreneurs' organization I belong to (EO) asked if I might have a story that would fit in with the theme "To hell and back." I told them I could do a talk on my PTSD journey. But I feared it might be too dark. The curator of the event, Sameera, asked me to elaborate, so I gave her the short version. She was moved and told me that she really wanted me to give this talk.

I usually embrace speaking opportunities, but this one was different. I accepted and even chose the topic, but I grew worried. You see, I had just graduated from Ginger's care. Would dredging up those feelings so soon after I had run the gauntlet be wise? What if I broke down onstage from reliving the pain? And what if standing up in front of all those people and sharing a story so painful actually hurt or haunted any of them in some way? I worked through all these fears and decided that the opportunity to help some people made it worth the chance.

Sameera wanted all of us speaking to do a run-through earlier in the day to verify that we had our thoughts organized. I arrived early at the beautiful old Belcourt Theatre in Nashville, relieved that they had decided to do my run-through last, thinking it would be easier with the other speakers gone. I saw this as not only good practice for me but also a chance for Sameera to see how dark and painful this talk was. Perhaps she would change her mind about having me give it. A part of me hoped she would.

I stood behind the curtain and clipped the microphone on, taking a deep breath. Then, I stepped out into the empty theater. I worked through the story in painful detail, barely holding it together even to an empty house. Fifteen minutes later I walked offstage to see Sameera had a pained look on her face.

"Oh, Scott, I am so sorry," she said.

I burst into tears, and she hugged me.

"Do you really still think I should do this?" I asked.

"Yes, I think it's important that you do," she replied emphatically.

"I don't want to just go out there onstage and rip everyone's heart out," I told her. "I don't want to hurt them."

"I think everyone can stand to hear this story," she said, "and more importantly, some people *need* to hear it."

I resigned myself to the task, still unsure that it was a good idea. On my way out of the theater, I passed by the sound man sitting in a back corner. I hadn't noticed him from the stage.

"Hey," he beckoned as I was walking by. I stopped and turned to face him. He nodded and spoke seriously. "You need to give this talk. I heard your doubts backstage. Your mic was still on. I unfortunately know something about PTSD. People need to hear your story."

I nodded and let out another sigh. "OK."

He smiled in affirmation. I walked out of the theater hoping he was right.

Already exhausted and knowing what this would take out of me, I took a rare midday nap. When I returned at the appointed time, I scanned the crowd from the back of the theater. There were well over one hundred in attendance already, many of them familiar faces. I decided that I would be better off alone until it was my turn. I went backstage, where I paced back and forth in an empty hallway.

I gathered my strength until the applause told me that the speaker before me had taken the stage. As I clipped the mic on, I felt my heart racing. While I had made great strides with my public speaking, I felt that old fear creeping in. No doubt it was the subject matter fueling my anxiety. I wasn't sure I could hold it together while recalling a story this painful.

As my name was announced, I steeled myself and walked out into the bright light to applause. I spoke from the heart, fighting back the tears. I found myself right on the edge of losing it, especially as I spoke about the Vegas shooting. In my emotional state, I was able to drive home the confusion and illogical feelings that came with my PTSD. The gravity of it all hung in the air, especially when I said the words, "I truly thought I was going crazy." I paused to let that settle in.

I then apologized for taking the audience to these darkest of places but explained that it was my strong desire to help them understand themselves, especially if they had some trauma manifesting, and even if they didn't. Then I spoke my final words. "If you are experiencing any of what I described, I promise you from experience that the difficult journey of reconciling it is worth the hard work. Take that journey."

As the applause rang out, I took a moment to look around. My eyes were adjusted enough to scan the house. I was rewarded by what I saw: some tears, but overall, faces filled with genuine appreciation. I exhaled a huge sigh of relief and walked offstage.

I think I helped.

I was thrilled when, over the next few days, some people who had attended my talk reached out to express their gratitude. Even better, some indicated they realized they could use help and asked to be introduced to Ginger. Two of those individuals said that prior to attending my talk, they didn't know what PTSD was. Best of all, one gentleman wrote me a letter about a month after he started therapy with Ginger. In the letter he noted that he, like me, had thought he was actually going crazy. He explained that when he heard me speak, it was a powerful revelation. Ginger had confirmed that he had PTSD, and he was well on the way to recovery. What he took the time to write next is the sort of thing that compelled me to write this book.

"You don't really know me," he wrote, "but I feel that you have arguably saved my life. You have saved my marriage, and possibly best of all, you have made me feel like I can be the dad that I want to be. Thank you."

Moments like this make every bit of facing the tough stuff worthwhile. This is what I mean by the silver lining.

Now that I feel the relief of getting through this chapter, let's review the tenacity within.

Fear

Fear itself is tenacious. Facing fear is not something you do once. It's something you will need to do again and again and again. Within this chapter, I had to be more tenacious than the fear generated by my PTSD. I was frightened that facing my PTSD might make it worse. That it would stir up all that evil, giving it a renewed hold on me. Once the truth of my PTSD was discovered, I had a choice. On the one hand, I could hide from it. Life had been going pretty well, so why rock the boat, right? That was not the choice that I made. Instead of turning my back on the shadows and scars left by my trauma, I faced them. This process proved to be painful, but I forged ahead tenaciously.

Speaking with the victims of the concert shooting hurt, but I had those conversations in the hope of helping them. The shooting brought back my PTSD, yet I still moved forward. I resolved to face it—to try and remove the bad wiring that had me so often on the edge of tears. This inward journey quickly revealed another dysfunction: my survivor's guilt. I faced that as well, daring to tinker with my brain through EMDR. My EMDR and traditional therapy with Ginger lasted well over a year. I didn't give up. I cried a lot and hurt a lot, but I didn't give up.

I hope you didn't grow weary of reading about my tears. They were very real. I felt broken and small, but I didn't quit, despite the pain. I probably could have ignored the needs of others and denied the existence of my darkest shadows. Instead, I spent two years working through these challenges. By taking the hard road, by trying and never giving up, I not only helped myself but made a difference in others' lives too. It's funny, but the chapter where I hardly felt like saying the word *tenacity* is arguably the most tenacious chapter of this book.

All of this is to say: Do the hard things even when they get harder—*especially* when they get harder. I suspect you, too, will discover wonderful silver linings when you dare to peer into your grayest clouds. Now, a few years later, with the benefit of hindsight, I find myself grateful for the struggle. The memories of the pain are over, replaced by the pride I feel having faced my fear and having positively impacted others. This is tenacity's silver lining!

Author's Note:

I haven't written in a few weeks. Digging up these painful memories is indeed hard. By immersing myself in this chapter, my PTSD came back a bit. I expected it might. It's impossible to get that deep into the violence and pain and not be affected. I didn't have any crazy visions, but I was depressed and noticeably off center. I feel strongly that the dark place I took myself to and the funk I have been in is totally worth it if reading this helps even one person. If I have helped you, I would love to hear about it. Please reach out to me via social media or at tenaciousbook.com.

This seems like the right time to introduce my next guest. He was a Navy SEAL for an incredible thirty years. During three decades and nineteen tours of duty, he operated at the highest level in the military in incredibly dangerous situations. I am so glad he has chosen to share some of his journey and the beautiful place where it has led him. Ladies and gentlemen, my friend Jason "Hendo" Henderson.

Welcome in, Hendo!

JASON "HENDO" HENDERSON
ON BEING TENACIOUS

I was in the service for nineteen tours over thirty years. Sixteen in combat. Almost all of those as a tier one Navy SEAL, an operator at Naval Special Warfare Development Group. My job was to surgically remove terrorists and retrieve hostages.

I quite frequently went on incursions focused on high value targets or attempting to recover hostages. Night after night, you never know what you'll encounter. You'll kick the first door open, and it might be somebody going for a gun and you've got to shoot at them, or maybe a man is running away and you have to catch him. If it's a person of interest, you may have to fist fight them because they don't want to come with you. If they pull a knife, you might have to pull your own knife or hit them over the head with something. Behind that same door there could just as easily be a family, or some animals, or an empty room. Every door is spiking that adrenaline up and down. Maybe I just shot a man who shot at me in the room to the left, and as I move to the door to the right, I've got to mentally reset before I kick that door open because it may be a room full of babies.

I never once harmed a woman, a child, or an elderly person—ever. I only shot exactly who I needed to shoot. If I shot them, they were armed, and every shot was a surgical shot. Likewise with hand to hand combat I only used as much force as necessary. If I felt like I could subdue them and get them handcuffed, I would do that. I would only pull a knife or go to extreme ends if they themselves had gotten a hold of a weapon. I didn't let any emotion become a factor whatsoever; I was just there to do a task. If you start letting emotion become involved, then you start making mistakes. I don't like to live in chaos. I like to live in order. I stay completely focused on what I can control. A Taliban fighter once hit me in the face with a shovel, and still, my emotion didn't change one way or the other.

I saw a lot of horrific things. I saw innocent people get killed by both the enemy and by the US military. I myself nor anybody who worked for me ever excepted collateral damage. I was a stickler for it, but seeing things like that can affect you.

After about my third tour, I started to feel like this whole thing was kind of a scam. Like, *why are we here?* The counter insurgency effort that the generals were mandating was extremely ineffective because they were treating the Afghans, Somalis, and Iraqis like Germans and Japanese post WWII. Germans and Japanese people are incredibly productive who are engineering masters. They could rebuild their own nation in a very short period of time with some help, and they did. But that doesn't work in third world nations. All we were really doing was making a long-term enemy. We're killing people so their children can then become the next generation's enemies. The big-picture reasons as to why we were there didn't make any sense to me. But while I was there, I can assure you that I was getting rid of horribly evil people—the worst of the worst. These were men who were doing heinous things—raping children. I mean, you name it; they were pure evil.

Then just like that, the US pulled out of Afghanistan and let the Taliban erase whatever progress we had made. They released all the prisoners that my brothers and I had put our lives on the line to detain. Many of my friends died doing that work, and we just pulled the plug and left. With this, I knew it was time for me to retire from service.

At the end of my career they sent me to Bethesda for a couple of weeks of testing. A place called N.I.C.o.E. (the National Intrepid Center of Excellence). It's where the Department of Defense provides advance care, research, and education about traumatic brain injury. They did lots of MRIs, brain scans, and body scans. Not surprisingly, I was diagnosed with PTSD (Post-Traumatic Stress Disorder), although now I think they only call it Post-Traumatic Stress. They took the "disorder" out of it as if somehow deleting that word or letter is going to fix everything. Anytime I hear people saying that it's not a disorder, I'm like, *shut up*. We're messed up. We've got some problems we need to get fixed. You can call it whatever you want. Call it sissy-itis, I don't care. I just want some help fixing whatever is wrong with me.

I was specifically diagnosed with having hyper vigilance. I was constantly hyper aware and relentlessly scanning for possible threats. Everything I saw around me was something coming to kill me. I would think, *Oh, if this person cuts me off and comes out with a gun, I'm going to do this and shut him down like that.* Or as I was going for a run, I'd think, *If somebody jumps out of the bushes, then I'm going to get them this way.* Or worse, *if somebody attacks my family, or somebody is a public shooter, or if riots break out, then this tactic is how I'm going to eliminate the threat.* My whole mindset was perpetuating the state of how I was going to kill people around me. I became really worried about it because I just really saw the world as a black place, a very dark thing. Because of this, I also had issues with sleep, anger, and depression.

I never would have thought that I was a depressed person. I didn't think I had any reason to be depressed. Granted, I had lost like thirty of my friends, which, of course, will make you depressed to a certain degree. I still think about those guys a lot, and I do what I can for some of their kids now.

Then there were the drugs. In the field, the way they kept us performing at such a high level was with a ton of pharmaceuticals. You needed medicine to sleep because you always had to sleep at random times. Mostly I was going to bed during the daytime post operations. I needed stuff to help me sleep then. I also needed stuff to help with all the pain that was in my body. I needed mood enhancers to keep me from becoming enraged. I had to take something to help me stay awake and push myself higher. So you use all these pharmaceuticals on this performance enhancing regimen. And then when you retire and you no longer have your mission, now you're just a junkie or an addict.

Every day was like this, and having insomnia meant I was not sleeping at night. When I would finally sleep, I'd have recurring dreams of demons coming to get me—night terrors. And it was always kind of the same thing: A demon would come in and drag me towards hell. As a man of strong faith, this was terrifying.

It's like you literally come from killing somebody one day, and then all of a sudden you're at home going out to dinner with your family. And it's quite a psychological transition that you have to make. I would have to sit in my driveway before I'd walk into my house. I'd be like, *Okay, I'm no longer a SEAL. Now I'm a father and a husband. Just go inside and take out the trash and wash dishes and hug your children and do whatever you need to do.*

My timing wasn't great either. When I retired, it was 2020, in the middle of COVID. With COVID you couldn't work or go to the gym. Everything was shut down. Plus there were riots breaking out over George Floyd, so I was just kind of pacing around my house drinking pints of wine in the morning, wondering what I'm going to do with my life.

I realized I needed a purpose. There were all of these riots—maybe I could help train the police in deescalation of force. Few people, if anyone, have the experience I have with this. I was like, okay, well, I need to get my own shit right first. I immediately threw away all my pills, and I cut my alcohol down to one and a half or two and a half drinks per day. OK, now what?

I went out and created a nonprofit, Four Pillars Collective, so I could get out and start training law enforcement in then underfunded and defunded cities. This brought me joy. I immediately had lots of law enforcement hitting me up, saying, "Hey, we need help. We're struggling." I was training these officers, but then they started sharing that they had experienced a lot of violence and horrible things too. Shootings, investigating pedophile cases. They were also struggling with PTSD. I wasn't just helping them with training; we were supporting each other through that understanding as well.

At times, in cities like Chicago and New York, their senior officers were saying, "Hey, we don't want Navy SEALs weaponizing

> our law enforcement and coming in here." Well I was training them to only use the exact amount of force they needed to safely detain people, but I guess the brass was afraid of the optics. As such, I would have to train them almost secretly. But, you know, those guys would show up on their day off and would train hard. We would work on things like how to extract violent people out of vehicles safely or what they should look for within mobs to keep the situation from getting out of hand. I also started doing some bodyguarding and self-defense training with women and girls going off to college. I have daughters, so I am passionate about keeping women safe. All of this was, as Scotty says, the silver lining. Everything I had endured equipped me to help these people. And helping them was helping me.
>
> Since I've retired, I've found that the real, true internal premium you gain from service to others is much better than self-service. I am so fulfilled when I focus on service to others, helping and lifting others up, and being strong enough to carry others. That's when I'm doing what I was put on Earth to do. To me, this is why I've been blessed with strength, perseverance, and tenacity. It is to help and lift others up, no longer focusing on myself. Maybe that was what I had to go through to come to that realization and be the servant I am today.

What a shiny silver lining. Hendo, buddy, thank you for being the warrior, protector, and man that you are. We are all grateful.

Isn't it wonderful to hear that Hendo has found helping others to be a medicine for their struggles *and* his own?! There is more to his amazing story, though, as you'll discover a bit later in this book.

Sadly, a surprising amount of people have some PTSD from trauma earlier in their life. If that's you, you can get help. A week after first turning this chapter over to the editor, I saw Ginger for the first time in a long time. I feel better now. I allowed myself the necessary time to recover, process things, and seek further guidance. With her help and this grueling chapter behind me, I'm ready to keep writing! Thank you so much for reading this and sharing in my struggle. I feel a great sense of satisfaction for getting through it tenaciously.

(Heavy chapter, funny picture! Dr. David Haase and I in our lederhosen at Oktoberfest the day before the Vegas tragedy. Lee Griffin at a stadium show. Hendo camoed up with a compound bow, a formidable combo I'm sure.)

*All photos and supplemental material can be found on TENACIOUSBOOK.COM

INTERLUDE III
The Spoils!

Every gray cloud has a silver lining. In the previous chapter, we explored the silver linings of tenacity—the good that comes with the struggle. Let's look at that concept and broaden it a tad to include what I like to call *the spoils of tenacity*.

What do I mean by that? Using tenacity to achieve a remarkable goal might get you more than you expect. For example, as you read earlier, Thomas Marshburn used his tenacity to overcome obstacles and fulfill his dream of becoming an astronaut. But tenacity didn't stop paying off there. As hard as it is to imagine, he attained something well beyond his dream. He's back again here to share what that special something is. Take it away, Tom.

> ### THOMAS MARSHBURN'S SPOILS
>
> Making your way around on the outside of the space station is really quite perilous. Of course, one misstep or missed grip could be tragic. In the icy cold, your hands and feet can get numb, and that massive suit's inertia can even pull you off the station if you

aren't careful. Beyond that, you are towing your safety tether, and while it does attach you to the station, it can also get hung up on the station's many protuberances or around you or your backpack in some way. We train relentlessly and are masters of mitigating those concerns. But there's no getting around the fact that it's dangerous.

As such, we have a surprising work-around, a shortcut that we employ for longer trips. We use the fifty-eight-foot robotic arm to swing us safely away from the station along our path. If you climb on the arm at full extension in one direction, and then do a full swing to the other, it replaces a good one hundred feet of treacherous travel—a simple move that has far fewer variables. You step into the footholds, clip in, retract your tether, and off you go. This is appropriately nicknamed the windshield wiper move.

Now, space walks are hectic affairs. NASA always wants to maximize your time because you have a lot to accomplish. Couple that with the dangers, and your mind is running hard the entire time. Every seemingly free moment is actually internally hectic. You are assessing your immediate safety, planning your next move, and occasionally thinking back and triple-reviewing what you have done.

One of my walks included four windshield wiper maneuvers, three of them in icy darkness with the sun on the far side of the earth. The moment I want to share occurred on the last of these maneuvers.

As the arm started its slow climb, I could feel my feet in the foot restraint, but that was my only sense of being tethered to something. And even then, my feet were floating around inside the boot. So sometimes I'd have to look down to prove that I was still locked in. You can't help but have this profound sense of falling. This was near the end of a successful walk, so I didn't have too much to review. My safety wasn't in question, so this allowed me a little time. I was canted back so I had to bend at the waist to see anything—a few external lights on the station, dim city lights on nightside Earth. There were the occasional lightning flashes, too, which are really quite gorgeous, but you have to look for a while to catch them.

I straightened up and stared into the void. My eyes hadn't adjusted, so it was just this nothingness. No stars or planets. Nothing. A profound sense of exposure and solitude came over me. There had never been a time in my existence when I was not connected to something—not even on the highest mountaintop, as you can certainly feel gravity's pull there. Nor while scuba diving, where you are floating, but you've still got structure and objects around you. You can feel the viscosity of the water on your body. Even when skydiving, with the ground rushing toward you, you feel the pressure of the air whipping around you as you reach terminal velocity. But not here in the blackness, as I floated in my boots. Here, there was nothing. I felt what nothing feels like. Experienced what nothing looks like.

But it wasn't exactly nothing. No, the blackness was infinitely three-dimensional and palpable, enormous beyond imagination. It was completely icy in a sense. I can't find the right words—perhaps "as inhuman as you can get." I had the clear feeling that it didn't care about me at all. The sun on a nice sunny day—oh, the sun cares. It gives us warmth and light. The earth, even if you're in the desert, holds you, and you know where you can go to get water. But in this expanse, it feels like any kind of human or living existence is an afterthought that can be shrugged off in a second, and it wouldn't matter. Engulfed by this void, you get an idea of your place in the universe. And it's tiny. I struggled to

> process this deep, deep feeling, and all I could come up with were these words by Nietzsche:
>
> I looked into the abyss, and the abyss looked into me.
>
> I was forever changed by that moment. And although the picture I painted may not convey this, it was a beautiful change. We are tiny... fragile. But somehow in my mind, this means we are more precious and wonderful.

Wow, Tom. Just wow. Thank you.

The perspective Tom received was not expected. And it's something he never could have received without the tenacity to work toward his dream of leaving Earth. Remember, as you chase your dreams, you are setting yourself up for so much more than you even know.

Fascinated, I was compelled to look up the Nietzsche reference Tom made earlier. It was inspired by a larger quote that includes the following, "And when you gaze long into the abyss, the abyss also gazes into you." Digging a little deeper, the all-knowing Internet had this to say about it. The "abyss" in Nietzsche's quote is a metaphor for the dark, dangerous, and often unfathomable aspects of human existence and the world. I keyed in on the word *unfathomable*. Tenacious Tom has experienced a great many incredible things in his life, and to us his abyss may be unfathomable, but it is less so thanks to his taking the time to share. For this I am so grateful.

THE SPOILS!

(Thomas on an EVA with the earth 250 miles below him. Another pic of me doing zero G training.)

*All photos and supplemental material can be found on TENACIOUSBOOK.COM

CHAPTER 10
A Look in the Mirror

Grow through what you go through.
—Unknown

I laid down and awkwardly fumbled with my headphones and blinders. "Are you ready?" the stranger asked.

Terrified, my head swirling under the influence of the psychedelics, I mustered a response. "Yes, I am ready to see me." I took a deep breath as the blinders plunged me into darkness. A moment later, headphones covered my ears, enveloping me in a cacophony of sound. I took a deep breath, and suddenly . . .

. . . my world exploded. Or did I?

The Mirror

Three years had passed since that day I stood onstage and shared my PTSD journey with a group of fellow entrepreneurs. I had remained in a happy place overall until the global pandemic. We all endured that awful time, so I will spare you the details of my experience beyond a summary paragraph or two to set the stage.

As you might recall, fear of failure was the first and biggest challenge I faced on my path to tenacity. I beat it like an alcoholic beats alcoholism. It was still there, but day after day I overcame its influence.

Then, the pandemic shut down the entire concert industry, bringing all of my company's income to virtually zero. This made it impossible to properly take care of my people. I knew logically there was nothing I could do to change that reality, but being the one to tell my employees I had to reduce their pay—or cut it off entirely—gutted me. For eighteen months this process repeated time and again until payroll eventually receded to less than 10 percent of what it had been. I felt that I was personally failing them. Even though I had overcome my fear of failure years earlier, the pandemic forced me to confront that old fear again, day after day. No matter what I did, I couldn't seem to find a way to help my team of people win. The old fear found a new foothold in me.

My friend Dennis could tell I was struggling and reached out to me. He had some experience with old trauma and shared his solution with me. Dennis told me about something he had tried that worked on his trauma all the way back to its core beginnings. I recalled my EMDR work addressing Lee's death. While rummaging around in my brain we had come across some PTSD related to my dad from my childhood as well. It was likely the source of my fear of failure. I had shelved the prospect of diving into that issue in favor of focusing on the PTSD I experienced around Lee's murder. Was it time to go deeper? I was already beat up. It was not like I'd be throwing shade on a sunny day. I listened intently.

Dennis began sharing his story, and right out of the gate red flags started popping up for me. Although Dennis is grounded and logical, and possesses a science-oriented brain, he shared that his experience had gifted him a conversation with his soul. He spoke about it as a spiritual experience. This was out of character for Dennis, making my science brain skeptical. More red flags flew up when he spoke about the medicine that opened up this opportunity.

I asked, "What medicine?"

He replied that he didn't know—that he wasn't supposed to know. OK, now every alarm in my head was going off. "Wait, are you talking about drugs?" I asked.

"Well, let's call it medicine," Dennis replied calmly. "Throughout history, medicine like this has been used by many cultures to gain insight and understanding about the nature of our existence."

"Oh hell no," I retorted. I had managed to spend my entire life in the music business without doing drugs. No way was I doing them now.

Dennis respected my stance but asked if I would mind if he shared the rest of his story. I'm always interested in learning, so I agreed. I did, however, reiterate that I could never, ever do drugs.

The story was fascinating. The "journey," as he called it, was clearly powerful—an immensely positive thing for him. But there was still no way I was going to do drugs.

Dennis finished sharing, and I expressed that I had seen so many friends and coworkers struggle with addiction that I couldn't go there. I told him that my dad was a smoker and an alcoholic and that I wouldn't tempt fate for fear that I was wired for addiction as well. Dennis nodded, understanding my concern.

"These medicines aren't addictive," he quietly promised.

"I'd be afraid I might have a bad trip or break my brain," I countered.

Dennis smiled and said that wouldn't happen either. He tried to assure me that the place he visited made an art out of curating beautiful journeys. Seeing that I wasn't willing, he wisely held up his hand and expressed that he had no intention of talking me into it, reiterating that he was just sharing his experience and answering my questions. I thanked him for that, but I was ready to talk about something else.

This book's purpose is to encourage and empower you to have the best life you can have. You and your decisions drive the path of that life. As such, wouldn't you want those decisions to be made with as much clarity as possible? (Sigh.) The obvious answer is yes, but what my friend proposed scared me. That clarity scared me. I wasn't ready to fully tackle *me* yet. Does that resonate with anyone else? Read on.

Over the next few months, I was compelled to ponder the experience Dennis had described. My friend is brilliant and kind, and, as such, his opinion carried weight. Dennis had also shared his experience with another mutual friend, Michael, piquing his curiosity as well. Curiosity notwithstanding, I had to say no to drugs . . .

Though here's the thing that I kept wrestling with: A trusted friend described a way I might better understand myself and my life. He was offering me a chance to look in the mirror and see myself from a different perspective. I haven't gone into my childhood at any length in this book, as my path to being tenacious started at age eighteen. Thus, I have only once mentioned that, in my opinion, my father had borderline personality disorder. I think his frequent, irrational scolding and punishment did more than incubate my overdeveloped fear of failure. As I hinted in an earlier chapter, I think it also hardwired me to self-analyze. Throughout my formative years I was desperate to keep him from being upset or hurting me. I was hypervigilant about my actions in hopes of not triggering him. What I surmised, but didn't fully understand then, was that his lashing out and my desperate attempt to avoid those lashings made me prone to self-analysis. As an adult, this tendency helped me develop and grow into a version of me I feel good about.

Yet here I was, being offered a chance to see me more completely, and I was saying no.

I couldn't stop thinking about what my friend had shared, so I read a few books on "medicine" work. These books, notably including *How to Change Your Mind* by Michael Pollan, were fascinating, and I started asking Dennis questions. Months later, after many more heartfelt conversations with him and with others who also had "journeyed," I accepted that it would not break my brain if I tried it. All the evidence made this logical, but my fear remained.

Soon after coming to this conclusion, Dennis, Michael, and I were talking, and the subject came up again. Dennis asked if we were ready yet. My answer surprised me as it escaped my mouth: "Yes." Michael agreed that he was ready too. We grinned at the bold path we had just chosen, but I qualified my answer. "I'm doing this only because a mirror has been presented to me, and I can't bear not looking in it." The child in me still longs to understand myself and always will.

A month later, my friend Michael and I flew to the beautiful remote facility. We were shown to our rooms. I was surprised to find that we were the only guests. My room was gorgeous, with floor-to-ceiling windows overlooking a gentle stream. As promised, there were some pills waiting for us in our rooms. We were instructed to take them a few hours beforehand to "grease the wheels" a bit. As with all of the various medicines we would be given here, we were not permitted to know what these were. Not knowing was a hard pill to swallow (pun intended!) and unnerving.

As required by the facility, I had been counseled extensively on what to expect and guided through setting intentions for my "journey." I would be given medicine and laid in a bed referred to as a "nest." This consisted of body pillows snuggly placed on each side of me and a weighted blanket on top to cocoon me. Headphones turned to almost full volume provided a playlist developed by Johns Hopkins University for this kind of journey, while a blindfold blacked out all light. The blindfold was deep enough that it would allow me to keep my eyes comfortably open, as I was told this might put me in a different mental state. What I heard made sense.

Two people would watch over me, ensuring my well-being and potentially guiding me if needed. I would also have two microphones clipped to me to capture anything I had to say. It was explained that because I wouldn't remember much, transcribing and reviewing the audio of my journey was a required part of the process. It was stressed that working with our transcript after the journey was, in fact, what made much of the insight take hold. If this sounds scary, trust me, it was extremely so.

What if I had some sort of psychotic split? What if I did become addicted despite all evidence to the contrary? What if some dark, repressed memory came to light? What if I wet the bed?! Lastly—and this question was of some real gravity—what if I see me, and I don't like what I see? What if I discover I am bad (like I was told when I was a child)? What if I was bad like my father?

The Deep Dive

All of these fears were crashing into each other in my head as my friend Michael and I stood overlooking a beautiful pond at the facility. Today was Journey Day.

The two people who would be guiding us approached. I had met one of them, the man in charge of the facility, Carl, on the phone. He had been greatly reassuring, and I had already developed some comfort with him. The other guy, Charlie, was trying to get to know me, but I was too scared to focus on our conversation.

Carl finally spoke up. "Well, are we ready to get started?"

By the way, this facility employs a doctor and a nurse. This isn't a shady, fly-by-night situation run by some old hippies. These people take your mental health and safety very seriously. The four of us sat in my room, and my buddy and I were handed our medicine. We looked at each other and I could read Michael's mind:

Holy cow, are we really doing this?

Yup.

As we each partook of the mystery medicine, we reviewed our intentions and were told that the substance would work on us, and with us, in its own order, and that it had an intelligence that we shouldn't resist. Frankly, to my already high-strung self this sounded like absolute bullshit. It ticked my nerves up yet another notch. A quiet alarm chimed from one of the guides' phones and we were handed still more medicine. I tried to pay attention as our guides continued to talk of our intentions, but I was wound up. Not long after, another alarm sounded and more of a different medicine was doled out. This dose progression was not fully explained earlier (or, more likely, I had missed the explanation), and somehow loading up with multiple doses made me even more anxious.

"When will we know it's time?" I asked Carl.

He smiled. "Don't worry, you and I will both know at about the same time."

Despite my calm exterior, somewhere around here I went from high anxiety to full-on panic! *Oh God, we are breaking our brains.* Just then the medicine started to hit me. I took a quick, short breath and met eyes with my host.

"See," he said, smiling. "I told you we would both know simultaneously. Let's get you guys started."

Michael felt the medicine as well. He shot me one last anxious glance as Carl walked him out of the room, leaving me with the stranger who had assured me it was time.

Notably under the influence, I had difficulty walking to and getting in the nest.

"Are you ready?" he asked.

Terrified and disoriented, I managed a reply. "Yes, I am ready to see me."

My head was a swirling mess as he put my blinders on. The world went pitch black. The nurse arrived with one final dose. "This last one will hit you fast," I was warned. A moment later, music erupted from the headphones.

Oh, God . . .

Exploded

I wish I could explain the experience. I cannot. I can't even fully recall the feeling for myself. Certain experiences in life feel different because they are different. This felt different because *I* was different.

In my recording, you can hear the fear in my voice. At first I saw something I believed was the machine calculating space and time. This visual was fleeting, and I sense that it was nothing relevant. In other words, I do not think I actually got a glimpse under the hood of the universe.

As this image melted away, I found myself drowning in a black liquid. A terrifying fraction of an instant later, I broke the surface, finding myself to be extremely buoyant. I floated there for a bit, struggling to process the bizarre environment. In hindsight, I do not put any weight on this experience either. It was a hallucination without relevance, in my opinion.

Here is some of the transcript just as I surfaced from the black liquid. Forgive the choppy sentences; they are exactly as I uttered them while deep in the medicine that day:

"I'm frightened."

I can't stress enough how strong the fear in my voice was.

"I'm frightened, but I chase the fear."

Breathing deeply, I reassured myself that I was buoyant on the black fluid.

"It's like I just . . . It's like I just . . . came to the surface of a lake."

I paused while taking in the black lake with no end in sight.

"Oh, I'm floating. It's another level of consciousness. It's me, I'm with me. What an incredible journey."

There was a longer pause. The fear was still strong in my voice at first, but as I continued my tone shifted to more of a nervous excitement.

"Where will I go? What will I do!?"

"Oooohhhh . . . Wow, what am I doing?! Holy shit. So beautiful, I was not ready for this!"

This was not what I thought . . . how could anyone think . . . What is this? What is this? This was not what I thought. How could anyone think . . . what is this?"

About ten minutes in, my reality shifted from the lake and I found myself in a black sphere. I expressed curiously that something was in the middle.

"It's me," I said, a tone of wonder suddenly replacing all fear. *"It's me."*

Upon uttering those words I teleported to the middle of the sphere, where I perceived myself now to be sitting calmly.

"It's me. I'm here with myself."

Bolstered by the reality that my brain was working and I was no longer seeing bizarre visions, I continued questioning.

"What do I do with me?"

Remembering my guidance, I leaned into gratitude.

"I am so lucky to have my friend Dennis who told me about this. Gosh, how is Michael in the next room doing right now? What is his world? What is happening to him? I am very lucky to have these friends. I have friends—people to accompany me through this treacherous thing called life. I value my friends. I value me. I love me . . . I need to love me."

My voice found traction, my fog cleared, and I spent the next five hours and twenty minutes in a full-speed, run-on sentence coherently and methodically telling myself who I am, and why I am who I am. I spoke about what absolutely matters to me and why, who my father was and why, even who his father was, although I never knew him personally. The generational hurt seemed crystal clear as I saw it flow down through time into me. For over five hours I was deep, deep inside me.

Eventually, I felt normal-ish, so I pulled the blinders up and found that I was safe in my room. I was alive! My brain seemed to be working, and while my sweat soaked through the sheets, I could tell that I hadn't wet the bed! *Wow!* I did it!

I was momentarily surprised that I was alone, but just then someone from the facility peeked in my window and smiled. Seeing that I was up, he came in.

"How are you?" he asked.
"Great, I think! Hey! How is my buddy?"
"He's doing fine." *Relief.*
"How long has it been?"
"Over five hours."
"Wow."

As is so often the case, the fear outweighed the reality. I was fine, just as all evidence had pointed to. I found myself in an ecstatic state, fiercely proud of facing my fear of the medicine and also thrilled to be alive. I had a sense that I had done great work. I felt different about me.

Give that last statement the gravity it deserves. *I felt different about me.*

How can *you* take a good look in the mirror? Is there something about you that you should face? I dare you to tackle it. I bet you'll find that it wasn't anywhere near as scary in reality. More importantly, it's not as scary as your fear of it is right now.

Integration

Later, I sat in Michael's room as we compared notes. A realization struck me like a hammer. I'm going to give it its own line on the page as it's a big deal.

"I feel differently about my dad."

Indeed I did. The guides told us that the experience would likely rewire our brains. My transcript later revealed that I had spent most of my time working out my feelings about my father, and who he was relevant to me. In that moment, I just knew I felt different.

"Better or worse?" my buddy asked.

"Better. *Way* better. Somehow I'm not so angry. Somehow I just . . . feel sorry for him."

I feel like I could write a whole book on this therapy, and someday I might. While I don't feel that this medicine work would be merited or good for everybody, it was incredible and life-changing for me.

Let me sum up and highlight a few key things for brevity. I was promised that I wouldn't break my brain. Being the science-minded guy that I am, I had a brain-function test just before the therapy, and I had another afterward. The results? I didn't break my brain!

I was told that this would change me. The change scared me because I liked me just fine as I was, faults and all. The therapy did change me, but in my opinion it helped me be more of my true self.

I was terrified I'd become addicted, even though I was told that I wouldn't. I was promised that afterward I would have no desire to go right back under for at least a few months, and even then, only to continue the work, not because of any physical or psychological craving. This was exactly my experience; I loved my journey but felt no desire to go again for months.

It was, in summary, almost exactly as advertised. I might not have described it as a conversation with my soul. I would say something a bit more scientific, perhaps this: It downregulated the default-mode network in my brain. Thus, my ego, which resides within, essentially took a nap, during which time I was gifted with a new perspective on myself, my life, and the forces within it. That perspective was unclouded by the influence of behaviors and biases learned over a lifetime. Shy of these ever-present preconceptions, I reverted to an almost childlike purity, full of wonder. I was able to come to fresh and untainted conclusions about my life. Some of these beautiful observations really sunk in, allowing me to form new interpretations, new perspectives, and to better see and better be me.

Or maybe I just met my soul.

Diving into such deep therapy on the heels of the trauma the pandemic wrought felt right. I was hurting and ripe for change. I missed my father's eighty-ninth birthday, as that was the date the medicine facility could squeeze Michael and me in. My dad, never hesitant to throw guilt, heaped it on. I wondered what would happen with our strained relationship moving forward. The rule when dealing with people who have borderline personality disorder is to put up barriers so as to keep yourself a safe distance from their attacks. These barriers can be geographic or emotional. I used both with my dad. I loved him as he was my father. I really did. He had some great qualities that I embraced, but I paced myself in terms of how often I would see him. I did this for my protection, as his behaviors hurt me.

But now, I felt different. I knew he could still be emotionally damaging, but I didn't feel like I would be as sensitive to it moving forward. As frustrated as he was that I missed his birthday, this might have been the best present I could have given him. Sadly, we will never find out. Not long after the journey, and before I had seen him again, his lady, Ruthann, called choking back tears. "Scotty . . . Dad is gone." I felt gravity release and was suddenly lost.

Ernie

It is devastating to lose a parent. My dad loved me as best as he could, and I loved him a lot despite our struggles. He was so energetic and positive in many ways. He loved people and could make new friends with ease. He was a joker who enjoyed teasing others and being teased in return. But having what I believed to be borderline personality disorder, he also regularly slipped into hurtful behavior. I remember when he was in the hospital, two doctors had refused to see him anymore, and I had to have a serious talk with him to keep a third doctor from following through with his threat to leave too. It's the only time he ever owned up to his actions. He was mad as hell at me for accusing him of behaving badly, but I insisted relentlessly, and hours later he finally conceded.

"I hear the words coming out of my mouth," he said. "But I can't stop them."

"Dad," I replied, "if you lose this doctor, I'm afraid no one will help you. Please try and be kind." (Sigh.) He did not manage to be kind, but gratefully, despite threats to leave, that doctor stayed until Dad recovered.

It is interesting what happens when you couple the upheaval of a perspective-shifting medicine journey with the release of gravity that comes when the primary source of your trauma suddenly disappears. I was lost, but found myself buried in the inevitable details. I was the executor of Dad's will, tasked with the exhausting work of closing out his accounts—over two dozen of them. I wrote a speech for his funeral, and per his request, I sang "My Way," somehow managing to belt it out as tears streamed down my face. After everyone left the gravesite, I went back and alternated between crying and yelling at him. Exhausted, I finally returned from upstate New York to Nashville a couple of weeks later, emotionally bankrupt.

The phone rang. It was Carl, the guy who ran the medicine journey facility. "Hey pal, how are you?" he asked.

"I don't know."

"Well, I heard the news, I am so sorry. I was watching over you for much of your journey. I know it was all about your dad. Can I make a suggestion?"

"Sure."

"I think you should come back sooner than the five months you scheduled. I have a cancellation in a few weeks. I already called your buddy Michael, and he's game too. What do you think? Do you two want to come in sooner? I think you would benefit from the unique perspective, especially now."

I said yes and soon made the journey back to the facility with my buddy. This time we went during one of the facility's regular retreats with about a dozen other guests. They were amazing people—all different but with one thing in common: They wanted to be better and were willing to take a hard look at themselves toward that end. I took the medicine without the previous fear and dropped in with ease. The journey was wonderful, and I will share one interesting thing.

I kept describing seeing layers of something dimly lit above me. It appeared to be a cross section of something. I could see it at an angle.

Then, a good hour into my journey and after describing this vision a few times, it hit me: They were layers of dirt, as if dug by a backhoe. I was at the bottom of my dad's grave! With this realization, suddenly the casket walls formed around me. I was terrified, not because I am sometimes claustrophobic and was buried alive, but because I feared I wasn't in there alone. I slowly turned my head to the right, seeing only the white tufted fabric, and then to the left, where, with great relief, I found I was alone. Surprisingly, being there by myself in Dad's casket felt OK. I asked myself why I was there, and this is what I came up with:

I had just buried my dad—left him in the ground. Maybe I was in his casket to leave behind some of the fear that he had bequeathed me— the doubt and insecurity. The hard wiring that my brain had formed in my young mind, accepting the blame for his anger. That anger wasn't my fault. Could I leave behind all of that fear and guilt, here in my dad's grave? I decided that I could, and largely, I think I did. I'm not magically squared away in that department. Some of those old circuits can still be activated in weak moments, but I did leave much of it in the grave that day. I replaced that fear in favor of wiring that is more honest.

Who would think that a trip inside your dad's casket could be a positive experience?

John

Shortly after this journey, my stepfather, John, who was loyally married to my mom for thirty-eight years, fell into dementia. He had started seeing things. These hallucinations were harmless at first, but vivid enough that he couldn't ignore them.

"Aren't you going to feed them or something?" he would ask my mother. She would explain that the three children he saw in the house were not there.

Soon his delusions overwhelmed him, and one night, frightened by a man outside with a gun (who wasn't there), he became dangerously manic. He was taken to the hospital. While in the hospital, he contracted Covid and gave it to my mother. I caught it while taking care of her. We had the earliest form of the virus—bad Covid. I will never forget sitting in my stepfather's chair, deathly ill, watching over my sick, eighty-five-year-old mom to make sure she was still breathing. There had been too much loss and death; I was not going to lose her. Thankfully, I was able to locate some monoclonal antibodies, and a day later a nurse was infusing them into us. Mom and I were on the mend within twenty-four hours. Unfortunately, my stepfather was not as lucky. I lost a second father within just a few months.

The last few years with my stepfather were hard on my mom. Occasionally, his delusions would drive him to harsh behavior. This left some bad memories in her house. Mom announced that she was ready to get out of my beloved childhood home in favor of somewhere smaller where she could make some new memories. She found an idyllic little house across the street from the elementary school I attended as a child. We quickly purchased it and started the arduous process of downsizing.

Unfortunately, just as we were finishing, and before Mom could spend a night in her perfect new home, she had an accident. She fell down at the doctor's office and destroyed her ankle, breaking it badly in four places. Her recovery would require four procedures. At eighty-six years old, this was devastating. She would spend the next sixty-three days in the hospital, at times giving up and refusing to eat. I was told that given her age, the recent loss of her husband, and her injuries, she was unlikely to ever leave the hospital.

Somehow, defying all odds, my mother made it out of that place and into her beautiful home. My rock, my hero, had tenaciously fought through.

Have you ever had a period of such loss or struggle in your life? Are you in one now? Is it stealing your energy and keeping you from working toward being a better version of yourself? If so, I get it. Really, I do. But I would counter that deep in the struggle is actually a great time to work on you. These difficulties are going to change you anyway. Why not put some work into who you become? Why not dig deep and find the energy to see yourself and who you want to be? Why not be tenacious?

Throughout all of the death and struggle I experienced at this time, I didn't pause my introspective medicine work. I had every excuse to put it aside, but I am grateful that I didn't. After each session, my assigned counselor and I spent many weeks integrating the new and truer perspectives on my life. It became clear to me that if I didn't continue this work, the deep old ruts created by decades of misguided thinking would slowly draw me right back to who I had been before. I took that to heart and leaned into reinforcing what I had recently learned. I wanted to keep this new me.

I understand that there are always reasons for why now isn't the best time to address something deep within you. This experience was impactful enough that finally I committed to taking care of me. I think that was more powerful than the medicine itself, which is really saying something. As I write this chapter, two years have passed, and I am still continuing my medicine work. I see a real difference in me and, wonderfully, so do others. There will always be excuses, but truthfully, there is no time like the present to look in the mirror.

Angel

After that second, sooner visit to the facility, I decided that the recommended three months between medicine journeys was right for me. There were many insights I gained during the next two journeys, but one message rang clear. What came through was that I should help. More specifically, I should help this facility take care of the people they serve. Maybe I should volunteer as a caregiver myself.

Shortly after my fourth journey, I texted Carl at the facility announcing that I was coming to begin my training in two weeks. He laughed and replied, "OK." I happily made the trek to the facility and began learning what it is like to be on the other side of the process. The work felt like a natural fit for me. I *loved* helping others discover the magic of these medicines. I am fiercely proud to say that I made several trips to the facility that year and helped guide dozens through their journeys. They were beautiful, amazing people, each facing fear in the pursuit of discovery and truth. I will say this: If for some reason I had to leave music, this would be the industry that would receive my time. I loved it.

So why am I speaking in the past tense about this? I loved helping the people who came to the facility, but more than that, I loved my mom.

Mom

My mom, as I said earlier, is my rock. She was always my safe place. The security I felt with her contrasted the feelings my dad engendered. As a child, my dad was constantly putting me down. My mom took a different tack. She lifted me up and supported me with love. She looked at who I was and who I wanted to be and loved me down that path. She was and is my hero, and I did and do work hard to make her proud. As such, when the call came informing me that Mom had had a stroke, I was beside myself. I caught the very next plane to New York.

Mom lost her short-term memory with the stroke, but worse, she was diagnosed with vascular dementia. This was the disease that had taken not only her husband but both of her sisters. While other forms of dementia result in a gradual decline of cognitive ability, vascular dementia progresses more like a walk down stair steps. Subsequent small strokes would take more and more of her away. I told the medicine facility I could no longer volunteer there. Instead, I favored traveling home to be with my sweet mom every week.

I still look after her and, more importantly, relish every moment with her that I can. In less than a year I had lost my dad and my stepdad, and now through dementia, I was losing my mom too. I was overwhelmed by feelings of loss and helplessness. This was officially the hardest year of my life. It couldn't get worse . . . could it?

As usual, Moo TV was doing the production for Nashville's New Year's Eve celebration in 2023, and I was there with my sweet friend Laura. Suddenly I had a stabbing pain in my side. It grew and became all but unbearable. It persisted into the next day until I could barely get out of bed. I convinced myself that I had pulled a muscle and that all I needed was rest. I awoke the day after and conceded that it was time to go to the ER. I waited for eight hours to be seen. Everyone there was seemingly convinced that I had kidney stones. This wasn't OK. I had been through so much; I wasn't up for painful stones. They finally scanned my kidneys for the little buggers and found none. I wish they had, as what they found instead was a softball-sized mass in my right kidney. Dad died, my stepdad died, my mom had a stroke and dementia, and now this. Shit.

Mass Hysteria

My doctor is one of my two best friends. You know: David, the one I was with at Oktoberfest. Upon receiving my initial CT scans, he ordered a barrage of tests, including a PET scan, bloodwork, and an ultrasound. I spent all day being poked, prodded, and slid inside that damn tube. Could this be real? The ultrasound technician was a cute Asian lady—we'll call her Chen. I lay on my side as she ran the cool apparatus over my skin, peering into my body.

"Chen?"

"Yes, Mr. Scott."

"Do you see it?" I asked. She paused. She probably wasn't supposed to say.

"Yes, Mr. Scott. I see it." There was a sadness in her tone, and suddenly it was really real. Tears started to trickle down my face. God, please don't let me have cancer.

After the last test of the day, still in agony, I went to give a talk to a Leadership Music class. I had committed to it months before, and it was important to me, so I endured. I love giving back, sharing my knowledge. I made it through the hourlong speech and headed to dinner with Laura.

After dinner, we sat on my couch where the pain and fear finally broke me. Tears started flowing again. After a brief release, I pulled myself back together, trying to be strong for her. Dr. David texted me, asking if he could come up. He actually lives in my building. This didn't bode well, as it was 9:30 p.m. He was a super early riser, so this was past his bedtime. I started to fill with dread. He and Lindsay—his amazing friend, coworker, and now fiancée—walked in, and after hugs all the way around, David got right to it.

"Scott, you have cancer." Laura made the saddest little sound.

The words ripped me in two. I nodded yes, as once again my tears flowed. This time everyone was crying. *No!* My dad, my stepdad, my mom—so much illness, death, and loss. My tank was empty, and now this. Was I going to die? For the next ten minutes the good doctor explained everything the scans had shown him. The tumor was huge, and while there was a slight chance it wasn't cancerous, everything pointed toward the big C.

"What's next?" I asked.

"For you, my friend, it will be bright lights and cold steel." Surgery. He wanted it out of me ASAP. I let that settle in.

Pause here and think about what you would do if you just found out you may be about to die.

Pause again and realize that even if you don't have cancer, you, like all of us, have limited time—healthy time—to fulfill your wishes. That time is so very precious.

Today is a great day to work toward the things you dream of.

The things you might regret not doing.

Tenaciously.

Tenacious

I am very proud of what happened next. I nodded my head and declared that I not only was going to beat my cancer but also was going to use this as a catalyst for positive change. I hadn't been taking physical care of myself, and that was going to stop. I was going to eat right and in the proper amounts. I was going to focus on my physical health as much as my medicine work had me focusing on my mental health. I made a proclamation to the room: "Several years from now, I am going to be able to say that cancer saved my life! I meant it!"

I was supposed to go on vacation with my entrepreneurs group that week. The destination was Guatemala. It would have been the fiftieth country I visited—a cool milestone. My doctor David and my other best friend, Hunter, were supposed to be going as well. They both refused in favor of taking care of me. I hated that they missed the trip but was equally grateful for their love and support. I would be fighting for my life.

David pulled some strings so I could be operated on in six days. I met with my surgeon, whom I immediately liked. He was going to take my whole right kidney and as much of the fatty tissue around it as he could. It would all be shipped to a lab and carefully sorted through to verify the mass was cancerous and to see if it had spread to any of the surrounding tissue and lymph nodes. If it was cancer and it was found to be spreading, well, that would quite possibly be it for me. The good doctor also expressed that a lot of blood flowed through the kidneys, and thus there was a real chance I might bleed out. Cardiac arrest and stroke were also possibilities. I was advised to get my affairs in order. OK. I might die on the table. Got it.

Having heard the bad news, Carl from the medicine facility once again reached out. He suggested that if I wanted to take a journey to process my diagnosis, he would be happy to help. I told him I really didn't see where I had time. Ten minutes later my friend Michael, whom I had taken every journey with so far, called.

"Hey, can I suggest that you accept the offer of the medicine journey?" he said.

He was convincing, and the next thing you know we were both traveling to the facility. Instead of having a simultaneous journey with me this time, Michael asked if he could come and watch over me. Similarly, my friend Dennis, who first introduced me to the medicine work, also asked if he could make the trek and watch over me as well. I agreed. As I released myself to the medicine with two dear friends at my side, my gratitude overflowed.

I went in heavy and deep, and my transcript was beautiful. Within ten minutes I settled in and belted out the following in an authoritative tone:

"This cancer is just going to be a blip on the radar, a moment in my life of great gravity, but I will use that gravity to alter my course. I am going to start taking care of myself. I am going to be healthy, eat right, and get enough sleep. I am going to use this cancer to save my life!

Bright Lights and Cold Steel

The day came and Dr. David drove me to the hospital. My business manager, Alice, who as I have said is absolutely like a mother to me, met me in the lobby to hug me. The tears flowed.

"I'm not crying because I'm weak," I told her. "I'm crying because I'm strong and I am going to do everything I need to do to beat this. Including not holding anything in. I'm going to cry when I feel like it instead of holding tears back. And I'm going to save my strength to fight this disease."

Hunter and David were allowed to join me in pre-op. They should have been in Guatemala having an adventure. We all should have been there. David, like any dignified doctor, passed the time making balloons out of surgical gloves and writing a joke to the doctor on my skin near the primary incision point. I was grateful for the levity, but then the speaker squawked, "Code stroke in operating room 6." It was an unwelcome reminder of one of the possible pitfalls of my surgery. I was as ready as I could be. Could we please go already? A half hour later it was my time, but still no one came to get me. Once again the speaker squawked, "Code stroke in operating room 8." Another stroke. Great.

Brad Paisley called. Did I mention that almost nobody knew about my cancer? That is still true. When you run several companies, there is a benefit to projecting strength. This book is how most of my friends and employees will find out. I will say to them now: I hope you all understand why I didn't share this with you at the time. I just couldn't, for the sake of the company. I so wish that weren't true. I could have used your love and support.

Anyway, Brad knew and gave me a great pep talk. He told me about meeting with President Zelensky in Ukraine. (The US government had asked Brad to go.) Brad said someday we are going to perform there together. "How's that for another cool reason to survive?" he added. It sure is a cool reason, Brad. Thank you for being a great friend.

Almost three hours after I was supposed to be operated on, they finally came for me . . . just as a third stroke was announced on the PA.

This is where I might have given those around me a moving speech—a reflection of bravery and wisdom that would be a fitting goodbye in the event I didn't survive the surgery. You know, some heartfelt, inspiring words to remember me by.

Nope. I was overwhelmed to the point of speechlessness. Could this be it? I waved to my friends, tongue-tied, as I was wheeled out of sight.

David said, "See you soon, pal."

Hunter added, "You got this, buddy."

I reminded myself that I had a lot to live for.

The C-Word

I awoke in post-op . . .

Wait, let me repeat that: *I woke up*! I was alive. I didn't die on the table. I looked at the nurse and tried to move. She ran over and told me to hold still for a bit.

"I want to be with my friends," I groaned.

"OK, soon," she softly reassured me.

Modern medicine is pretty amazing. I hurt like hell, but within an hour or two of getting to my room I was asking if I could take a walk. I was ready, as Scott Hamilton so aptly put it, "to start getting strong." The orderly questioned if that was a good idea, but even though it hurt like hell I convinced him it was. I knew that moving would get me out of the hospital sooner and fend off pneumonia. It was a good idea, but whoops, I overdid it. About five minutes into our walk, I almost passed out. With all the incisions it hurt to breathe. I was taking tiny breaths, and they weren't delivering enough oxygen. I scared the heck out of the orderly as I almost fell, dizzily panting to catch my breath.

Back in my room, my best friend Hunter was great company. He all but refused to leave that first night and was back before I awoke the next day. I had one rule for him, and all of my guests, that was unique to this situation: Please don't make me laugh and rip my sutures apart. I had a pretty big hole in my gut since they needed to take the football-sized kidney and tumor out intact. Later that day my friend Richard stopped in and the no-making-me-laugh rule was explained. While talking to him, I locked up mid-sentence. Just as I was about to say the word *cancer*, I froze. Richard looked at me, concerned. I collected myself with watery eyes and explained, "I can't say the C-word. It triggers me."

He nodded in acknowledgment. "Scotty," he said, "in fairness, the C-word has been triggering women for a long time." I tried to fight it, but I laughed, unintentionally ripping at my sutures. I yelped in pain and then, remembering the joke, laughed harder. And so the cycle went! Richard jumped out of his chair, apologizing and begging me to stop. Eventually I did. I somehow managed not to tear myself open, and it's a pretty great joke between us now.

Go ahead, ask me how it's going! Per my initial prognosis, there was a 90 percent chance that I would live *if* I survived the surgery. That sounds like great odds until it's your life on the line. A 10 percent chance of death is really scary. With David's guidance, I started eating better and getting to sleep earlier. I hired a cook to make and deliver healthy meals. (This is surprisingly affordable, by the way.) And I have been getting exercise when I can. I was looking to achieve improved health, not necessarily weight loss. I wanted to eat things that wouldn't fuel cancer—healthy foods. No sugar, no carbs, no processed foods—and no alcohol! That last one was tough, as alcohol was such a staple of my social life.

As I write this chapter, I am eight months post-op. I eat well, sleep well, exercise when I can, and . . . I've had no alcohol other than five drinks on my birthday in July. I feel great, and I have slowly but surely lost fifty pounds. That's huge! Everywhere I go people tell me I look great.

Last week I saw Garth Brooks for the first time since the surgery. He asked, "Where's the rest of you?" while smiling and giving me a big hug. I have done the work, and here's the crazy thing: The first four days of the new diet sucked . . . but it was noticeably easier by the fifth day, and it got downright easy by the end of the month. I have created, learned, and reinforced healthy new habits, and now they are my default. Drinks are no longer tempting, nor is sugar until about 10 p.m. I'm not sure why that is, but I fend off those late-night cravings by distracting myself . . . or going to bed. I am well on my way to fulfilling my proclamation that in two years' time I'd be able to say that cancer saved my life!

This chapter touts the importance of looking in the mirror. I definitely took a good look at myself and my eating habits, and, thanks to the terror of cancer, I finally started making healthy decisions. Now when I look in the mirror, metaphorically *and* physically, I like what I see.

What if you didn't need a life-threatening brush with cancer to look at your health? The changes I made in my eating were hard . . . at first. But magically, once I endured the tough beginning, it got easy. Now it's even natural, much the way my journey to being tenacious has become natural. Look in the mirror. What do you want to change about you? I urge you to take the necessary steps. I am all but certain you will find that real and meaningful change is less scary than you think, and you'll see that it gets easier every day.

My subsequent doctor visits have produced stellar results. My prognosis rose to 95 percent, with David noting that my biological markers looked great in a dozen ways besides my lack of cancer. Then, at my six-month visit, with still no sign of cancer, my prognosis hit 99 percent. David looked at my charts and exclaimed, "Your body is healing itself. This is amazing."

I have had one medicine journey since my cancer, and it was beautiful. With these looks in the mirror, I now know myself better, and I feel I am operating as a truer version of me. One of the impossible-to-believe red flags when I was considering a medicine journey came when someone likened it to eight years of conventional therapy for every journey. I thought that was a wildly unrealistic expectation for spending five hours in the medicine. Well, guess what? In hindsight, eight years actually feels right. Mind you, I still embrace traditional therapy. When my cancer hit, I scheduled some time with Ginger as well. Her guidance was also invaluable.

Remember that your tenacity comes from you, whatever method you employ. Do the hard work of looking in the mirror. Take a journey of self-discovery so you can be your truest self. Apply the strength that understanding brings as you tenaciously run down your dreams.

Thanks for hanging in there with me for these last two chapters. Both were full of struggle. I love using tenacity to climb mountains and chase dreams. But as you just heard, you can also employ tenacity to scale some inner mountains. I invite you to explore yourself. Whether the journey is outward or inward, when the going gets tough there is no better ally in the fight than tenacity. Tenacity not only is responsible for the wonderful life I live but also carried me through this brush with death.

My next guest knows something about looking in the mirror. Please welcome back our pal Hendo.

JASON "HENDO" HENDERSON
ON A LOOK IN THE MIRROR

As I stated in an earlier chapter, I did everything that I possibly could to fix my PTSD and traumatic brain injuries. I was eating all the right foods. I was taking all the right supplements. I was completely off all pharmaceuticals. My drinking was under control. I studied everything there is to study about insomnia and hypervigilance and post-traumatic stress, and still, I was depressed. Privately, I was kind of fighting my own war.

As long as I was helping others, I felt good. But it was when I was alone at home that I was struggling. My family didn't know—I kept it to myself. I had tried everything, but I was still angry, depressed, and couldn't sleep. So, in desperation, I went and did what everybody else who is in the skills does nowadays when they retire. I went down to Mexico to see if psychedelics could help me. Mind you, it wasn't with a bunch of hippies at some random location. Like Scotty's story, this was a legitimate facility. I was hooked to an EKG, and I was on an IV with a doctor overseeing it all. This was actually done as part of a medical study from Johns Hopkins and Stanford, so everything was under heavy observation. They induced me and the other subjects with psychedelics to document how it might mitigate any of the signs and symptoms that we were struggling with.

I took two very serious medicines: Ibogaine on day one, and five doses of 5MEO DMT the second day. Ibogaine just emptied me out. I vomited every thirty minutes for twelve straight hours. It was incredibly challenging—one of the hardest things I have ever endured, and that is saying something. I guess it's not like that for everyone, but for me it was just a massive purge. It seemed to be productive, though, as I was purging things I needed to rid myself of, physically and emotionally. Then, just twenty-four hours later, I went back in and did five doses of 5MEO DMT.

As Scotty said, it's really impossible to describe what it's like in the medicine space, so I'll just tell you this: My depression vanished that weekend—completely gone. How incredible is that? The medicine didn't really tell me what the root of my depression was. Some of that would come with another medicine later, but the relief I received right then was miraculous. I cried like a baby for thirty minutes in this nurse's lap, and then my depression was gone. The locked-up emotion that I'd had throughout my entire life was released. I still get sad sometimes, but I don't lock it up anymore. If I get sad, I cry—or maybe I don't. I allow the emotions to flow wherever they're going to flow.

While I am not recommending them, and I am not a doctor, I think that psychedelics are an incredible tool when they're used for the right purpose. I wasn't an addict, so I don't know that Ibogaine was the right drug for me. I learned it's commonly used to cure addiction, and it has remarkable results in doing so.

Still, Ibogaine did put me in such a vulnerable state so that when DMT came in, it kind of worked its magic. It had a profound effect, so I guess I should accept the recipe.

Knowing there was something to psychedelics, I went off and tried them all. Every type, every variation. I found that a lot of the medicines expose what's hindering you from being your best self, and that's invaluable. But what's crucially important is what you do afterward, in the integration cycle, to rebuild and free yourself. If you look at your body as a receptacle, you will see that you filled it full of all the shit of life, but then, with help from the medicine, it was emptied. You need to be careful what you refill it with. It would be natural to refill it with the same shit that was dragging you down before and have the same anchors hinder you from being your best self. But alternatively, you could refill it with light and service to others and with righteousness so that you're now doing what you're supposed to be doing—or what I feel I've been put on earth to do, at least from my spiritual perspective. That's the path I choose to take.

I went and did ayahuasca too. I'm not a big fan of it because of the shamanistic aspect of it, but I am glad I tried it. Through the medicine it was exposed to me that a variety of child abuses were the root of my anger. And thanks to the medicine, I was actually able to go to myself as this beaten-down child and pick myself up and hug myself as the strong man I am today. I told my younger self, "Hey, it's going to be OK. You're going to be a big, strong person when it's all over. You are going to be OK." I did this and then kind of handed it off to the angels to release it from me.

After that, all of my anger was gone, but then I was in a quandary. OK, I've lost all my depression. I've lost all my anger, but my anger had been my fuel my whole life, so am I still a capable man? I went right back into the sports I had competed in while in the service—powerlifting, jiu jitsu, and judo. But now I was doing it not because I needed to quell the anger; I was doing it because I just love doing it, and I love the community. This time around it didn't matter if I won or lost. All that mattered was that I trained hard, and I went out and competed. I just liked being a part of it. I loved going out there and testing myself, not so much to knock others down, but instead to lift them up.

I've always wanted to be as strong as possible so that if I came across a mass-casualty event I could pick people up and move them to safety. You know, I don't feel that I would be much of a father to my two children if I couldn't pick them up and carry them out of harm's way. So I've always trained in that type of mindset where what I'm doing is not even for me. I'm trying to strengthen myself for others and for my own faith. You know, as a Christian—a Catholic Christian, to be specific—I know it's a narrow path to get into heaven, but really, as a servant, I want to push as many people in front of me onto that path.

When I was going out and training officers and families, so often one of them would say, "Hey, my cousin is struggling as a veteran [or a cop, or a medic, or a fireman], and they're having a really hard time. Do you mind talking to them?" I'd never told them anything about my struggles, but somehow they just knew to talk to me. I saw a need, so I created Northstar Ministries. Its purpose is to help people who have achieved at a high level but have fallen off to get back to being their best selves. We help them rebuild so that they can, in turn, help others and mentor them through their struggles. We have veterans, first responders, even a rock star. Some may be at the end of their careers; some are struggling with addictions; others are struggling with life or divorce and everything that comes with that. So we help them.

> I know that I need to be strong enough so I can move all of these people in front of me on that path to heaven—so that they can get there ahead of me. I feel, in a lot of ways, that this is why I've been given all these natural talents of strength and the ability to fight. It's so I can use them to battle against evil and to lift others up. There's a huge internal premium attached to that. There's no amount of money that can give you the same feeling as helping somebody else who is really struggling.

Hendo is a man of incredible strength, and I don't just mean physically. When presented with the chance to better see himself, he dove in. How beautiful is it that he found the truth he deserved by having the strength to look? How wonderful is it that he shares his strength as the warrior angel he is?

I hope that the psychedelic therapy described within this chapter didn't alarm too many of you. Also know that none of my guests other than Hendo were aware of this topic being included in the book. I recognize that this therapy isn't for everyone, and I'm not recommending that you all go out and do it. I am simply recounting a path that I chose that yielded amazing results for me. What I am recommending is that you recognize that you are the most important factor in your success and happiness. If you have some unresolved demons, working on yourself can yield amazing results. Whether it's EMDR or conventional therapy as we discussed in chapter 9, or something else that you feel works for you, I encourage you to look in the mirror. This book is about being tenacious enough to live your best life. Nothing I have done in all of my years was as impactful as being brave enough to look in the mirror. Doing this is scary at first, but wow, so very worth it.

Dare to look. I promise, you will *love* what you see, especially when you really look.

(Me in my hospital room; you can see the fear in my eyes. Cancer is terrifying. My dad and I skiing, my sweet mom and I at Christmas. She is the queen of Christmas! Hendo looking sharp and proud.)

*All photos and supplemental material can be found on TENACIOUSBOOK.COM

CHAPTER 11

Orchestrating Joy

Do not judge me by my successes; judge me by how many times I fell down and got back up again.

—Nelson Mandela

There is a distinct sound a really big audience makes. It's a hum. A thousand little conversations melding together. It's an unintelligible murmur, save the occasional squeal or a laugh rising above. It's low in volume, but you can, if you will, sense its volume, its scale. Standing behind the curtain, this meditative hum is currently the soundtrack for my stage jitters.

Will I remember the words? *Hum.* Will I hit the notes? *Hum.* Will they not like me? *Hum.* What the hell am I doing? *And the hum drones on.*

Somewhere in my rumination of doubt the music fades and, ready or not, it's time.

LADIES AND GENTLEMEN, PLEASE WELCOME SCOTT SCOVILL!

I bolt onstage, throwing my hands in the air, and cry out, "Let's do this!"

Incredibly, the crowd, nearly ten thousand strong, roars back! I draw a deep breath and fire up my baritone. It booms through the massive speakers. I know the words. I hit the notes.

The crowd swells, fears melt, and I find myself bursting with joy as it hits me. I am a singer! What a moment. What a life!

If you glean one thing from this book, I hope it is that tenacity has been the key to living an exceptional life for my guests and me. It has personally transformed me from someone afraid and ashamed of who I am into someone who is incredibly proud of myself and the life I live. As you have seen, being tenacious made all the difference. Employing the deceptively simple act of not giving up, I ran down dream after dream.

In the past two chapters, specifically, I showed you how I employed tenacity to look inward so I could be the best version of myself. Let's close out with one last unlikely dream I have been running down lately. Consider this a case study in the kind of unlikely magic tenacity has yielded for me . . . and can yield for you too!

Music

As a five-year-old, I used to lay the speakers down in our living room and slide in between them. There, as if wearing massive headphones, I would marvel at the sound. As I grew older, my Walkman and boom box were prized possessions. The music gave me a sense of not only identity but also shelter. When the going was tough, I would hide within familiar sounds. I could count on my music.

Every weekend, I would listen to Casey Kasem's *American Top 40* countdown. I was so invested in *my* music that I would get really upset when the wrong song climbed the charts. Conversely, when a song I loved hit number one, I would run around the house celebrating. It was, after all, *my* song!

When alone, I would sing along as loud as I could. I wouldn't sing in front of others; I knew I couldn't sing well. You see, one day in choir practice, a grade-school teacher locked eyes with me and sternly commented, "Someone over here sounds terrible." I was pretty sure she meant me. Message received. I started mouthing the words and got myself out of choir as soon as I could. This was no big deal to me. Back then, there was a lot I felt I couldn't do. I just added singing to the list.

But, as you've read, my love of music did find a beautiful outlet. Through my work with live shows, I could be a part of the music industry, helping others be seen and heard. I have happily dedicated my life to this work.

Still, despite what I was told, I sang. My voice would crack, unable to hit the higher notes, but I sang nonetheless. It just felt *right* to sing. It felt good. One night, not that many years ago, I was at a party with friends in Norway. Johnny Cash's haunting rendition of the song "Hurt" came on the radio. I was with trusted friends, and just buzzed enough to not care, so I started singing along, down low where Johnny had placed it. Unlike virtually every other song on the radio in the eighties, I could hit all of these notes. What I had somehow never realized was that I was a baritone.

Apparently, I made an impression because my friends, who were in a band, suggested that I join them onstage the next night to sing that song. I was scared to death, but, as you know, my tenacity had taught me to tackle fear, not run from it. Thus, I agreed.

Nervous as hell, I sang the song as best I could, but I was grateful to get offstage to the sound of what I deemed *polite* applause. I made a beeline to the bar for my first drink. I needed it after that embarrassment. The barmaid was a beautiful Norwegian girl with hair so blonde it was almost white. She reminded me of the dragon queen from the show *Game of Thrones*.

"I'll take *all* the beer, please," I begged, ruminating over my performance. *That wasn't good. No one needed to hear that. Why did I do that?* I thought to myself. Meanwhile, the lovely barmaid was frozen, not moving toward the beer I so desperately needed. I looked at her pleadingly.

After a pause, the following words rolled off her beautiful lips. "I have goose bumps."

I looked at her incredulously. Was she sincere? Goose bumps? Over my singing? A smile slowly formed on those pretty lips, and I felt mine respond.

The friends who'd asked me onstage finished their set. They also shocked me when they agreed that it was great. "You should join our band," they said, and they weren't kidding.

"Join a band in Norway?" I asked. "I live in Nashville. That's ridiculous."

Well, maybe. But let me tell you a little story.

Several years ago I was invited to be a part of a small conference called Summit Series. It was described to me as a collection of out-of-the-box thinkers gathered to inspire one another, all in the hope of making the world a better place.

I attended and was indeed inspired. Of note, I met Tim Ferriss, the influencer and author of the *New York Times* bestseller *The 4-Hour Workweek*. In the book, Tim teaches us how to maximize our time with the goal of increasing not only our monetary wealth but also, more importantly, our experiential wealth. The latter part made it a real page-turner for me, as Tim shared unbelievable adventures from living abroad while still running his company. To say the things Tim did were unbelievable is an understatement. They were absolutely nuts! (Intrigued? Good! Read his book too.)

Because I had found real value in the conference, I made it an annual pilgrimage, each year spending some time with Tim. Mind you, I'm not claiming to be his buddy; I just found him fascinating. Three years in (and several drinks into the evening), I dared to ask him a question.

"Tim, you don't need to answer, but I feel compelled to ask: Did you really do all of that crazy shit you wrote about in *The 4-Hour Workweek*?"

Tim hesitated long enough before answering that I worried I shouldn't have asked. It was a bold question, as he and I were just casual acquaintances. I waited uneasily. When he finally spoke, his answer was fascinating. It's been years, but here it is to the best of my recollection.

"I did it all," he paused. "But I will say this. You have heard me tell the story of my fiancée leaving me and the subsequent drunken binge in England. When I came back, I was shocked to see that my company had done just fine without me. I realized I needed to run an experiment. The rest of the book was that experiment—one where I intentionally pushed boundaries to collect data. I did this knowing I would write about it and that it would greatly affect my decision-making process."

Great answer, I thought, and I let the conversation turn to subjects he was probably more interested in talking about.

I awoke the next morning with a start and sat straight up in bed. I do this a few times a year when I've had an epiphany in my sleep.

"I'll be damned," I literally said out loud. Then I thought, *Tim lived an incredible life because he was writing a book . . . He didn't write a book because he had an incredible life. It was the other way around.* That said, I know Tim had a fascinating life prior as well, but his experiment and the book were his inspiration for taking it to the next level!

I made myself a promise right then that I was going to start living my life like I was writing a book. Not because I intended to be an author—at that time I had no such aspirations. No, I was doing this so that I could live my most interesting life. What has that looked like in execution? Well, when posed with an opportunity—maybe even a crazy one—I have asked myself a simple question: Would this make the next chapter more interesting? Would this decision make for a story I would love to read? If the answer is yes, and it wouldn't totally blow up my life, then I set out to do that thing, even if it's a bit crazy.

For example, years ago I sponsored a hockey team, the Nashville Iceholes. After watching the first game with their jerseys emblazoned proudly with Moo TV logos, I was asked to go out with the team for drinks. *Sure, why not?* At the bar I was asked to make a toast.

After I expressed how fun playing looked, someone shouted, "You should join the team!"

"I don't know how to ice skate," was my quick reply.

Well, three drinks later, they posed the question again. This time I asked myself if being an Icehole would make my life more interesting. Yes, learning to ice-skate at thirty-five to become an Icehole certainly would.

When I said yes, the whole team cheered. I bought all the gear the next day and dove into learning how to skate. I skated three hours a day, four days a week, and twenty-eight days later I pulled on the jersey and hit the ice. I was terrible, but I used my size to disrupt the goalie's vision at the front of the net and incredibly scored the third and fourth goals in our 4–3 win! I was hooked!

My love of hockey grew and became a big part of my life, providing some remarkable experiences. I endeavored to buy a part of the Nashville Predators NHL team. While I was unsuccessful, it was fun! I got to ride on the team jet to games several times. For a few years, the team after-hours party was often held at my condo whenever the boys won. Amazing memories—all because of Tim's inspiration.

I also used this principle when deciding to go on an Antarctic expedition. Even simple decisions, such as wearing crazy suits (I have over fifty!) to make each day more interesting, are weighed with this in mind.

My life is a story, and I want to write that story to inspire myself and others—a story that I can proudly reread when I get older. And hey, that story actually became a book!

It is my strong wish that this book will start you down the path to a more tenacious life.

> Live your life like you are writing a book.
> Ask yourself what will make the next
> chapter more interesting, then do it!
> This is the book you will read every
> day when you are older,
> make it a real page turner!
> —Scott Scovill

Did I just quote myself in my own book? Oh, the vanity! Forgive me, but the message I received has been transformative.

Thank you again for the inspiration, Tim, and forgive me if I got some of the conversation wrong. It was a long time ago, but the message has made such a difference in my life I had to give you credit for it. I will also say that Tim's life was very interesting before his experiment, but he sure did take it to extremes afterward. Seriously, read *The 4-Hour Workweek* if you haven't already.

OK, I sidetracked us again. Back to my story. Three drinks later and the prospect of singing in a Norwegian band seemed like it would absolutely make the next chapter of my life far more interesting.

"Sure! Why not," I replied.

The band cheered, and just like that I had joined the Norwegian band Spinning Wheels.

This was indeed a crazy decision. I'm not a singer—the probability for embarrassment was overwhelming. But I did love to sing, and my track record with tenacity gave me the confidence to do hard things. Heck, I had become *great* at doing hard things! If I failed, I knew I would keep going so long as it was something I wanted to do. And my love of music made it an exciting possibility. Make music? Yes! There's my first step.

Is there something in your life that you are afraid to do? Some step that just seems too crazy to be worth trying? If it's something you love the way I love singing, then employ your tenacity to at least take that first step.

So to recap: I love music, I just discovered that I could sing (as a baritone), and I just said yes to being in a band. Now, you've got to hear where this crazy first step took me . . .

Spinning Wheels

Shortly thereafter, I found myself flying over the Atlantic for our first gig, a huge festival called Countryfestivalen nested in a beautiful valley in Seljord, Norway. Amazingly, even though I was a guest performer, my name was listed on the T-shirt. That was cool, but I was already nervous, and this recognition just cranked up the pressure even more. I was so afraid of embarrassing myself—or, worse, embarrassing my bandmates. Remember my fear of public speaking? Thank goodness I tackled that tenaciously all those years ago. If I hadn't, I don't see how I could dare to do this now.

My heart was pounding as Spinning Wheels member Stian said my name, inviting me to join the band onstage. I walked out to mild applause from the couple hundred in attendance and clipped my iPhone to the mic stand. The iPhone was embarrassing. Despite my best efforts, I couldn't seem to remember the words to the songs. Thus, I would largely be reading along. I would love to tell you my performance was amazing; it was just OK, but it wasn't awful. I had a lot to learn about singing and, moreover, entertaining. This crowd was more critical than the prior crowd at the little bar I first sang at, but I did receive some cheers. Later that night, several people told me they liked my voice. That felt good.

Time for a few big questions. Just getting by was OK but not great. Did making music matter enough to me to keep trying? Did I love music enough to work at getting better? Toughest of all: Was I willing to endure the pain of delivering more less-than-stellar performances?

My answer to all three: *Yes!*

Thankfully, my bandmates were happy for us to keep doing gigs together as well, and I worked hard to justify their support. I do have a strong voice; it's just that as a baritone most songs are out of my range. We could pick deeper songs, or transpose higher songs to a lower key. Down there I found I had real power (as I'd discovered on "Hurt").

Over the next few years I frequently flew to Norway for gigs with Spinning Wheels. I didn't tell anyone in Nashville. I figured my peers and artists would laugh at my taking up singing this late in life. Music was, after all, a business for them. I didn't want my music hobby to confuse my industry friends and clients into thinking I was trying to be an artist as a career. This remained safely my secret, as no Google search in America would pick up show reviews written in Norwegian.

As much as I loved singing, it was hard for me. Beyond the glossophobia I faced every time I walked onstage—I continued to be terrible at remembering words. That's not OK when you are the singer. Still reading from my iPhone, I bought a Bluetooth foot pedal that advanced the lyrics, so the audience didn't see me doing this by hand. It was nonetheless embarrassing. Years in, I still knew only a few songs by heart.

I sometimes had a bad night, or at least a bad song, missing notes or losing my place in those darn lyrics. The feeling of letting down my bandmates was awful. Still, when it was good, it felt great. Thus, I endured these painful failures. I brushed off the dirt and tried again, working hard at not making the same mistakes twice. You know: tenaciously.

As Spinning Wheels' popularity climbed, I got a call from the band. We had been asked to come back to perform at the Seljord festival, but this time on the massive main stage. This was a big deal—the biggest gig we ever had! I confirmed that I could do it . . . and immediately started getting nervous. Two weeks later my phone blew up as Norway awoke to an announcement. Typically at Countryfestivalen, a band like ours would open for a big Norwegian band. All that changed this year. To my horror, they announced we would be opening for my good friend Brad Paisley. *Shit!* Again, nobody in Nashville knew I was singing in Norway, not even my buddy Brad. My secret was about to be out.

Before I get into just how terrifying that was, now seems like a good time to speak about Brad for a second. As I've mentioned, Brad has become one of my very best friends. Of all of the amazing artists I've worked with, the relationship he and I have is singularly special. Arguably, it started with Brad seeing an Alan Jackson show I did all those years ago and deciding video would be a big part of his show someday. It was exciting when his career reached a level where I got the call. Of all the artist-onboarding meetings my team at Moo TV and I have been a part of, his stands out for one dominant reason. Of course, honorable mention goes to Garth, who is also an incredible motivator, but the fact that Brad started with us when he was just hitting the big time, as opposed to Garth joining twenty years into his success, made Brad's introduction especially meaningful for us all.

Most artists are overwhelmed as they arrive at the point in their career when years of herculean effort have landed them in arena-sized shows. Many defer creative and technical decisions to other members of their team. Not Brad. He invited four of us to a preliminary meeting where he laid out exactly what his goals were. He exuded confidence that we were the team to make his dreams come true. His trust was inspiring, his excitement contagious. A couple of hours later I walked out of that room ready to run through a brick wall for Brad Paisley! His goals, as I recall, were to sell the big arenas within two years, sell out those arenas within three, and win a major award within five. We did this, notably with Brad working as hard if not harder than all of us. True to his plan, he was selling out the big arenas in two years, and within five he won *many* awards including the *big* one, CMA Entertainer of the Year!

Designing and providing creative direction on his shows was always a labor of love. A million ideas bounced around and were tried. There were, of course, many sleepless nights, but uniquely, Brad was up at all hours, shoulder to shoulder with us. He taught himself to edit, build graphics, and even create animated cartoons. He is an incredibly driven worker, and we bonded over that work—and over the pride we had in its result. As he was awarded Entertainer of the Year, I won Visual Designer of the Year. It was fantastic!

I have tremendous respect for his creativity and work ethic, but his generous spirit also quickly became apparent. In one of many examples of this, Brad featured William Shatner in his music video for the song "Online." I asked Brad what it was like to work with Bill (as his friends call him); he was my first hero as Captain Kirk on *Star Trek*. He told me Bill was just great. Then, about a month later, Brad asked me to come to his concert in Kentucky.

"Why?" I asked.

"Because Bill is going to be there. We're going to hang out. Since he was your hero, I thought you'd enjoy being with us."

Hell yes, I would!

Several days later, I found myself hanging with Brad on his bus in Kentucky when Bill walked aboard. What we didn't know yet was that he and his horse, Thunderbolt, had just won the Amateur

Roadster to Bike Championship at the 2013 Kentucky State Fair World's Championship Horse Show. Without so much as a hello, Bill dramatically dove into the story.

"It was a moment between a man and a steed . . ." His tone was serious as he theatrically gestured. "A hush fell over the crowd. It was time . . ." (I'm sure I'm not getting Bill's words exactly right, but you get the idea. All I could think as this master of engagement spun his tale was, *Pinch me, Captain Kirk is telling me a story!*) Bill wrapped up his account with something like, "As I released the reins the crowd erupted, and I knew we had won the day!"

"Holy cow, you won?!" exclaimed Brad.

Wow—what a storyteller! Bill, like so many actors, brings much of himself to the characters he portrays. I realized that *Star Trek*, arguably my favorite source of entertainment and dreams from childhood to this day, was hugely shaped by this man standing in front of me. In that role, he wasn't just acting like Captain Kirk; he was filling that character with his own charisma and bravado.

I had an incredible time with Bill and Brad that day. Thanks to Brad's willingness to share his friendship, I had a remarkable day with a hero, and thanks to Brad, I have, in fact, had the honor of spending time with Bill many times since.

In addition to frequently rolling my bus down the highway to visit Brad on the road, he and I have done lots of fun things in our free time too. We both bought Lotus sports cars and went racing in the Nevada desert. He's a great driver. Together we have had some amazing times with artists such as B. B. King, Charlie Daniels, Carrie Underwood, and Jimmy Dickens. It's just interesting to be Brad's sidekick.

On a more serious note, we started a charity together. The Store, a grocery that provides a dignified shopping experience for those in need, was completely Brad and his wife, Kimberly's, vision. They funded its launch and leaned in with their star power, and when it came time for the initial planning, I was honored that Brad asked for my help. I then proudly sat on the board of directors for the first six years.

Probably the most important thing, though, is that we both have been there to deliver the hard truth to each other when we needed to hear it—something, I can tell you, that he did with great care on a few occasions for me. He has been a true friend, and I am so thankful.

When people ask me what he's like, I say, "Brad hasn't let the fame go to his head. He comes across like, 'Hey, you aren't going to believe this, but somehow I'm really famous and my life is amazing. Rather than describe it, come with me and see. We'll have a blast!'" And I do come along, and we do have a blast!

Now here I was, about to be his opening act, and even though we are great friends, he had no idea that I could even sing.

Two days after hearing about being Brad's opener, I coincidentally found myself alone with him and his manager. "Norway," I blurted out.

"Yeah!" Brad replied, smiling. "We just announced that show. Come with me, it'll be fun! You always go to Europe with me." I do—I always tag along when Brad does Europe. We have a blast traveling together.

"I'll be there," I replied. "I'm your opening act."

Brad looked confused. "Why is that funny?" he asked.

"It's not a joke. It's not funny. It's true, and it's terrifying."

"I don't get it," he said, still puzzled.

"I have been singing in a Norwegian country band for years, and we've gotten pretty good. They booked us to be on the main stage a few weeks ago. To my terror, I just found out that we are your opening act."

Brad was still completely confused. "You don't sing," he stated matter-of-factly.

"I *do* sing. I have been singing in Norway for years."

He shook his head no. "What do you sing?"

"A lot of things. They say I sound like Johnny Cash."

"No you don't," he paused. "Sing then. Sing me some Johnny Cash."

"Right now? No."

"If you sing, then show me. Sing," he insisted.

So here I am being asked to sing a cappella in front of an entertainer of the year. Great.

🎝 "I HURT MYSELF TODAY, TO SEE IF I STILL FEEL," my voice boomed forth.

Brad looked stunned. "Holy cow," he mused. "You *are* my opening act."

"Yes, and I need a favor from you."

"What's that?" he asked, still in shock.

"Realize that I am having fun and that's all. I know you are a perfectionist. Just embrace that I am nowhere near perfect." My friend Brad smiled, still processing this news, but he happily agreed.

I was really nervous about the show. Actually, *frightened* would be a better descriptor. I decided that I was going to start seeing a vocal coach and that I was going to somehow find a way to learn the words. I took two or three lessons a week for the next six months. Three wonderful things happened. First, I got better. I developed improved control, better pitch, and more range. Second, with this frequency of practice, I actually beat the lyrics of a few songs into my head. I got to where I just needed the first word of every verse to help me remember. This was way better than reading. But the third benefit was the best: I felt ready. So much of life is mind over matter. Remember that quote I have repeated ad nauseam? "Whether you think you can, or you think you can't—you're right." Better than thinking I could, I *knew* I could!

The day came and I found myself in Norway, standing behind the upstage curtain with my band. I was a swirling combination of super excited and terrified. Would I embarrass myself in front of Brad? Once again, Stian from Spinning Wheels called my name. Here we go!

I ran onstage in front of thousands of fans and belted out the opening line to "Folsom Prison Blues."

"'I HEAR THAT TRAIN A COMIN' . . .'"

The Norwegians love Johnny Cash, and they lit up. I noticed Brad standing on the side of the stage watching. He and dozens of my friends on the crew were hearing me sing. My secret was out! For the first time since I started performing with this band—and for only a moment—I didn't feel like an impostor. I felt like a singer. And the cheers were intoxicating. I looked out into the crowd and saw something amazing . . . smiles. Happy people being entertained by me!

Just think about all of the tenacious little steps that got me here. I tackled my fear of public speaking years earlier. Without doing that, I never could have done this. The tenacity that produced a lifetime of work in the music business took me to Norway. It made me brave enough to sing that first night at the bar. Then it made me, crazily enough, game to say yes to being in this band. All these decisions were fueled by the confidence being tenacious brought me.

Next, I tenaciously spent countless hours in humbling lessons working at being the best singer I could be. None of it was easy for me, but I made those efforts and took those steps, and I finally ended up in an unbelievable place. I was singing in Spinning Wheels, the band that was Brad Paisley's opening act, onstage in front of thousands of happy Norwegians!

Please ask yourself what little steps you could be making toward something you love to do. What unexpected magic might come from that? Be tenacious!

My Name Is Christmas

Also among those in attendance that night in Norway was Luke Wooten, Brad's producer, who happens to be one of my favorite people and best friends. Luke and I often go to hockey games together, and a few weeks later at a Preds game in Nashville I asked him a question.

"Luke, what if I wanted to make an album? How would I go about that? Where would you point me?"

"Johnny Cash covers?" he assumed.

"Sure, but I would also love to try some originals."

Luke smiled. "I will produce your album!"

"Oh, no," I replied. "I don't deserve you! I was thinking there was somebody less . . . awesome."

Luke smiled a huge smile. "Scotty, I heard you that day opening for Brad. When you stepped up to the mic I was like . . . Damn, Scotty can sing! I'm going to produce you. This will be fun!"

I thought for a minute and conceded, "OK, but only if it is fun. I need for you to enjoy it."

Luke and I started brainstorming and worked out a few songs, but I reiterated that I wanted to do a Christmas album first. Why Christmas? Because everybody loves Christmas, especially me. I reasoned that potential skeptics in the music industry would embrace a Christmas album as something joyful, whereas a country album might be viewed with more of a side eye. I wanted to avoid anyone thinking that I had delusions this would be my career. I just loved making music.

I listened to a ton of Christmas songs and noticed that almost all of my favorites had the backing of a full orchestra. Could I do that? I did some research and discovered that I could afford to hire the City of Prague Philharmonic. Whoa, that would be amazing.

Next, I reached out to a songwriter named Madeline Stone. I asked her if we could try writing together. She happily agreed. I told her I had never written but that I loved music and hoped that I could write. I arrived at our first session and was greeted with the sweetest hug. She had an amazing energy about her.

"What are we going to write about today?" she asked.

I laid out my idea for a song and explained how each verse would carry the singer's journey forward. We wrote the first verse pretty quickly. It came naturally. Madeline jumped up and clapped her hands. "You're a writer!" she exclaimed. This was music to my ears.

I worked hard at songwriting with Madeline. Three of my Christmas originals made it to the album. I cowrote two of those songs with Madeline, and I wrote a very personal one solo. It is called "Mom at Christmas," and, as the title suggests, it was for my mom.

All three originals were duets. Would you believe a young Lainey Wilson sang with me on my demos? I would have loved to keep her on those tracks, but her label head, Jon Loba, asked that I not, stating that she was about to do big things and he didn't want to muddy the waters. Boy, that's an understatement. That sweet lady is now a multiyear Entertainer of the Year! What a wonderful human and talent.

Honestly, I had her in the sessions because I was trying to get Dolly Parton to do a duet with Lainey. Dolly's answer was so Dolly. She expressed that Lainey was so good she didn't need any help and that if she did a duet with her, Lainey might never realize that she could make it on her own. A perfect response from a perfect lady. I knew Lainey was special, so I understood John's request. In the end, it was all OK because I did get three other amazing ladies to duet with me on my originals: Kinsey Rose of *The Voice* fame; Hanne Sørvaag, a household name in Norway; and the amazing Lindsay Ell. Those ladies are all phenomenal. Oh, and I put a kids' choir on "Mom at Christmas." Give that a listen!

Luke put together an incredible band for me. Most sessions were led by the legendary Brent Mason, a Grammy Award–winning, multiyear Musician of the Year guitar player, who has been called one of the ten best studio musicians of all time. I thought Luke must be kidding when he said Brent would be the band leader. Nope. There I was in the studio with the prodigious picker.

In about half a dozen sessions we laid down the foundation for the songs. Working in the studio is incredible, particularly with originals. Watching Nashville's world-class musicians interpret my songs was euphoric. Their instincts were strong, and they were happy to change anything I felt was off my vision. Thanks to Luke and this wonderful team, I was making music. *My* music! Oh, and I almost forgot to mention: Brad Paisley himself even played on "Here Comes Santa Claus." Wow!

With the foundation laid, it was time to put some icing on the cake. In keeping with our rule that it had to be fun, I informed Luke that I was taking him to Prague to oversee the orchestra. He happily agreed, but I added a second rule.

"What's that?" he asked.

"We have to wear Christmas clothes."

"But it's July!" he retorted, laughing.

"I know," I smiled. Luke returned the smile, and it was done. I have an amazing picture of Luke in the town square, grinning in the July sun while wearing a Christmas shirt with the words "Don't Get Your Tinsel in a Tangle!" emblazoned across the front. This shirt I bought for Luke actually inspired me to write a song titled "Don't Get Your Tinsel in a Tangle" for my mom. Give it a listen when you get a chance.

I love the Czech people, the city, and the food. Luke and I made the most of our time, visiting everything from the massive Prague Castle, which broke ground in AD 970, to an amazing rock bar called Harley's, where the insane bartender taunts customers by blowing fire and spraying water on them. I have spent my life traveling, and I have never been to a crazier bar than Harley's.

Best of all, we made music. Our engineer, Vitek, and the team at Smecky Music Studios were wonderful. We Zoomed in my arranger, Chris Boardman, and made quick work of the songs. The absolute greatest moment, though, came as we were doing "Mom at Christmas."

In three passes we had it down but decided that we wanted a safety pass just in case we'd missed a mistake. The wonderful musical interpreter, Stanislava, asked if I wanted to stand in the orchestra for the safety pass.

"In the middle of the orchestra? Hell yes!"

I sprinted down there as quickly as I could, bursting into the big hall. My evident enthusiasm was greeted by smiles and laughter from the huge orchestra. Conductor Richard pointed his baton at where he thought was the best spot for me to stand. With a wave of that same baton, the incredible musicians struck the first chords I had written for my sweet mom. The sound pressure from the more than sixty instruments was unexpectedly powerful. First I had goose bumps, then goose bumps on my goose bumps, and finally tears started streaming. I was in Prague, making my music for my sweet mom, with a full orchestra.

Along with opening for Brad, this was one of the greatest moments in my life—one I will cherish forever. Remember, tenacity is the path to a life full of adventure, and you get there, wherever that adventure lies, one tenacious step at a time.

I thought about ending the chapter here, but the fun kept building, even as I was writing this book. Brad asked Spinning Wheels and me to open for him again, this time in Oslo at the arena—basically the Madison Square Garden of Norway. Running out onstage in that cavernous venue was amazing! I continued to make music, and I released a country album titled *I Hold the Light*. To my joy, a few tracks were featured on Spotify's prestigious "New Music Friday Country" playlist. People were listening! As you know, I wasn't chasing commercial success, but when you create something—when you make some music—it feels wonderful to know that people are gleaning enjoyment from it.

Brad went on yet another European tour, and this time he asked us to open in Norway *and* Sweden—two huge shows in each country!

I was excited but commented to Brad, "Nobody knows us in Sweden. Maybe you shouldn't have us open there."

"Not yet, they don't," was his sly reply as he walked away.

Wow, opening in Sweden too! I was expanding thanks to Brad's faith in me. I decided to triple down on my efforts and started seeing vocal coach Kristin K. Smith several hours a week. This rapid reinforcement poured rocket fuel on my continuously developing tone, range, and control. Most remarkably, I was starting to remember lyrics too. My brain responded to the repetition by developing capability. I wasn't just finally remembering the words to the few songs we always played; I found I could remember new songs as well. Not stressing over lyrics was a huge deal for me!

I spoke with Spinning Wheels, and they happily agreed to do all four shows . . . until the drummer texted a couple of weeks before the gigs that they weren't going to be able to do the two in Sweden. Crap! Over ten thousand fans were coming to these shows, and I don't have a band! I spent about five minutes not knowing what to do, and then I had a thought. I had directed Brad Paisley's music video for the song "No I in Beer" and remembered Brad having me include a Swedish guitar player who he said was awesome. I fired off a quick text to Mikael (Micke) Stromqvist.

"Hey, want to put a band together and support me opening for Brad Paisley in Gothenburg and Gavle?"

"Hell yes!!!" flashed on my screen, then a moment later, "I will have an amazing band together for you by tomorrow!"

And so it was. I was poised to do my first shows as Scott Scovill, not just as a guest of Spinning Wheels. The next day I found myself on a Zoom call with three really excited Swedes, all fans of Brad, especially Micke. They seemed perfect. As terrifying as it would be to take the stage in front of ten thousand people with strangers, I liked these strangers. I had sent them a list of several songs to learn. Wonderfully, within a week they sent me a video of them performing them all perfectly. *Wow!*

I did the two shows in Norway with Spinning Wheels. Incredibly, I no longer needed to read the lyrics. What a massive change that made; the shows were so much fun. After the second show I said goodbye to my friends in my longtime band. (Thank you, Tom, Stian, Ole Roy, and John!) Then I rode Brad's bus to Sweden for our first show day. There, just a few hours before the massive show, I met my new band in person for the first time—Micke on guitar, Daniel on drums, and Martin on bass. They all had great energy. In a few short hours we found ourselves on the side of the stage in a huddle. I gave a quick speech that went something like this:

"Nobody knows me here, so there is no expectation other than this: *Have fun!* If we screw something up, as we are likely to, the rule then is to *have even more fun!* Thank you for sharing this amazing opportunity with me, guys."

Before breaking the huddle, I made eye contact with each of my smiling bandmates. My first show as Scott Scovill, with my very own band, was about to begin. I stepped away for a minute to collect myself.

There it was, that sound a really big audience makes. That hum. A thousand little conversations melding together. Standing behind the curtain this meditative hum was the soundtrack for my prevalent stage jitters.

Will I remember the words? Will I hit the notes? Will I be awful? What the hell am I doing? The hum droned on.

Somewhere in my rumination of doubt, the music faded, and ready or not, it was time.

LADIES AND GENTLEMEN, PLEASE WELCOME . . . SCOTT SCOVILL!

I bolted onstage, threw my hands in the air, and cried out, "Let's do this!" Incredibly, the nearly ten thousand attendees roared. I drew a deep breath and fired up my baritone, belting out the first line. *I know the words! I hit the notes!*

The crowd swelled, melting my fear, and I found myself bursting with joy as it hit me: I am a singer! What a moment, what a life!

It seems only fitting that the guest for this final chapter is Brad Paisley himself. Brad, thank you for helping make some of my dreams come true and for being an amazing friend.

What do you think? Has being tenacious made a difference in your life? Please do tell!

BRAD PAISLEY
ON BEING TENACIOUS

If there's one word that sums up Scott Scovill, it's *tenacious*. It's the perfect way to describe his focus on creative endeavors, and it's definitely the best way to describe what it's like to collaborate with him.

The first time I met Scott, we were talking about adding video to my live show. I was just beginning to headline, and I had some big ideas about what video could do. In my head, I thought I was being pretty innovative. Then I met Scott, and I realized very quickly that I'd just bumped into someone who not only matched my excitement but had an even bigger vision. From that day on, I knew I'd found a partner in crime for all things visual.

What makes Scott different from most people in his field is that a lot of video content at concerts is about atmosphere—swirls of color, moody images, those abstract things that set a tone. And there's nothing wrong with that, but Scott and I share a love for storytelling. Not just telling it with music but with pictures, humor, and quirkiness. We figured out early on that you can film strange, funny, unexpected things and weave them into a show in a way that sticks with an audience.

Take our mascot, for example. We dreamed up this giant, plush, bobbleheaded version of me. I'd tossed out the idea: "What if we had a sports-mascot version of me?" That was all Scott needed. Next thing I knew, he was down at the mascot factory in Nashville—the same one that made the Phillie Phanatic—ordering up a custom, oversized, Muppet-like version of me. To this day, that big foam-headed guy shows up in the show, and it never fails to get laughs.

We've put that mascot through all kinds of stunts. We've sent him down Broadway on a pedal tavern. We've had him smash guitars. We even rigged him up to swing on a wrecking ball in a nude suit—which, trust me, is something you can't unsee. The beauty of it is, all I had to do was float the idea, and Scott ran with it like a kid at Christmas. That's his gift; he takes an idea, no matter how crazy, and makes it real. And he doesn't stop until it works. That's his tenacity.

Now, I'll admit, I'm the kind of guy who will stay up all night chasing down a creative idea. I'll pull an all-nighter just to make sure something feels right artistically. And what's remarkable is, Scott has the exact same drive. I can be working on an edit at 3 a.m., and he'll text me a video clip from his basement where he's filming a stop-motion car chase with toy cars for my song "Mr. Policeman." That's just who he is. He's tireless when there's a vision to bring to life.

That tenacity has made us not just collaborators but lifelong friends. There's nothing quite like working side by side, exhausted but grinning, and then watching an audience react to something you cooked up in the middle of the night.

One of the first times I realized how far this partnership could go was when I asked Scott about animation. I've always loved drawing and thought, *Why not incorporate cartoons into the show?* So I asked him, "What program should I learn if I want to make animation?" Without hesitation he said, "Toon Boom."

So, I went off for two weeks and taught myself how to use Toon Boom. With Scott's editing help, we debuted my very first cartoon during a live instrumental break. The crowd went wild. There I was, playing the guitar, pouring my heart into the song, and suddenly the biggest cheer of the night was for a cartoon I had drawn. That moment cemented what Scott and I try to do: Take what people already love and then surprise them with something new and unforgettable.

Scott's not just a guy with technical know-how. He's an artist who genuinely loves the process. He gets joy out of making things, out of entertaining people, out of seeing that reaction when an audience is surprised or delighted. And he's built an entire company around that idea, producing tours across America and Europe that push the boundaries of what a live show can be.

We've done some wild things together. We once created a *Star Wars*–inspired laser animation, complete with spaceships flying through a three-dimensional battle during an instrumental. We pulled off a virtual Carrie Underwood that was so convincing, the night the real Carrie surprised me onstage, people weren't sure which was which. And yes, we've even staged an arcade-inspired video game sequence for the song "Ticks." These are the kinds of things that make Scott light up, because they're about fun. They're about making the show more than just music.

Now, don't get me wrong—we've hit plenty of roadblocks along the way. Technology fails. Files get corrupted. A video wall doesn't fit. Contractors hand over something that looks terrible. And the big one: Our rehearsal space was once flooded with eight feet of water. We lost almost everything. Most people would've said, "Well, that's it. Guess we're done." Not Scott. He literally went in wearing scuba gear to see what he could rescue. That's not dedication—that's insanity. And that's Scott.

That attitude—never stopping when the road gets rough—is what makes him unique. Every time we've faced a problem, he's been the one to figure out how to work around it. He doesn't fold. He doesn't say, "It wasn't meant to be." He barrels through until it works.

And that's why "The Scoville Scale" is such a fitting name for measuring the heat of peppers. Scott Scovill himself is the ghost pepper of creativity: fiery, relentless, and guaranteed to leave an impression.

Over the years, Scott's tenacity has made us partners, but more importantly, it's made us friends. We've stayed up late chasing impossible ideas. We've laughed until our sides hurt at the mascot's antics. We've pulled off things that seemed undoable. And through it all, Scott's been the guy you can count on to keep pushing until the vision is reality.

For Scott, it's never been about money, or awards, or recognition—even though he's earned plenty of that. It's about the thrill of entertaining, the satisfaction of making something that didn't exist before, and the joy of seeing a crowd light up. That's what drives him. And it's why I know we'll be doing this together, in some form, for the rest of our lives.

So if I had to sum him up in one word, it's the word that titles this book: *tenacious*. Scott Scovill doesn't stop. He doesn't give up. He doesn't take no for an answer when it comes to creativity. And that's why he's not only my collaborator but one of my closest friends.

Man, thank you, Brad. The assignment was to talk about *your* tenacity; choosing instead to write about us as a team makes me feel like a million bucks! You continue to be one of the most impactful people in my life! Thank you for being a great friend.

Brad asked me over to his house not long after the Swedish shows. He told me, "You ran onstage that first night in Sweden and grabbed the audience. You were awesome. I was amused to find myself thinking, *Damn, Scott is really bringing it*." Brad also expressed that in his mind, I had gone from trying out Johnny Cash covers to being a full-fledged artist, singing originals with a command of the stage. I was fiercely proud of his praise, but I will say this: He has more talent in his pinky than I could ever hope to cultivate, but still, I appreciated the kind thought.

I was bursting with pride when Brad added one last thing. "I think you should open for me in all of Europe in 2024." *Wow. That sounds scary . . .*

"Hell yes!" was my ecstatic reply.

It merits saying again: This story is crazy. Through tenaciously beating my fear of public speaking, relentlessly working on my vocals, learning to write music, and spending thousands of hours honing my songs, I dared to dream, and I backed it up with a million tiny steps. I also dared to fail! At times, I stood in front of thousands and forgot the words to songs I was singing. Other nights my voice was so tired and strained, it let me down on all the high notes. I even hit sour notes on nights I didn't have an excuse. But I also learned from each instance. Failure hurts. But it hurts less when tenacity teaches you that failure isn't final—it's just a stepping stone. With each disappointment, I brushed off the dust and got back up to belt out powerful lyrics that came from my heart. I have seen, heard, and even felt the crowd react. I am a singer, an artist on an incredible adventure, because I never gave up.

Where can being tenacious lead *you*?

(Brad and I onstage performing at a sold out Oslo arena in front of fourteen thousand fans! An epic live picture of Brad. A couple more pics of me performing.)

*All photos and supplemental material can be found on TENACIOUSBOOK.COM

EPILOGUE

How about that? You've made it to the end of the book—how are you doing? Has anything in particular sparked for you yet? Is there something you are working toward tenaciously?

Think of this last example as you struggle: It took me seven years to finish this book! Granted, I had a few other full-time jobs, but still. A better writer might have finished it in a year. That better writer likely has a natural talent for this kind of work, never requiring much review or revision. They might excel at organization and focus, making them a factor more productive than I am. They might have been more persuasive in getting guests to contribute or less timid about asking for that favor. Perhaps, unlike me, they would have been content to let AI or a ghostwriter write parts of it—or all of it. For this imaginary writer, it might have been an innately easy endeavor. This is exactly my point! Tenacity is the tool we use to do the things at the edge of our reach, the hard-to-achieve dreams.

Yes, it took me seven times longer to finish the book than this imaginary person. But would I want to read their book? Maybe. Clearly they are impressive. But in all of my favorite books and stories, the lead character is challenged. What makes their journey exciting is that the odds are stacked against them. Their shortcomings make them relatable. After we see them get beat down, we thrill as they get back up. When they somehow win the day against all odds, well, that's just magic. Those are the stories I want to read. This is the kind of story I suggest you write with your life. A tenacious one.

My invitation to you is to live that kind of life so that as you get older you can metaphorically flip through the pages of your own story and smile. This is my hope for you and the reason for this book.

Writing it has been scary. I struggled with the question, Will anyone want to read it? Even now, seven years in, this fear rears its head often. There were huge periods when I got nothing done and felt guilt. At the five-year mark, I submitted a draft that was twenty-one chapters long to a previous editor and endured the heartbreaking directive that I needed to cut the book in half. I spent an entire year whittling away at my stories, throwing away experiences I had thought worthy of sharing. There were five chapters I threw out entirely. That was so painful, but I did it, and I do think the book is better for it.

Oh, the favors—I'm not one to ever ask for help, so you can imagine how hard it was for me to approach my famous and fascinating friends about contributing to the book. I know their time is so precious. Wonderfully, so many friends said yes, but as they are busy people, at times I waited over a year for their submissions. Some said no, making me feel embarrassed that I had asked. (This was not their fault, mind you.)

I had a few editors along the way, and while I am grateful for all of them, some reversed the advice of their predecessors. With their permission, I moved on from my pay-for-help publisher with the dream of landing a major deal. Two years later, six years into writing, I still didn't have a publisher, and therefore I had no idea if anyone would really even know about my book. I also questioned whether the book would really help anyone. I feared that I would fail, embarrass myself, and waste time I could never retrieve.

If you live in fear . . .

But, as my song "Try" declares, "If you live in fear, it'll chain you, and you're never gonna fly, so I try." I was scared, but I tried, and I kept trying, and little by little this book came together. Dear friends took time out of their crazy lives to share stories with you, the reader. My literary agent and friend Kathy Armisted read my first few chapters and declared that she was going to take me on, boldly claiming that she would find us a great publishing deal and strong distribution. How? She has worked with many authors before, none as unknown as me, though.

It took her a bit over a year, we had a great meeting with Forefront Books. We loved them, and to my joy we signed with them. We were also thrilled that Simon & Schuster would be distributing the book. It will now surely find its way into readers' hands! With Forefront came a real angel in the form of Hope Innelli, the remarkable human they assigned to be my editor. She brought incredible experience, having edited many bestsellers, but the really exciting thing was that I agreed with damn-near every suggestion she made. We made a great team, and I gained another lifelong friend. I love Hope's big heart! Now, with an amazing team behind me, I made that push to get the final 10 percent of the book done. That last bit is always as hard as the first 90 percent. With their help, I am allowing myself to finish.

"Allowing myself to finish" is an odd way to put it, so permit me to explain. I have done some soul-searching regarding why finishing has been so hard, and, as odd as it sounds, here is my theory. My mom, who is my rock, has been saying for the past few years, "Hurry up and finish the book before I die." She's kind of kidding, but at her age and condition, she kind of isn't. I honestly think that some of what's been holding me back these past two years is the thought that if I finish the book, my mom will feel as if she can pass away. As crazy as this sounds, I feel there's some truth in it. Once I made this odd connection, I was somehow better able to work effectively again. Isn't the mind a funny thing? I am so grateful that my team was patient while I struggled. Thank you all.

Well I am finally finishing the book, and, as I stated in the beginning, the first copy off the press is dedicated to my sweet mom.

So, what now? This book is done—what's next? Well, I've always had an interest in film. I dabbled in it a while back, executive and co-executive producing a few movies—one even starring Jennifer Garner, *The Tribes of Palos Verde*. Jennifer is wonderful. Maybe it's time to write and make my own movie?

There is always music in my heart, and, as such, I have several new songs I want to bring to life. This next album will broach some deep feelings. There's a song called "Six Feet Down and Starin' Up," which I wrote imagining I was in my dad's coffin, and another titled "To the Moon and Back," expressing my love for my mother. I wrote one song about psychedelic therapy, although it absolutely seems like it's about something else; I wonder if any of you will figure out which one. Then, to lighten things up, I wrote a raucous party song about hangovers. That last one has gone over well; I tried it out live while headlining a festival for a few thousand Swedes last week.

Speaking of live shows, we did open for Brad's European tour in 2024. It was incredible. Check out the behind-the-scenes series posted on my YouTube channel (@scottscovill1511) sometime. We played Iceland, Switzerland, Germany, Denmark, Sweden, and Norway to crowds of over ten thousand some nights. We even had our own bus with my name emblazoned across the side. After the tour, the band flew back to America and we played Nashville and Chicago, a fun encore to our world tour.

I also wrote a song about my cancer journey. I am two and a half years past that nightmare as I write this in 2025. Crushingly, we did just lose Alice (Momma Moo) to the disease, but I'm grateful to say that I am cancer-free and continue to make better decisions about my health. I am still on track toward fulfilling my promise that I will someday say that "cancer saved my life." Oh, and despite my hangover song, I'm still not drinking either! Shockingly, I really don't miss it!

In business, Moo TV was once again named the best in the business at the 2024 Pollstar Awards. I'm particularly proud of my team. Their willingness to step up allows me the time to do things I love, such as writing this book.

All of that is exciting, but the biggest endeavor I'm undertaking these days is one far more personal. For six years, a lady named Katie Groshong was my assistant. Then, just before the pandemic hit, we parted ways. For the next four years, we fell out of touch. As I have mentioned, the pandemic broke me down in so many ways. At the same time, Katie's marriage ended, leaving her a bit broken as well. A casual encounter four years later landed us in a huge hug, an embrace of two dear friends who had so missed each other. But there was something more in that hug. Something was different. Something wonderful. We decided to get dinner, and that felt wonderful too. Dare I explore if Katie and I could be more than friends? The answer was simple—my heart, in fact, never gave me a choice.

As I write this, sweet Katie, her two dogs, Kona and Kea, and I are living together. Next week is our one-year anniversary. As we navigate building a life together, we both are doing the hard work of being the best and truest versions of ourselves we can be. With my parents as the relationship examples of my formative years, this is scary territory. But with Katie, I face that fear gladly. I adore her smile, her silliness, her creativity, and her huge heart. She makes me laugh and cry. She certainly is, as I like to say, making the next chapter more interesting. I love her so very much.

Seven years of writing is a good chunk of my life. In that time, I invested my most valuable currency—time—into this book. I invested it in you, too, hoping that sharing what I have learned may help you along your path. If I am lucky, this book itself will be one of my greatest rewards for living tenaciously—for living a life worth writing about. I believe I have done so, even if I am the only one who will read the full book of my life. This smaller volume in your hand, titled *Tenacious*, can be thought of as a chapter of my life. A chapter I am so very proud to share with you. I pray it helps inspire you to chase a dream—and to dare to live your best life.

For the hundredth time, my friend, I invite you to do just that.

See your dream.

Break the inertia and take that first step.

Quiet the voices of doubt and get past your own hard wiring.

Embrace failure; see it as a stepping stone, not a wall.

Be flexible enough to go around obstacles.

Do all of this learning from the struggle.

Try and keep trying, no matter what.

Be tenacious.

(My family! From left to right: Kona, myself, Santa, Katie, and Kea. All dressed up for the holidays! Katie and I on camels in Morocco. An early vision board for the book, 3x5 cards for the win!)

*All photos and supplemental material can be found on TENACIOUSBOOK.COM

Lyrics to the song TRY (2020, Try again), written by: Scott Scovill, Victoria Shaw, and Madeline Stone

(v)
THERE ARE TIMES WHERE I FEEL FROZEN IN THE PLACE WHERE I AM STANDING CAUSE THAT MOUNTAIN SEEMS IMPOSSIBLE TO CLIMB
THERE ARE TIMES I HEAR THE WORDS SAYING CAREFUL WHERE YOU STEP
AND I REALIZE THAT VOICE INSIDE IS MINE
BUT I'M NOT LISTENING, I'M NOT LISTENING . . .

(c)
YOU MIGHT BE SCARED AS HELL, BUT THE ONLY ONES WHO REALLY FAIL ARE THE ONES WHO NEVER TRY
IF YOU LIVE IN FEAR, IT'LL CHAIN YOU, AND YOUR NEVER GONNA FLY
SO I TRY, OH I TRY

(v)
I REFUSE TO LET MY FEAR HOLD ME DOWN JUST LIKE A PRISONER
I'D RATHER MAKE MISTAKES THEN JUST STANDING STILL
I MIGHT FALL FLAT ON MY FACE , BUT TELL ME MAN, WHO HASN'T
AND THE WAY I GOT BACK UP WAS BY SHEER WILL
I'M NOT GIVING IN, I'M NOT GIVING IN. . . .

(c)
YOU MIGHT BE SCARED AS HELL, BUT THE ONLY ONES WHO REALLY FAIL ARE THE ONES WHO NEVER TRY
IF YOU LIVE IN FEAR, IT'LL CHAIN YOU, AND YOUR NEVER GONNA FLY
SO I TRY, OH I TRY

SOLO
(bridge)
JUST KEEP MOVING FORWARD WHEN YOUR KNEES ARE SHAKING
JUST KEEP MOVING FORWARD WHEN YOUR KNEES ARE SHAKING
JUST KEEP MOVING FORWARD WHEN YOUR KNEES ARE SHAKING

(c)
YOU MIGHT BE SCARED AS HELL, BUT THE ONLY ONES WHO REALLY FAIL
ARE THE ONES WHO NEVER TRY
IF YOU LIVE IN FEAR, IT WILL CHAIN YOU, AND YOUR NEVER GONNA FLY
YOU MIGHT BE SCARED AS HELL, BUT THE ONLY ONES WHO REALLY FAIL ARE THE ONES WHO NEVER TRY
IF YOU LIVE IN FEAR, IT'LL CHAIN YOU, AND YOUR NEVER GONNA FLY

SO I TRY

I REFUSE TO LET MY FEAR
HOLD ME DOWN LIKE A PRISONER

Copyright 2022 Scott Scovill Publishing/ASCAP, Victoria Shaw Songs/SESAC, Deana Do Music/ASCAP

ACKNOWLEDGMENTS

I would very much like to thank literally everyone; consider this short list a start.

My mother, father, grandmother, and grandfather, thank you all for guiding this curious kid into adulthood and beyond. I know my path took some turns that must have made you cringe. As you have read, I was scared too, but hey, it worked out to be the adventure of a lifetime! Thank you for the love and attention you poured into me when it mattered the most.

Lee, who was like a father to me, and Momma Moo, (Alice) who was definately a mother, I miss you both so very much. I do believe that I will see you again.

Everyone who has been a part of Moo TV, Moo Creative, and The Steel Mill, staff and clients. It's been quite a ride; you all are a second family to me.

My friends . . . too many to do more than scratch the surface really, but Hunter, David, and Lindsay. The Ocho (Eric, Marty, Mose, Jimmy, and Ian). The QCPP. Luke, Kristin, Brad, and Kendal. The Brotherhood. Shawn, Craig, and Mikey. Lastly, life-long friends Dave, Ken, Matt, and Mark.

My love, Katie, for my present and my future.

ACKNOWLEDGMENTS

Thank you to everyone who tried to help me remember the facts. This story starts over forty years ago; I know I didn't get it all straight, but I did my best, and it was wonderful reconnecting with so many of you.

The team for this dream: My agent and champion, Kathy Armisted, my wonderful publisher Forefront books (Johnathan, Jennifer, Becky, Landon, Rylee, and Caroline), my amazing editor and dear new friend Hope Innelli, and early proofreader, Sarah Crawford. Launch manager, affiliate guru Matt McWilliams, Triple Seven PR (Shannon Leigh, Tori, Ryleigh, Carrie, Ashley), and last but not least, my right hand Brandi Simms.

My incredible contributors who somehow found the time to invest in you. Storme, Scott, Colin, Jonathan, Dierks, Mom, Chris, Tom, Kate, Cam, Cady, Crispy, Peter, Alan, Garth, Hendo, and Brad. Thank you for shining your inspiration our way.

There are so many people I love who are somehow not in this book. People who are so important to my heart. If this was an autobiography you would all be in these pages; please know that, and if you would, this next line is for you.

Thank you to everyone who has ever touched my life. You have taught me so much, and I am so grateful for you all.

This book was written because I love to live, learn, and share what I experienced. At heart, I am a storyteller who both selfishlessly wants to be heard and generously hopes he can make life better for those around him. My wish of being heard has been granted. Thank you. Now all that remains is my wish that I have helped you help you. Your move.

(More pictures, more gratitude, and whatever else I can think of that might help you can be found through this link, and on tenaciousbook.com)

*All photos and supplemental material can be found on TENACIOUSBOOK.COM